THE LOFTUS DELUSION

–

Why Atheism Fails

and

Messianic Israelism Prevails

David Reuben Stone

B.S., M.S. UCLA

www.loftus-delusion.com

Published February, 2010 by David Reuben Stone.

ISBN: 978-0-557-32063-9

To all who seek truth.

CONTENTS

PREFACE

The Loftus Delusion could not have been completed without the faithful encouragement and support from my friends and family. I thank them for their understanding and patience. In writing the book, I have benefited from the published works of many others, both atheists and theists. I am indebted to them for their efforts to understand and explain their views. Finally, I apologize for any errors, and I encourage your feedback to help ensure that future editions contain the modifications needed to correct them. Please visit http://www.loftus-delusion.com for author contact details.

David Reuben Stone

February 2010, 1st Edition

INTRODUCTION

The question of the existence of God is an issue of fundamental significance. If it is reasonable to not believe that God exists, then shall we live our lives however we prefer? If God exists, and in particular, if the Biblical God exists, then how shall we live? The importance of determining the answers to these questions can not be underestimated. Our answers carry with them not only practical implications for the manner in which we live our daily lives, but our answers may also seal our conscious and eternally unending fate. Such consequences are of truly utmost and limitless significance.

The purpose of this study is to continue the project of answering these critical questions by further exploring the nature of my theistic arguments[1] in the context of an examination of a critique of Biblical theism published by John W. Loftus.[2] Chapter 1 is a defense of probabilistic *modus tollens* reasoning, and includes examples of the application of such reasoning to the Intelligent Design (ID) debate. Chapter 2 presents an explanatory filtration procedure useful in the justification of my Argument From The Laws Of Physics (AFTLOP) and my ID arguments. My ID arguments and AFTLOP are then fused together, in conjunction with the explanatory filtration procedure, to justify an agent-caused version of physical-event occasionalism (ACPO). Chapter 3 explores the implications of the Human Ignorance Principle for the problem of evil as it relates to the theism-atheism debate, and includes a critique of Loftus' perspective on the problem of evil. In Chapter 4, Loftus' views on rationality, morality, control beliefs, and the Outsider Test are critiqued. I provide a brief summary, in Chapter 5, of an evidentialist apologetics approach to justifying a conservative Biblical worldview. Chapter 6 is a critical response to Loftus' views on the Bible. Finally, in Chapter 7, I frame the theism-atheism debate in the context of a newly developed test (STONE) useful for attaining debate resolution between advocates of the opposing viewpoints.

Please be sure to obtain a copy of John W. Loftus' book, *Why I Became an Atheist: A Former Preacher Rejects Christianity* (ISBN: 978-1591025924), so that my critical analysis will be understood in light of the original context of the referenced text.[3] The atheistic arguments in his book are refuted in detail, and theism is shown to be strongly confirmed by my theistic arguments. Also, my approach to justifying fundamental Biblical beliefs is immune to his objections to such beliefs. The reason I have became no atheist is, thus, due to my perception that the case for theism in general, and for conservative Biblical beliefs in particular, is strongly confirmed by considerations investigated in this (and an earlier[4]) book, and is eminently more plausible than the case for any alternative worldview I know.

If ten well-informed conservative Biblical theologians, each representing distinct theological inclinations and philosophical approaches, addressed the arguments examined in *The Loftus Delusion*, then a diverse body of results would surely obtain. Readers should bear in mind, therefore, that the specific approach in this book depicts only one of a wide range of options available to the conservative Biblical theologian.

The following convention will be used to document quotes from other reference sources. References in the form (p. X) document page number X. A reference in the form (p. X-Y) documents pages X through Y. References in the form (p. X:Y) document the sentence appearing on line Y of page X. ("Line" refers to a horizontal line of text on a page, and does not refer to titles, subtitles, blank space, or text in headers-footers.) A reference in the form (p. X:Y-Z) documents the sentence(s) on page X that range from line Y to line Z. Finally, a reference in the form (p. W:X-Y:Z) documents the body of text that ranges from the sentence beginning on line X of page W to the sentence ending on line Z of page Y. This convention is adopted for the purpose of avoiding excessive direct quotations, and for the purpose of reducing the total length of *The Loftus Delusion*. Thus, identification of a specific reference in *The Loftus Delusion* will generally require access to that source, unless the complete quote happens to be provided.

For the record, I personally embrace conservative Biblical theology, and this, of course, entails I accept theism. However, theists of all stripes will likely find my natural theology compatible with (and supportive of) the components of their worldview which entail there exists a personal creator-sustainer-designer of the physical world. Also, I submit that my approach to justifying distinctively Biblical theological beliefs is likely to be compatible with (and supportive of) many central components of the views of members of the largest branches of the Christian tree, including Orthodox, Catholic, and Protestant/Evangelical. It is surely important to ask which system (if any) within these major branches is best, but I do not focus in detail upon this question here, as my primary focus is the targeting of atheists (as well as other skeptics critical of essential Biblical beliefs[5]) with reasons for embracing theism and a conservative Biblical worldview. For those who may be interested, however, I do provide a brief summary of my favored theological system (Messianic Israelism) in the Appendix.

Atheists and other critics of conservative Biblical theology must modify their worldview so as to account for my position defended here. Also, I look forward to the critical review of my work by others so that I might improve the quality of my analysis by removing any possible blind spots of my own. All comments and suggestions are welcome and encouraged. Please visit http://www.loftus-delusion.com for author contact details.

Projects of this magnitude are challenging, time-consuming, and expensive. Any assistance readers might provide would be welcome and appreciated. Again, please visit http://www.loftus-delusion.com for more information.

NOTES

1. Stone, David Reuben (2007). *Atheism Is False: Richard Dawkins and the 'Improbability of God' Delusion.* Morrisville, NC: Lulu Press, pp. 14-60.

2. Loftus, John W. (2008). *Why I Became an Atheist: A Former Preacher Rejects Christianity.* Amherst, NY: Prometheus Books.

3. Throughout this volume I provide detailed references to the *second* printing of Loftus (2008). The second printing contains corrections to many (but not all) typographical and formatting errors. The result is that the second printing contains changes on a few dozen pages, including the following: 70-77, 81, 109, 111-112, 116, 153, 163, 213-214, 219, 266-280, 309, 312, 321-322, and 391. Also, the second printing has a thicker font size with darker blue coloring on the front cover. The ISBN numbers are the same on both printings. To determine which printing you possess, note that the first printing erroneously lists Craig and Moreland (2003) in the Bibliography, whereas the second printing contains the correction with Moreland and Craig (2003) in the Bibliography; the author order is corrected in the second printing. Note, too, that the second printing incorrectly shows "Anslem's" on p. 345. Other errors persist in the second printing, but I will refrain from publicizing them so as to better facilitate the tracking of subsequent printings. The reader is encouraged to purchase a copy of the *second* printing of Loftus (2008), thereby insuring that my references to distinct lines of text are linked to the correct printing.

4. Stone (2007).

5. For an introduction to conservative Biblical theology, see Grudem, Wayne (1994). *Systematic Theology: An Introduction to Biblical Doctrine.* Grand Rapids, MI: Zondervan. Also, see McKee, J.K. (2009). *Introduction to Things Messianic.* Kissimmee, FL: TNN Press. Also see Huey, William and McKee, J.K. (2009). *Hebraic Roots: An Introductory Study.* Kissimmee, FL: TNN Press.

CHAPTER 1

Intelligent Design and Modus Tollens

Abstract: *Intelligent Design (ID) critic Elliott Sober has alleged that ID is grounded in an unjustified probabilistic modus tollens argument form. This allegation is here disputed, and both quantitative and qualitative probabilistic modus tollens argument forms are developed. A central component of the Probabilized Modus Tollens Theorem of Carl Wagner is shown to provide independent confirmation of the accuracy of the qualitative form, and investigations by ID proponents are examined in the context of that inductive logical structure. A recent analysis by ID critic Jordan Howard Sobel fails to account for the ID argument here defended.*

I begin with an analysis of the structure of an argument form known as *modus tollens*. The deductive form of this argument may be expressed as follows:

(1) $A \rightarrow B$
(2) $\sim B$
(3) $\sim A$

This argument form is well known and widely used. If A entails B, and if B does not obtain, then A is not true.

Frequently, however, the nature of our epistemic state is not always so clear. For example, it may be the case the A entails B is likely, yet A does not guarantee B certainly obtains. Also, there may exist instances in which $\sim B$ is probable only to some degree. The presence of such uncertainties entails that $\sim A$ may be less than certain, and in fact, $\sim A$ might possibly be false, even given that (1) and (2) are likely. It is useful, therefore, to examine in greater detail the nature of *modus tollens* reasoning, as the results of such analysis will prove to be a significant epistemological development in general, where the ID hypothesis is but one particular case in which these results may be applied.

A probabilistic (inductive) modus tollens argument form may be expressed as follows, where $0.5 < k < 1$, and where $0.5 < i < 1$:

(4) $P(B|A) = k$
(5) $\sim B$
(6) $P(\sim A) = i$

It is indeed true that (6) does not follow from (4) and (5), and an opponent of probabilistic *modus tollens* reasoning, Elliott Sober, has provided examples to support this claim.[1] However, this is not the end of all such reasoning, as my development of a *quantitative probabilistic modus tollens* (QTMT) and a *qualitative probabilistic modus tollens* (QLMT) will show.

QTMT

I begin with the QTMT, which will show that (4) and (5) do jointly entail (6), provided P(B) is sufficiently small. First, consider the four distinct cases in which (4) could be true:

Case 1: $P(A) = P(B)$

Case 2: $P(A) < P(B)$

Case 3: $k = [\,P(B)\,/\,P(A)\,] < 1$

Case 4: $k < [\,P(B)\,/\,P(A)\,] < 1$

Then use Bayes' Theorem to express P(A) as follows:

(7) $P(A) = [\,P(B)\,P(A|B)\,]\,/\,P(B|A)$

So, given (4) and (5), we have:

(8) $P(A|\sim B) = [\,(1-k)\,P(A)\,]\,/\,P(\sim B)$

Substitution of (7) into (8) yields:

(9) $P(A|\sim B) = P(A|B)\,[\,(1-k)\,/\,k\,]\,[\,P(B)\,/\,P(\sim B)\,]$

13

It is important to observe that (9) is true in all four cases. Now consider the following:

(10) $P(A|\sim B) + P(\sim A|\sim B) = 1$

Given (4), (5), and (9), we may now use (10) to identify the condition under which $P(\sim A|\sim B) > P(A|\sim B)$. This may be seen as follows. First, (10) entails that $P(\sim A|\sim B) > P(A|\sim B)$, if $P(A|\sim B) < 0.5$. This, in turn, implies that $P(\sim A|\sim B) > P(A|\sim B)$, if:

(11) $P(A|B) \, [\, (\, 1 - k \,) \, / \, k \,] \, [\, P(B) \, / \, P(\sim B) \,] < R$

Here, $R = 0.5$. We may now solve for $P(B)$ in each of the four cases, assuming $0 < P(B) < 1$. First, consider *Case 1*. In this case, substitution of $P(A) = P(B)$ into (7) entails that $P(B|A) = P(A|B) = k$. This fact may be used to simplify (11) as follows:

(12) $(1 - k) \, P(B) \, / \, P(\sim B) < R$

Then, after substituting $P(\sim B) = 1 - P(B)$ into (12), we may solve for $P(B)$ to obtain:

(13) $P(B) < R \, / \, (R + 1 - k)$

Thus, in *Case 1*, given (4), (5), (13), and $R = 0.5$, we may conclude that $P(\sim A) > P(A)$.

Now consider *Case 2*. In this case, $P(A) < P(B)$, and we may establish $P(A|B) < k$ by reasoning as follows, where $0 < P(B) < 1$:

(14) $P(A) < P(B)$
(15) $k \, P(A) < k \, P(B)$
(16) $P(A \text{ and } B) < k \, P(B)$
(17) $P(B) \, P(A| B) < k \, P(B)$
(18) $P(A|B) < k$

Note that (15) follows from multiplication of (14) by k. Also, note that (16) and (17) follow from the definition of k and the definition of conditional probability. And, (18) follows from division of (17) by $P(B)$.

So, given (9) and (10), we find that $P(\sim A|\sim B) > P(A|\sim B)$, if (11) is true, where $R = 0.5$. After substituting $P(\sim B) = 1 - P(B)$ into (11), we may express $P(B)$ as follows:

(19) $P(B) < R / [R + (1 - k) P(A|B) / k]$

Observe that (18) entails that the expression in (19) is greater than that in (13). It follows that (13) is sufficient to infer that (11) is true in *Case 2*. Thus, given (4), (5), (13), and $R = 0.5$, we may conclude that $P(\sim A) > P(A)$ in this case.

Now consider *Case 3*. Here, $P(B) = k\, P(A) = P(A \text{ and } B) = P(B)\, P(A|B)$, which, given $0 < P(B) < 1$, entails:

(20) $P(A|B) = 1$

As in the previous two cases, (10) entails that $P(\sim A|\sim B) > P(A|\sim B)$, if $P(A|\sim B) < 0.5$. This, in turn, implies that $P(\sim A|\sim B) > P(A|\sim B)$, if (11) is true, where $R = 0.5$. After substituting both (20) and $P(\sim B) = 1 - P(B)$ into (11), we may solve for $P(B)$ to obtain:

(21) $P(B) < Rk / (Rk + 1 - k)$

Thus, given (4), (5), (21), and $R = 0.5$, we may conclude that $P(\sim A) > P(A)$ in this case.

Now consider *Case 4*. In this case, we may establish that $P(A|B) < 1$ by reasoning as follows:

(22) $k < P(B) / P(A)$
(23) $k\, P(A) < P(B)$
(24) $P(A \text{ and } B) < P(B)$
(25) $P(B)\, P(A|B) < P(B)$
(26) $P(A|B) < 1$

Here, (22) follows from the definition of *Case 4*, and we assume $0 < P(A) < 1$. Multiplication of (22) by $P(A)$ yields (23). Given the definition of k and the definition of conditional probability, (24) follows from (23). The definition of conditional probability may then be used to express (24) as in (25). Finally, (26) follows from division by $P(B)$, where $0 < P(B) < 1$.

Now, as in the other cases, (10) entails that $P(\sim A|\sim B) > P(A|\sim B)$, if $P(A|\sim B) <$ 0.5. This, in turn, implies that $P(\sim A|\sim B) > P(A|\sim B)$, if (11) is true, where $R =$ 0.5. After substitution of $P(\sim B) = 1 - P(B)$ into (11), we may solve for $P(B)$:

(27) $P(B) < Rk / [Rk + P(A|B) (1 - k)]$

So, (26) implies that the expression in (27) is greater than the expression in (21). Thus, given (4), (5), (21), and $R = 0.5$, we may conclude that $P(\sim A) > P(A)$ in this case.

We have, therefore, identified the case-specific conditions in addition to (4) and (5) which, if satisfied, entail that $P(\sim A)$ is more likely than $P(A)$. Note that $P(\sim A)$ is negatively correlated with $P(B)$ in this context.

QTMT and Probability Kinematics

The analysis above includes the assumption that (5) is true, which entails that an instance of $\sim B$ is known with certainty to exist. In fact, there may arise situations in which $\sim B$ is not known with certainty, but is known to be probable only to some specified degree. We may use a procedure known as Probability Kinematics (Jeffrey Conditionalization)[2] to account for situations in which the probability is J that a particular observation X is an instance of $\sim B$:

(28) $J = P(X \text{ is } \sim B)$
(29) $P(A|X) = J P(A|\sim B) + (1 - J) P(A|B)$

Substitution of (9) and $P(\sim B) = 1 - P(B)$ into (29), and further manipulation, yields:

(30) $P(A|X) = P(A|B) [1 - J (k - P(B)) / (k (1 - P(B)))]$

Note that (30) is true in each of the four cases in which (4), X, and (28) could all be true. Now, for each case, we may identify a condition which, if satisfied, entails $P(\sim A) > P(A)$, assuming $0 < P(B) < 1$.

First consider *Case 1*. Recall that substitution of $P(A) = P(B)$ into (7) entails that $P(B|A) = P(A|B) = k$ in this case. Consider the following:

(31) $P(A|X) + P(\sim A|X) = 1$

Given (4), X, (28), and (30), we may now use (31) to identify the condition under which $P(\sim A|X) > P(A|X)$. This may be seen as follows. First, (31) entails that $P(\sim A|X) > P(A|X)$, if $P(A|X) < 0.5$. This, in turn, implies that $P(\sim A|X) > P(A|X)$, if:

(32) $P(A|B) [1 - J (k - P(B)) / (k (1 - P(B)))] < R$

Here, $R = 0.5$. After substitution of $P(A|B) = k$ into (32), we may solve for $P(B)$ to obtain:

(33) $P(B) < [Jk - k + R] / [J - k + R]$

Thus, in *Case 1*, given (4), X, (28), (33), and $R = 0.5$, we may conclude that $P(\sim A) > P(A)$. Here, we assume $J - k + R > 0$. Note that (33) simplifies to (13), when $J = 1$.

Now consider *Case 2*. Again, since (31) entails that $P(\sim A|X) > P(A|X)$, assuming $P(A|X) < 0.5$, it follows that $P(\sim A|X) > P(A|X)$, if (32) is satisfied, where $R = 0.5$. We may solve (32) for $P(B)$ to obtain:

(34) $P(B) < [Jk - k + Rk / P(A|B)] / [J - k + Rk / P(A|B)]$

Here, we assume $J - k + Rk / P(A|B) > 0$. Observe that (18) implies that $k / P(A|B) > 1$. This, in turn, implies that the expression in (34) is greater than the expression in (33). In this case, therefore, given (4), X, (28), (33), and $R = 0.5$, it follows that $P(\sim A) > P(A)$, if we assume both that $J - k + Rk / P(A|B) > 0$, and that $J - k + R > 0$.

Now consider *Case 3*. As in the previous two cases, $P(\sim A|X) > P(A|X)$, if (32) is satisfied, where $R = 0.5$. We may substitute (20) into (32) and solve for $P(B)$ to obtain:

(35) $P(B) < (Jk - k + Rk) / (J - k + Rk)$

Here, we assume $J - k + Rk > 0$. Note that (35) simplifies to (21), when $J = 1$. Thus, given (4), X, (28), (35), and $R = 0.5$, we may infer that $P(\sim A) > P(A)$ in this case.

Now consider *Case 4*. Again, $P(\sim A|X) > P(A|X)$, if (32) is satisfied, where $R = 0.5$. Recall that we may solve (32) for $P(B)$ to obtain:

(36) $P(B) < [Jk - k + Rk / P(A|B)] / [J - k + Rk / P(A|B)]$

Here also, we assume $J - k + Rk / P(A|B) > 0$. Observe that (26) implies that the expression in (36) is greater than the expression in (35). Therefore, given (4), X, (28), (35), and $R = 0.5$, it follows that $P(\sim A) > P(A)$ in this case, assuming also that $J - k + Rk > 0$.

At this point in our analysis, given (4), (5), (9), and $R = 0.5$, we have shown that the additional case-specific condition which entails $P(\sim A) > P(A)$ is (13) for *Case 1* and *Case 2*, and (21) for *Case 3* and *Case 4*. Also, given (4), X, (28), (30), and $R = 0.5$, the additional case-specific condition which entails that $P(\sim A) > P(A)$ is (33) for *Case 1* and *Case 2*, and (35) for *Case 3* and *Case 4*. Thus, provided the relevant set of case-specific conditions C is satisfied, we may proceed to structure QTMT as follows, where $k < 1$ and k is close to one:

(37) $P(B|A) = k$
(38) C
(39) $P(\sim A) > P(A)$

Note that it is $R = 0.5$ that guarantees $P(\sim A) > P(A)$.

Now, assuming all quantities remain well defined, $P(\sim A)$ increases as R decreases. Furthermore, observe that (38) implies $P(A) < R$, which may also be expressed as $P(\sim A) > 1 - R$, substituting $P(A) = 1 - P(\sim A)$. These considerations suggest that we may further generalize QTMT by reasoning as follows:

(40) $P(B|A) = k$
(41) C
(42) $P(\sim A) > 1 - R$

Here, we do not impose the constraint $R = 0.5$, but permit R to vary as determined by our key parameters. Clearly, it would be useful to identify R as a function of k, J, and P(B), since the strength of the conclusion (42) could then be quantified, given those variables. $R(k, J, P(B))$ is a case-specific function and is easily determined from the functional relationships suggested by (13), (21), (33), and (35). Thus, given (4), (5), and (9), in both *Case 1* and *Case 2*, we obtain:

(43) $R = (1 - k) P(B) / P(\sim B)$

Given (4), (5), and (9), in both *Case 3* and *Case 4*, we obtain:

(44) $R = [(1 - k) P(B)] / [k P(\sim B)]$

Given (4), X, (28), and (30), in both *Case 1* and *Case 2*, we obtain:

(45) $R = [P(B) (J - k) - k (J - 1)] / P(\sim B)$

Given (4), X, (28), and (30), in both *Case 3* and *Case 4*, we obtain:

(46) $R = [P(B) (J - k) - k (J - 1)] / [k P(\sim B)]$

In general, therefore, given k, J, and P(B), we may infer $P(\sim A)$ from the relevant case-specific formula for R in my QTMT argument form as outlined above, assuming all quantities are well defined.

For a simple example of the QTMT in action, consider *Case 2*, where A represents "it is now raining outside", where B represents "it is now completely cloudy outside", where $P(A) < P(B)$. Suppose further that $P(B|A) = k = 0.91$, and assume we observe $\sim B$ with $J = 1$. Now, if we desire $P(\sim A) > 0.8$, then $R = 0.2$. Substituting k and R into (13), we obtain that P(B) must be less than approximately 0.69 to conclude $P(\sim A) > 0.8$. Alternatively, if we know P(B) is less than approximately 0.69 (say, from weather forecasts), then $P(\sim B)$ is approximately 0.31, and we may substitute k, P(B), and $P(\sim B)$ into (43) to obtain $R = 0.2$, which entails $P(\sim A) > 0.8$ (from (42)).

QLMT

Thus far, we have considered the QTMT, in which $\sim B$ is either known with certainty or known to be probable to degree J. An alternative (and more qualitative) approach is to explore such reasoning on a theoretical basis, where specific observations need not even be explicitly considered as in the QTMT. The QLMT may be expressed as follows:

(47) $P(B|A) = k$
(48) $P(\sim B) = m$
(49) $P(\sim A) = i$

Here, $0.5 < k < 1$, $0.5 < m < 1$, and $0 < i < 1$. There may arise situations in which (48) may be discovered, independent of any specific observations. In such situations, (49) may be established without consideration of conditions such as C or quantities such as R.

Thus, given (47) and (48), we may immediately conclude that (49) is true, since (49) follows from (47) and (48) in each of the four previously identified distinct cases in which (47) could be true. This may be easily shown, assuming each of k and m is close to one. In *Case 1*, for example, $P(A)$ is small, since $P(A) = P(B)$, where $P(B)$ is small. In *Case 2*, $P(A)$ is small, since $P(A) < P(B)$, where $P(B)$ is small. In *Case 3*, $P(A)$ is small, since $P(A) = P(B) / k$, where $P(B)$ is small, and where k is close to one. In *Case 4*, $P(A)$ is small, since $P(A) < P(B) / k$, where $P(B)$ is small, and where k is close to one.

Another way to show (49) follows from (47) and (48) is by simply noting that $P(A) = [P(B) P(A|B)] / P(B|A)$ entails that $P(A)$ is small in this context, since $P(B)$ is small, $P(B|A)$ is close to one, and $P(A|B) \leq 1$. Also, there exists yet another demonstration that (49) can follow from conditions such as (47) and (48). This may be found in a previous publication of mine.[3]

Clearly, given (47) and (48), it would be useful to determine i as a function of m and k, since the strength of conclusion (49) could then be quantified for each of the four cases in which (47) could be true. We may begin the task of identifying $i(m, k)$ by substituting i, m, and k into (7) to obtain:

(50) $1 - i = (1 - m) P(A|B) / k$

Solving for i, we find the general equation for i, using the substitution $P(A|B) = P(A \text{ and } B) / (1 - m)$:

(51) $i = 1 - P(A \text{ and } B) / k$

Even given (47) and (48), the value of $P(A \text{ and } B)$ may not be known in general, and the expressions for $i(m, k)$ above might not appear to be useful for quantifying the case-specific value of i. Nevertheless, given $P(A) + P(\sim A) = P(B) + P(\sim B)$ in *Case 1*, we easily obtain:

(52) $i = m$

Thus, the problem of determining $P(A \text{ and } B)$ in (51) may be avoided in *Case 1*.

Given $P(A) + P(\sim A) = P(B) + P(\sim B)$ in *Case 2*, $P(A) < P(B)$ implies:

(53) $i > m$

Thus, a lower bound for i may be identified in Case 2, even if P(A and B) is unknown.

In *Case 3*, we may use k = P(B) / P(A) = (1 − m) / (1 − i) in (51) to establish P(A and B) = 1 − m, which may then be used to simplify (51) as:

(54) $i = (k + m − 1) / k$

In *Case 4*, k < P(B) / P(A) = (1 − m) / (1 − i) may be used in (51) to show that P(A and B) < 1 − m, which may be used to simplify (51) as:

(55) $i > (k + m − 1) / k$

So, given (47) and (48), (49) immediately follows, where i is given by (52) in *Case 1*, (53) in *Case 2*, (54) in *Case 3*, and (55) in *Case 4*. Additionally, we may note that m − 1 > (m − 1) / k, which implies m > 1 + (m − 1) / k and leads to:

(56) $(k + m − 1) / k < m$

Therefore, given (47) and (48), we may draw the following case-independent necessary conclusion:

(57) $i \geq (k + m − 1) / k$

This result has been independently discovered by Carl Wagner,[4] although his derivation follows a considerably different approach than my own. Indeed, I genuinely thought it plausible that I was the first to discover this result, but subsequently learned that Wagner had already published it some three years before my independent discovery. To my knowledge, my derivation above is new to the literature. This result is of profound significance for inductive reasoning, as it is useful for quantifying the degree of confidence with which we may employ probabilistic *modus tollens* arguments in any context.

For an example of the QLMT, let A represent "the moon is made of cheese", and B represent "A is scientifically established as highly probable". William Dembski claims that a hypothesis such as A can be rejected without consideration of possible alternative hypotheses.[5] I submit that implicit in this claim is the QLMT. Since P(B|A) is high and P(~B) is high, it follows that P(~A) is high. More specifically, since both P(B|A) and P(~B) may be conservatively approximated as at least 0.99, we may use (57) to immediately infer P(~A) ≥ 0.99. Explicit consideration of alternative theories of lunar composition is not required in this reasoning, and we may, thus, reject the exclusively comparative conception of evidence embraced by Sober.[6]

The QLMT is, therefore, an inference form which establishes that if the probability is likely that we make observations contrary to expected observations conditional upon some theory, then the theory is, itself, improbable. Although a theory is not necessarily rendered improbable due to specific observations unlikely on the theory, a theory is rendered improbable if likely observational evidence is unlikely on the theory. Thus, consideration of the degree of compatibility of likely observational evidence with a theory may be sufficient to establish the improbability of that theory, even if no comparison to alternative theories is considered. Rejection of the exclusively comparative conception of evidence is in order.

Response to Elliott Sober

Counterexamples provided by Elliott Sober are not relevant to the QLMT. Consider the "seven of hearts" example.[7] Here, we may let A represent a normal deck with a random draw, and B represent not drawing a seven of hearts. Sober is right that ~B does not entail ~A is likely, even given that $P(B|A)$ is high. However, the QLMT applies to cases in which $P(B)$ is less than 0.5 (see (48)), whereas $P(B)$ is not known to be less than 0.5 in the present example. Therefore, although we may grant that this example is sufficient to counter the claim that (6) necessarily follows from (4) and (5), it does not establish that (49) does not follow from (47) and (48). Yes, (49) does not follow from (47) and (48) in this example, since (48) is not known. This fact is not a valid counterexample to QLMT, however, since my inference applies when (48) is known.

The "seven of hearts" example is also not relevant to QTMT. We know that $P(B|A) = k = 51/52$, and we know that $J = 1$, since ~B is assumed to be known with certainty. However, since $P(B)$ is not known to be small, we do not know (41) is true. Again, we see that this is not a valid counterexample.

Likewise, Sober's "roulette wheel" counterexample[8] is not applicable to QTMT or QLMT. Let Z denote the probability that precisely 100 double-zero outcomes would occur in 3800 spins of the wheel. It is true that the small value of Z does not justify rejection of the theoretical considerations T that are used to evaluate Z. Nevertheless, this consideration is not applicable to QTMT or QLMT for the simple reason that Z is small, whereas this probability would need to be large so as to be pertinent to a probabilistic *modus tollens* formulation of an argument against the likelihood of T. My formulation assumes condition (41) or (48) is satisfied, whereas these are not known to be satisfied in the present example.

Sober has more recently affirmed his rejection of some versions of a probabilistic *modus tollens* inference form.[9] He also acknowledges (without dispute) the existence of Wagner's theorem[10] and, by implication, he may be taken to have acknowledged the existence of the QLMT. Unfortunately, he fails to appreciate (as shown above in the discussion of the cheese-moon hypothesis) that the QLMT may be used to refute his thesis that proper (inductive) hypothesis testing must be contrastive.[11] Also, he fails to address the critical role that QLMT-structured inferences may play in the ID debate, as detailed in the following section.

QLMT and Teleology

Now I shall demonstrate how probabilistic *modus tollens* reasoning may be used in the context of the results of investigations by some ID proponents. I begin with the investigation by Hugh Ross, where the probability of finding a planet which could support carbon-based life is examined.[12] Let N represent naturalism, defined as the hypothesis that the laws M of physics are the impersonal causal explanation of the set Q of physical events, where M represents the set of all presently known laws of physics, and where Q represents the set of all physical events presently known to be described by any member of M. C represents the set of all physical conditions[13] necessary for the naturalistic origin of a planet on which L is true, where L represents the hypothesis "physical Earth-like life exists". Let A represent the conjunction "N and $(C \in Q)$", and let B represent "$P((C \in Q)|N) \approx 1$". The QLMT argument form may be used to argue as follows:

(58) $P(B|A) = k$
(59) $P(\sim B) = m$
(60) $P(\sim A) = i$

Premise (58) is true, and k may be conservatively estimated at $k \approx 0.9$. Premise (59) is the critical probability calculation that is provided by Hugh Ross,[14] where $m \approx 1 - 10^{-144}$. Then, the formula in (57) may be used to establish that $i \approx 1$, which entails either N is unlikely or $C \in Q$ is unlikely, and this result is a key component of an argument in favor of ID (see Chapter 2).

The QLMT may also be used to express Michael Behe's argument for ID at the level of cellular protein-protein binding sites.[15] Let A represent "Known Darwinian evolutionary mechanisms are known to be a necessary condition of any cellular structures S that require a total of more than two different kinds of proteins at protein-protein binding sites". Let B represent "The probability is approximately 10^{-40} that there exist a total of more than two different kinds of proteins at protein-protein binding sites in S." The symbolic representation in premises (58), (59), and (60) might again be used, here representing Behe's argument that known Darwinian explanations of S are highly implausible. The evidence one may offer in support of (59) is the observation that it is very likely the case that S exists. Then, (60) is the conclusion that it is very likely that A is false, and this conclusion may function as an important component of an argument in favor of ID.

We may also structure Behe's argument using Q, M, N, and S as defined above. We may let A represent the conjunction "N and (S ϵ Q)", and let B represent "P((S ϵ Q)|N) $\approx$ 1". Premise (58) is then true, and k may be conservatively estimated as k $\approx$ 0.9. Premise (59) is the critical probability calculation provided by Behe, where m $\approx$ 1 – 10^{-40}. Then, the formula in (57) may be used to establish that i $\approx$ 1, which entails either N is unlikely or S ϵ Q is unlikely, and this result is a key component of an argument in favor of ID.

William Dembski's ID argument may also be recast into a QLMT argument form using (58), (59), and (60). Dembski has argued that instances of complex specified information (CSI) are generated only by intelligent agents.[16] The QLMT could be employed in Dembki's argument structure designed to filter physical events with a natural cause from intelligently designed physical events. Here, use Q, M, and N as defined earlier, and let R represent structures (e.g., the bacterial flagellum) manifesting CSI. Let A represent the conjunction "N and (R ϵ Q)", and let B represent "P((R ϵ Q)|N) $\approx$ 1". Premise (58) is then true, and k may be conservatively approximated as k $\approx$ 0.9. Premise (59) is inferred from the vanishingly small probability (as calculated by Dembski) that known physical laws describe impersonal CSI-generating instances; thus m $\approx$ 1. It follows that (57) may be used to establish that i $\approx$ 1 in (60), which entails either N is unlikely or R ϵ Q is unlikely, and this result is a key component of an argument in favor of ID.

Response to Jordan Howard Sobel

Sobel provides a critique of a QLMT ID argument of the form (58), (59), (60), where A represents "Pure Chance", and where B represents "~AsIfFineTuned".[17] It should be apparent that my use of QLMT ID arguments does not assume this structure, as my "A" and "B" represent considerably different quantities than Sobel considers. Even if Sobel's critique were sound, it would not be applicable to my ID arguments.

Sobel argues that a 'rigidity condition' must be satisfied in order for a person to properly update one's belief states in accordance with a QLMT argument structure. In my ID arguments, the ridigity condition is satisfied for a person P if and only if (58) is true both before and after discovery of (59) such that there is at most a negligible change in the value of k for P by virtue of that discovery. To refute my QLMT-formulated ID arguments, Sobel would need to show that (58) does not remain true after discovery of evidence that (59) is true, thereby establishing that the 'rigidity condition' is not satisfied. That is, he may be interpreted to maintain that if one's discovery of (59) leads to one's rejection of (58), then (60) does not follow for that person as specified in (57).

In my ID arguments, it is of critical importance to note the *satisfaction* of the rigidity requirement that (58) remain unchanged even after knowledge of (59) is acquired. This requirement is satisfied in my representation of the positions of Ross, Behe, and Dembski. For example, in the Ross case, (58) remains unchanged even after knowledge of (59) is acquired, where A represents the conjunction "N and (C ∈ Q)", and B represents "P((C ∈ Q)|N) ≈ 1. Indeed, it is difficult to imagine how (58) could be false (regardless of one's perception of the value of m in (59)), since (58) is apparently necessary in this case.

Sobel's concern that rigidity may not be maintained, given that one may perceive that non-human intelligent interventions are "all but incredible as he cogitates the who's, and especially the how's of these interventions,"[18] reveals an apparent confusion between the mere identification of intelligently designed entities and the fuller identification of the nature of the designer. We may detect design, yet know precious little regarding the identity or nature of the designer.

The presupposition that intelligent design may be detected only if the fuller identity or nature of the designer is also understood is a knowledge-stifling and needless requirement in scientific discovery. One could hypothetically envision Sobel's discovery of himself appearing before the Divine Judgement Seat and cogitating, "This can't be happening...I simply can't understand how a God could exist and judge me; therefore, I must reject this evidence of supernatural reality in favor of some naturalistic alternative." Clearly, we must not resist new discoveries on the grounds that we don't understand the details of processes relevant to them. There is no good reason to suppose that if some physical features of reality are known to be intelligently designed, then Sobel (or any of us) should understand much at all of the "who's and the how's" of those designed interventions. Therefore, Sobel's ignorance of the "who's and the how's" of those designed interventions does not justify rejection of such interventions as improbable on the grounds that he is so ignorant, given my QLMT-formulated ID arguments. We may postulate a cause of observed phenomena even if we know virtually nothing regarding the nature of that cause, save the fact that the cause caused the observed phenomena. We may adduce inductive support for "all ravens are caused to be black", even if we have little or no clue as to how or why some unknown process leads (via intelligent agency or not) to the causal production of black ravens. We may postulate "the sun shines", regardless of whether we have any particular understanding of how it shines, why it shines, or who may (or may not) cause it to shine.

We may disregard Sobel's Bayesian updating procedure in the context of the ID debate.[19] For example, consider the set Gp of possibly existing gods. The prior probabilities in the Bayesian updating formula either account for possible actions of members of Gp, or they do not. If so, then no justification has been given for beliefs regarding the likely actions of members of Gp. If not, then the priors are not justified, since relevant theories remain unconsidered in the computation of the priors. Either way, explicit justification of priors is not provided.

Furthermore, the guessing probability (principle of indifference) of 0.5 might be applied to members of Gp whose likely actions are unknown. In this case, then, the computation of priors is based on a potentially devastatingly large measure of guesswork, and the resultant Bayesian update is evidently not helpful, since it is not shown to be determined from sufficiently precise computations.

Granted, the expanded form of Bayes' theorem shown by Sobel provides a correct relationship between the various quantities in the formula. The problem is that in practice, the quantities are not always easily determined (or reasonably possible to determine). In addition to the problem of the priors mentioned above, how can we justify P(AsIfFineTuned|~Chance)? This calculation also appears difficult to assess, since insufficient evidence is available to justify beliefs regarding likely actions of members of Gp. This consideration serves to further emphasize the limited utility of Bayesian updating as depicted by Sobel. Fortunately, one need not rely on such an updating procedure. Rather, one could, for example, simply apply the QLMT or a probabilized version of *modus ponens* to newly acquired evidence. Updating via Bayes' theorem is not a necessary condition of one's acceptance of QLMT-formulated (or of probabilized *modus ponens*-formulated) inductive arguments.

To his credit, Sobel is at least aware of the strong potential for the use of the QLMT in support of ID. So far as I know, this potential has not yet become generally well known.

Summary

It is not my position here to defend Ross, Behe, and Dembski in all details of their arguments. However, given the key results of their investigations, the logical structure of the QLMT may be used to justify a critical premise in an ID argument, and there remains, then, only the task of identifying the rational status of the ID hypothesis by using an explanatory filter to verify the superiority of ID against all possible alternative explanations. I have, thus, justified a logical structure that may be defended against critics of probabilistic *modus tollens* reasoning in the context of the ID debate.

NOTES

1. Sober, Elliott (2002). *Intelligent Design and Probability Reasoning.* International Journal for Philosophy of Religion, v. 52, pp. 65-80.

2. Jeffrey, Richard C. (1983). *The Logic of Decision.* Chicago: University of Chicago Press, Chapter 11.

3. Stone, David Reuben (2007). *Atheism is False: Richard Dawkins and the Improbability of God Delusion.* Morrisville, NC: Lulu Press, pp. 48-50. A correction to the argument, there, is that "k – 1" be replaced by "1 – k" on p. 49:5. I apologize for the typo.

4. Wagner, Carl G. (2004). *Modus Tollens Probabilized.* British Journal for the Philosophy of Science, v. 55, pp. 747-753. See Wagner's equation (9) in Theorem 1 of section 3.3.

5. Dembski, William A. (2002). *No Free Lunch: Why Specified Complexity Cannot Be Purchased Without Intelligence.* Lanham, MD: Rowman & Littlefield Publishers, Inc., pp. 101-102.

6. Sober (2002).

7. Ibid., p. 67:25-29.

8. Ibid., p. 69:10-23.

9. Sober, Elliott (2008). *Evidence and Evolution: The Logic Behind the Science.* Cambridge: Cambridge University Press, pp. 48-58.

10. Ibid., p. 53, footnote 30.

11. Ibid., p. 52:20-24.

12. Ross, Hugh (2001). *The Creator and the Cosmos: How the Latest Scientific Discoveries of the Century Reveal God.* Colorado Springs, CO: Navpress, 3rd edition, pp. 175-199.

13. Ross, Hugh (2008). Why The Universe Is The Way It Is. Grand Rapids, MI: Baker. On pages 213-214, Appendix C cites several hundred relevant physical conditions.

14. Ross (2001).

15. Behe, Michael (2007). *The Edge of Evolution: The Search for the Limits of Darwinism.* New York: Free Press, p. 146.

16. Dembski (2002).

17. Sobel, Jordan Howard (2009). *Modus Ponens and Modus Tollens for Conditional Probabilities, and Updating on Uncertain Evidence.* Theory and Decision, v. 66, pp. 139-141.

18. Ibid., p. 140.

19. Ibid., p. 141.

CHAPTER 2

Theism and Explanatory Filtration

Abstract: *I have previously published both a theistic argument from the laws of physics (AFTLOP)[1] and a set of theistic fine-tuning design arguments.[2] In both arguments, the theistic inference is established in the context of an elimination of alternative possible explanatory hypotheses. The identification of an explanatory filtration procedure is an essential task in my theistic arguments, and is first clarified and published here.[3] These arguments are then conjoined to formulate the basis for my agent-caused physical occasionalism (ACPO) theistic metaphysics.*

Given some physical event P, there exist the following possible knowledge claims regarding P:

(1)   It is known that P has an impersonal causal explanation in terms of a law of physics.

(2)   It is known that P has an impersonal causal explanation in terms of no law of physics.

(3)   It is known that P has an impersonal acausal explanation.

(4)   It is known that P has a personal causal explanation.

(5)   It is known that none of the above four explanations is likely both best and good.

These five mutually exclusive possibilities represent the live explanatory options available for P. I define "V causes W" as "V generates (produces, makes, brings about that) W". So, it follows from my definition of "cause" that a cause makes an effect happen.

The AFTLOP

In my AFTLOP I argue that (4) is always the best explanation of P. Given this conclusion, we may note that since most physical events are not caused by human persons, it quickly follows that most physical events are caused by a non-human person(s) whose power and knowledge far exceed that of man, where this non-human person(s) may be referred to as "God". In this manner, theism may be simply and swiftly established.

The reasoning in my AFTLOP is somewhat lengthy and detailed, and I will not repeat all of it here. Its essential core, however, may be expressed as follows:

(6)   P is a physical event.
(7)   All physical events are caused by persons.
(8)   Therefore, P is caused by a person.

In my terminology, "person" and "agent" are synonymous; I define "person" as an entity with beliefs and desires. I mention (6), (7), and (8) here for the purpose of providing a distilled presentation of the argument; this may be useful for less philosophically sophisticated audiences. In fact, justification of (7) comprises a significant portion of the AFTLOP, and the reader is referred to the material in my previous publication on this topic.[4] What follows is a brief overview of some key considerations which help provide inductive support for (7).

Let CP represent "All physical events are caused by persons." Either the probability $P(CP)$ is determined or undetermined. But, it is undetermined only if no available evidence confers a probability on CP. In fact, available evidence confers a probability on CP (see below). Therefore, $P(CP)$ is not undetermined.

If $P(CP) < 0.1$, then we have evidence that ~CP. However, it is unlikely that we have evidence that ~CP (see below). Thus, it is unlikely that $P(CP) < 0.1$.

So, minimally, $P(CP) > 0.1$. In fact, $P(CP) > y$, if the following obtain:

(A)   The number of known CP-confirming events is large and increasing.
(B)   No consideration is known to be sufficiently CP-disconfirming to the extent that it is false that $P(CP) > y$.
(C)   Given (A) and (B), for every case in which a cause of a physical event is identified, the cause is known to be a person. Thus, absent sufficient evidence to the contrary,

we infer (inductively) that all physical events are likely caused by persons.

(D)   Further examination of possible CP-disconfirming reasons reveals that such reasons are not known to be sufficiently CP-disconfirming to the extent that it is false that $P(CP) > y$.

I define y to be the critical probability threshold such that individual J knows proposition x if and only if J experiences the belief B that x, where J perceives that the probability $P(B$ is a true belief$) > y$. As a matter of practical approximation, I generally assume $y \approx 0.9$.[5]

Support for (A) comes from a number of considerations. First, I am a person with the power to initiate event sequences which result in the causation of physical events. Also, many other (and presumably the vast majority of) persons throughout the world presently possess this same power, and this measure of power may be reasonably said to be possessed by persons who have lived throughout human history. The number of physical events caused by persons in this sense is, thus, large and increasing. Clearly, there is known to be a very large total number of such caused physical events, and we may conservatively assume this number exceeds 10^{15}.

Next, note the nature of physical events described by physical laws. Most known physical events are described by physical laws, and the number of physical events known to be described by physical laws is increasing. To the extent that one is inclined to accept that it is intuitively plausible that uncaused physical events would likely be patternless (and, thus, be unable to be described in terms of physical laws), one may infer that the physical laws (patterns) that describe most physical events constitute evidence that the physical events described by those laws are not uncaused. So, since physical events described by physical laws are likely caused, it is confirmed that physical events described by physical laws are likely caused by persons; it is of critical importance to note how this inference is considerably strengthened when taken in conjunction with the support for (B), (C), and (D). Even if one is inclined to take the position that uncaused physical events are not known to be likely patternless (perhaps on the grounds that since no uncaused physical events are known to exist, there are no available observations from which we may experimentally infer the properties of uncaused physical events), the force of my AFTLOP remains, as the nature of human-caused events is a sufficient body of data to justify (A). Thus, even if all possibly existing uncaused physical events are not known to be likely patternless, (A) remains justified.

Support for (B) includes the key consideration that there is no evidence that any caused event is caused by anything other than the free exercise of a person's power. It is logically possible that some caused events are not caused by the free exercise of a person's power, but this logically possibility constitutes only a negligible measure of disconfirmation of CP, and this possibility is not sufficient to establish that it is false that P(CP) > y. Some other possible objections to (B) will be examined in the discussion of support for (D) below.

Support for (C) comes from (A), (B), and the support already provided for (A) and (B). Also, the inductive inference to the claim that all physical events are known to be caused by persons is further strengthened by virtue of the absence of sufficient evidence to the contrary, and also by the support for (D) provided below. In addition, the uniformitarian assumption in science may be interpreted such that local properties of physical conditions are also possessed by nonlocal such physical conditions, further confirming that *all* physical events throughout the universe are caused by persons (given the absence of sufficient evidence to the contrary), not merely those physical events, in the vicinity of Earth, whose cause is identified to be personal.

Support for (D) may come from the blocking of anticipated attempts to provide compelling, substantive instances of CP-disconfirmation. For example, one could imagine a naturalist appealing to the great scientific accomplishment of the identification of physical laws that describe an immense body of physical data ranging from galactic-scale cosmological processes to quantum processes. The naturalist could take this accomplishment as evidence that, in fact, every instance in which a physical law L describes a physical event E, E is causally explained in terms of the impersonal L without need of personal agency in that causal explanation. In response to this objection, it must be emphasized that the mere identification that L incorporates E into an observed physical event pattern is insufficient as a causal explanation. "L describes E" does not entail "L causes E". Physical laws are descriptive, and the attribution of causal powers to physical laws is a huge metaphysical claim in need of support, yet none is available.[6] Therefore, the well known success of science in recent human history indeed provides strong support for the claim that the scientific community has identified a very large number of classes of physical events which can be understood as manifesting physical event patterns (i.e., physical laws), but the mere identification of such patterns, in and of itself, does nothing to support the claim that the causal origin of instantiations of physical laws is those very laws themselves. In short, physical laws *describe*, not *cause*. Therefore, appeal to physical laws provides no causal explanation of physical events described by those laws. The widespread descriptive success of modern science does not disconfirm CP.

One could object to (D) by assuming that many physical events (whether described by any known or unknown physical law or not) cause subsequent physical events. For example, it could be claimed that physical precipitation (e.g., rainfall) is an impersonal cause of the erosion of mountains. In response, physical precipitation is indeed correlated with mountainous erosion, but "A is correlated with B" does not imply "A is the cause of B", since G could be the cause of the correlation between A and B such that G is always the cause of both A and B, while A is never the cause of B, and B is never the cause of A. Therefore, we must reject this widespread (yet unjustified) metaphysical claim that physical events possess causal powers. In fact, in science, we merely observe physical event patterns, but we do not directly observe physical events *causing* physical events, nor do we have indirect evidence that any physical event is caused by a physical event. CP is thus not disconfirmed by this objection.

One might object to (D) by claiming that my inductive support for CP is an instance of the Hasty Generalization Fallacy, where the untested portion of a sample is wrongly presumed to possess the same properties as the tested portion. In response, this fallacy can be known to apply only if there exists sufficient evidence that the untested portion of a sample is unlikely to possess the same properties as the tested portion. In the context of my case for CP, we may assert that my claim "physical events not caused by human persons are caused by non-human persons" is an instance of the Hasty Generalization Fallacy only if there exists sufficient evidence R that there are not non-human personal causes of physical events not caused by humans. The problem with this objection is that anticipated alleged examples of R do not actually qualify as examples of R. For example, the claim could be made that an example of R is that there exists no independent evidence in support of any such non-human personal causal agents. In response, one need not possess independent evidence of x as a necessary precondition of making an inductive inference to the existence of x. For another example, the claim could be made that an example of R is that it is implausible (in terms of presently understood physical laws) that a non-human personal cause of most physical events could exist. In response, this objection carries with it the presumption that if there is a non-human personal cause of most physical events, then that cause must be plausibly explained in terms of presently understood physical laws; this objection is unjustified not only because explicit justification is not provided (nor is it available), but also because my inductive support for CP is, itself, evidence that the objection is unfounded. This objection should also be rejected due to its obviously question-begging unacceptable implication that, more generally, newly hypothesized entities may be invoked only if those entities are already known to be explained in terms of known physical laws.

One might object to (D) by appealing, in part, to Michael Martin's atheistic teleological Argument from Embodiedness.[7] In this argument, Martin uses the theistic supposition that the (physical) universe is a created entity, together with additional considerations, to inductively infer that the universe was created by one or more beings with (physical) bodies. Given the implausibility of self-causation, one could envision an atheist subsequently rejecting the claim that a being with a physical body could be the cause of the physical universe, since such a being could not be the cause of itself. Thus, an atheist could, in turn, infer that the theistic supposition is false that the physical universe is a created entity, disconfirming CP.

In response to this anticipated objection to (D), an inductive inference from a tested portion of a sample to an untested portion of a sample should proceed so as to be minimally restrictive in its conclusion, absent evidence that additional restrictions are likely to lessen the probability that the conclusion would be false. Granted, an inductive inference that asserts less (i.e., is more restrictive) is known to be less likely false, if it is known that a less restrictive inference would be more likely false. However, if it is unknown whether a less restrictive inference would be more likely false, then limiting inductive inferences to more restrictive conclusions unjustifiably presumes it is known that less restrictive inferences are more likely false. So, Martin's inductive inference I1, "The universe was created by one or more beings with bodies", is more restrictive than the inductive inference I2, "The universe was created by one or more beings". Furthermore, Martin fails to appeal to any background knowledge which entails that the more restrictive I1 should be favored over I2 for the purpose of lessening the probability that the inductive inference yield a false conclusion. Thus, we may reject Martin's I1 in favor of I2, since I2 is least restrictive, not imposing unjustified constraints on the probable nature of the creator of the universe, given the supposition that the universe is a created entity. But now, favoring I2 over I1, we no longer face the problem of implausible self-causation, since the creator of the physical universe need not be unjustifiably presumed to be a being with a physical body, but is simply inferred to be a being, period. A being could create the universe, yet not be part of the universe. The basis for rejecting the theistic supposition that the physical universe is a created entity is hence eliminated. In turn, we find that Martin's corrected inductive inference I2 leads to the conclusion that if the physical universe is a caused (created) entity, then it is probably created by a being (person). Since the physical universe is described by physical laws that describe physical events that are likely caused (from (A) and the uniformitarian assumption), it then follows that the physical universe is likely caused (created) by a person. In this manner, I2 confirms CP. Martin's Argument from Embodiedness, properly reformulated to be minimally restrictive, turns out to support CP, given the above considerations.

One might object to (D) by claiming that there exist uncaused events (e.g., quantum events). In fact, John W. Loftus apparently assumes[8] that David Ramsay Steele's unjustified assertion in this regard[9] is correct, yet fails (along with Steele) to account for causally determinist theories of quantum mechanics which even an atheist may accept.[10] The problem, here, is the lack of justification for making the inference from "Physical event F has no known impersonal physical cause" to "F is uncaused". Some people (including, frequently, naturalism-minded scientists) assume that physical events presently causally explained in terms of no known law of physics are likely to be causally explained (in the future) in terms of a physical law not presently known. Given this assumption, such people should reject the above inference to "F is uncaused", thereby eliminating these grounds for maintaining that CP is disconfirmed by the existence of allegedly uncaused physical events. Some people assume that the non-deterministic (probabilistic) nature of some physical laws (e.g., quantum laws of physics) implies those laws describe uncaused physical events. This assumption may be rejected, however, since it entails that we accept the unjustified claim that a person can not be (or probably is not) the determining cause of events described by probabilistic physical laws. Thus, probabilistic laws in quantum physics (or in any other discipline in the physical sciences) do not disconfirm CP by virtue of an apparently probabilistic nature.

One could conceivably object to (D) on the grounds that the exercise of human free will exemplifies instances of uncaused physical events, where person J freely causes E if and only if J's causing E is uncaused. In response, human free will exemplifies instances of uncaused physical events only if the exercise of human free will is, itself, a physical event. We need not assume, however, that J's free choice to raise her hand is an instance in which the raising of J's hand is an uncaused physical event, since the raising of J's hand (a physical event) may be viewed as the effect of J's exercise of free will (a nonphysical event). (Or, perhaps, God freely causes the raising of J's hand in response to J's free choice to raise it, but I won't argue for this possibility here, even though some versions of occasionalism might entail such implications as this.) Therefore, we need not accept that human free will disconfirms CP.

We have no known instances in which a physical event has an impersonal cause, and we have no known instances in which a physical event is uncaused. Given my support for (A), (B), (C), and (D), it follows that P(CP) > y. Thus, we know CP and we know (7). We may then infer that (4) is, in general, the best explanation of P, and a very good explanation indeed, since it is much more probable than any known rival explanation. Since most physical events are not human-caused, it follows that most physical events are caused by a non-human person(s). The non-human personal cause of most physical events clearly possesses power and knowledge much greater than that of man. Therefore,

God exists, where God is identified as that non-human personal cause. In this manner, the AFTLOP may be used in conjunction with my explanatory filtration procedure to confirm theism.

Ravens, CP, and Enumerative Induction

The case for CP may be expressed in terms of the logic of enumerative induction. To illustrate the nature of such reasoning, consider the set of all Earthly ravens now living. It is commonly accepted that all such ravens (or at least, all non-albino ravens) are black, yet it is also likely that no human has observed all ravens now living. How, then, can we be confident that all ravens are black? Clearly, a deductive proof is not available to me (since I am not presently observing all ravens), and, if someone else claimed to be presently observing all ravens, I could reasonably dismiss such a claim as delusional. In other words, I can mount a convincing case that all ravens are black, but I don't seem to have absolute certainty that my position is correct. Nevertheless, I maintain that it is likely that all ravens are black, and such a claim must be grounded not in certain deductive logic, but in uncertain (though not utterly arbitrarily construed) inductive logic. How, then, shall we structure our reasoning?

Enter enumerative induction. First, Let R denote the claim "All ravens are black", and let us disregard exceptions (of presumably negligible significance) to this position such as albino ravens, variously colored spray-painted ravens, green ravens (sick from excessive consumption of fries accidentally dropped on grounds near play structures at fast-food restaurants), genetically altered fluorescent ravens, etc. A good inductive argument will conclude that R is likely. Such an argument need not conclude that R is certain. It would appear that our degree of confidence in R should be a function of the number of observed ravens known to black. In particular, as the number of observed black ravens increases, our confidence in R would be expected to increase, provided no other considerations arise to defeat our inductive reasoning in conjunction with those observations. In addition, if no non-black ravens are observed, then our confidence in R would be even further strengthened, provided (again) that no other R-defeating considerations have arisen.

Even without a formula equating our degree of confidence with the various relevant parameters, it seems intuitively evident that a large (say, n > 1000) observed sample size with all black (and no non-black) ravens would provide a great deal of inductive support for R. As n approaches, say, 10,000 or more, our inductive support strengthens even much more firmly, provided no counterbalancing considerations are available to significantly oppose this reasoning. Thus, we may infer (inductively) that R is likely true, even absent a formula that quantifies the degree to which R is likely true. Reasonable and rational persons use enumerative inductive inferences in their lives, I submit, routinely and almost unconsciously and automatically.

To formalize, somewhat, an enumerative inductive logical structure, we may assert that it is likely that all members of the set X of K-type entities have property P, if the following conditions are satisfied:

EI_1:   The number of members of X observed to have property P is large.

EI_2:   No member of X is observed to not have property P.

EI_3:   There is no good reason to suppose any unobserved member of X does not have property P.

In support of the black ravens inference, K denotes ravens, X is the name of the set of all ravens, and P represents being black. Thus, it is likely that all ravens are black.

In support of the CP inference (recalling the considerations detailed in my AFTLOP), K denotes physical events, X is the name of the set of all physical events, and P represents being person-caused. Thus, it is likely that all physical events are person-caused.

I presume that R is not controversial. So, those who wish to object to this argument for CP must identify a logical structure which can be used to support R, but not CP. It's not sufficient to merely identify an alleged counter-example to my logical structure. Rather, critics must find a structure (or set of conditions) leading to R (but not CP), and which is not grounded in prior unjustified considerations which beg the question in favor of the anti-CP position.

As clear as my argument appears to be, it would be helpful to find a way to quantify the probability (i.e., our personal expectation of the belief) that all members of X (observed or not) have property P in a proportion that is approximated by Z, given that we have observed only a subset of the members of X, where the proportion of observed members of X with property P is defined as (and approximated by) Z. James Hawthorne's presentation of the Simple Estimation Theorem[11] may be used to measure the degree to which we may confidently assert that the proportion of observed members of X with property P approximately corresponds to the actual proportion of all members of X with property P. He argues that so long as it is not very highly likely (prior to consideration of the properties of observed members of X) that the proportion of all members of X with property P is approximately Z, then the observation of a large number (in quantifiable terms) of observed members of X manifesting property P in a proportion approximated by Z renders likely (in quantifiable terms) the inference that all members of X manifest property P in a proportion approximated by Z. Indeed, so long as one's prior probability is not exceedingly strongly oppositional, and so long as we have no reason to suppose that our observations are not non-randomly selected so as to bias the observed proportion of members of X with property P with a significant measure of deviation from the actual proportion of members of X with property P, we find that a surprisingly small (and quantifiable) number of observations of X renders likely our conclusion that Z approximates the proportion of members of X with property P. Given a conservative estimate of a trillion instances in which physical events are known to be observed to be person-caused, the reader is encouraged to supply the relevant parameters (including those which account for one's prior probabilities) in the formula expressing Hawthorne's lower probability bound to verify the high degree of confidence with which we may use this enumerative inductive inference to establish that CP is extremely highly likely.

The aforementioned technique leads to convergence upon the conclusion that CP is very likely, even in cases in which all informed inquirers might not initially agree upon an accepted prior probability that Z approximates the proportion of members of X with property P. If persons with distinct prior probabilities agree to set those prior probabilities aside for the purpose of investigating the path upon which this enumerative induction leads us from a mutually agreed upon neutral starting point, then the strength of a quantified measure of confidence could be even further amplified regarding the conclusion that Z approximates the proportion of members of X with property P.

So, just as all ravens are inferred to be likely black (even though we don't actually directly observe that all ravens are black), we likewise infer that all physical events are likely caused by persons (even though we don't actually directly observe that all physical events are caused by persons). It quickly follows that the human inability to cause most physical events entails the likely existence of a non-human personal cause of most physical events, and the term "God" seems as good as any for such a person(s), since this term is typically associated with a person whose power and knowledge far exceed that of man. Perhaps the author of Romans 1:20 had in mind some kind of inductive reasoning along these lines. God's power and knowledge are evident from what has been made.

The Fine-Tuning Design Argument

My theistic design argument is actually a set of fine-tuning arguments which may be used in conjunction with my explanatory filter to justify the theistic inference.[12] These arguments do not require that we begin with the assumption that all stages in the AFTLOP are sound. Rather, the strategy here is to begin with the (typically naturalistic) assumption that known physical laws describe physical events that have an impersonal cause, and then show this assumption entails the likely nonexistence of such a cause of specific physical conditions essential for the naturalistic origin of a planet on which Earth-like life exists. In this connection, following the use of the QLMT logical structure shown in Chapter 1, I use the results of the investigation by Hugh Ross I have there discussed[13] to establish that N is unlikely or C ϵ Q is unlikely. This result entails that (1) is a highly improbable explanation of physical event C, where C is represented by P. (In the discussion that follows, C is represented by P in (1), (2), (3), (4), and (5)).

Next, we observe that neither (2) nor (3) is true. This observation is further supported by just those stages in the AFTLOP which entail that each of (2) and (3) is an unlikely explanatory possibility in general.[14]

There remain (4) and (5) as available options. However, (5) can be true only if a subset of two or more of the first four options contains no clearly superior member. It is not the case that a subset of two or more of the first four options contains no clearly superior member, since each of (1), (2), and (3) has been rejected. Therefore, (5) may be rejected.

Thus, we infer (4) by default, and since human power and knowledge is incapable of producing events such as C, the exercise of power by a non-human person with much greater knowledge and power than humans must be the cause of C. Theism is hence confirmed.

Theism is yet further confirmed via consideration of the fact that the existence of conditions represented by C is a necessary, but not sufficient, condition of the naturalistic origin of Earth-like life on a planet in the universe. The significant improbability of a naturalistic origin of such life persists, even given C. Thus, even given C, the origin of life and its diversity on Earth further confirms theism, as my explanatory filtration procedure may again be used to isolate a personal being (far more powerful and knowledgeable than man) as the cause of that life.[15]

It is worth emphasizing that my fine-tuning design arguments are not grounded in a fallacious god-of-the-gaps form of reasoning in which the nonexistence of a scientific explanation of C in terms of known physical laws is the only consideration used to infer a theistic explanation of C. Rather, as shown above, my theistic design inference is established by an eliminative argument structure in which alternative possibilities are shown to be unlikely. In fact, appeal to an as-yet-unknown impersonal causal explanation of C in terms of an as-yet-unknown law-based physical pattern would exemplify a fallacious *naturalism-of-the-gaps* tactic. Naturalistic responses such as this are more fully explored in the following section.

The Naturalistic Response

Those inclined to embrace a hard-core acceptance of the existence of an impersonal causal natural explanation of C, despite my adduced evidence to the contrary, may be likely to reject my theistic design inference and insist that the naturalistic assumption (9) is true:

(9)   It is known that P (here, representing C) has an impersonal causal explanation in terms of an unknown law of physics.

The grounds for this insistence are likely to be that since future scientific discoveries can not be predicted, and since many scientific discoveries have provided physical law-based descriptions of events not so described prior to those discoveries, rejection of (1) is unjustifiably presumptuous and likely to hinder future scientific progress.

In response to this objection, it must be emphasized that rejection of (1) is grounded not in ignorance of unknown naturalistic explanations, but in the knowledge of the limitations on such explanations as entailed by probability estimates grounded in scientific *knowledge*, not ignorance. So, rejection of (1) is not unjustifiably presumptuous regarding possible future discoveries of naturalistic explanations, but is a justified response to the unlikelihood of such discoveries, given known naturalistic limitations on such explanations. Granted, the possibility of future unexpected discoveries is real, and the pursuit of such possible discoveries may be a useful component of a scientific research program designed to minimize hindrances to such discoveries.[16] Such possibilities, however, do not justify rejection of probabilities established by presently available knowledge. This may be shown by exposing the internally inconsistent consequence of assuming (1) is likely, when the probability of (1) is known to be unlikely:

(10)   Premise (1) is unlikely (from my fine-tuning arguments).
(11)   It is known that P has an impersonal causal explanation in terms of an unknown law of physics (from naturalistic assumption (9)).
(12)   Premise (1) is likely (from 11).

In other words, acceptance of (9) in the face of compelling evidence to the contrary is self-contradictory and simply unjustified, since (12) contradicts (10). The situation is even worse, however, for those who blindly hold on to the possibility that (9) could be true. Consider the following, where N represents "Known physical laws describe an impersonal causal explanation of all physical events known to be described by those laws":

(13) $P(\sim(1) \mid N) = k$
(14) $P((1)) = m$
(15) $P(\sim N) \geq (k + m - 1) / k$

Here, k is very close to one,[17] and may be conservatively estimated to be 0.99, and m = 0.9 can represent the blind assumption that (1) is known to be likely. Premise (15) follows from Premise (51) in Chapter 1, using my QLMT argument structure, and entails that $P(\sim N) \geq 0.9$. In this context, the more strongly one blindly assumes (1) is likely, the more strongly N is disconfirmed. Furthermore, the more strongly N is disconfirmed, the more confidently we may reject (1), where physical event P in (1) may represent any physical event known to be described by a physical law. In other words, acceptance of (1) in the face of my fine-tuning arguments (where physical event P is represented by C) leads to rejection of N, and this in turn opens wide the door to theism which naturalists so desperately seek to keep closed, since rejection of N entails rejection of any impersonal causal explanation of any physical event in terms of any physical law. In seeking to plug up a hole in the filter, blind-faith naturalists open wide a gaping chasm, where that chasm remains unexplained by their naturalism. Thus, such naturalists who adamantly insist upon accepting (1) via (9) are found to inadvertently support theism, since theism enjoys superior explanatory power in that it provides a justified personal causal explanation of what atheistic naturalism (given that blind faith) does not explain. In addition, if atheists must reject what is scientifically established in order to support their atheism, whereas theists find their theism confirmed by what is scientifically established, then clearly theism is the better explanation, given these considerations.

Furthermore, it is arbitrary and unjustified to reject my inference to (4) merely on the grounds that future scientific discoveries might establish (1) and thereby render (4) unlikely. After all, we could instead arbitrarily choose (without justification) to always reject any inference to (1) merely on the grounds that future scientific discoveries might always continue to disconfirm (1) and thereby continue to render (4) likely. So, the mere possibility of future unknown scientific discoveries does not justify rejection of what is established by presently known naturalistic limits to explanations in terms of physical laws.

In general, we may not reject "X is presently known to be likely" merely due to the logical possibility that "X will be known to be unlikely in the future", since this would require acceptance of a self-refuting principle R that would largely preclude knowledge, where R represents "we may reject that which is presently known to be likely, since it may be shown unlikely in the future". After all, if R is known to be likely, then we may reject R, since R may be shown unlikely in the future. The very act of accepting R leads to rejection of R, implying R is not true. Therefore, we may not reject what is known to be likely merely because it might, in the future, not be known to be likely.

The objection may be raised that it is true that many physical events not previously explained in terms of physical laws are now so explained, implying that physical events not presently so explained may be likely so explained in the future. In response, the AFTLOP entails that all such explanations are personal causal explanations, so atheists do not avoid a theistic inference by this objection. Also, even if one is unaware of the theistic implications of the AFTLOP, we may examine trends in scientific discovery to reveal that known physical laws are evidently persistently incapable of explaining such features of physical reality as: (a) the origin of conditions necessary (but insufficient) for life on Earth; (b) the origin of life on Earth; (c) the origin of the diversity of life on Earth; and (d) the continuing existence of physical reality in accordance with physical laws. Granted, many categories of physical events continue to be explained in terms of newly discovered physical laws, but the persistent explanatory failure of known physical laws can diffuse allegations of inductive support for the probable discovery of future explanatory success of presently unknown physical laws in these cases. Such allegations are further diffused by the improbability of unknown physical law-based explanations, as confirmed by the presently known improbability of such explanations in terms of presently known physical laws.

It is the fourth case that is most fundamental here, since a physical law describing (a), (b), and (c) would hardly help the case for atheism unless an atheistic explanation of (d) were also provided. Granted, there is a recent attempted atheistic explanation of some physical laws that is given by Victor Stenger,[18] but I have previously shown the failure of that attempt,[19] and so far as I know, Stenger has not yet responded to my position. Also, Quentin Smith has considered a non-theistic origin of some basic physical laws,[20] but his argument is grounded in the unjustified assumption that subsequent physical states are caused by prior physical states,[21] and the implications of the AFTLOP are not taken into account there.

Natural Theology

My explanatory filtration procedure may be used in conjunction with my fine-tuning design arguments and my AFTLOP, leading to the confirmation of theism. These arguments may be fused together, and a condensed expression of the key conceptual components follows, where E is defined as the set of all physical events not caused by earthly persons. I use the definitions of C, L, M, N, and Q given on page 23 in this brief statement of an instance of my natural theology:

(16) $P(\,(\,P(\,(\,C \in Q\,)\,|\,N\,) \approx 1\,)\,|\,(\,N \text{ and } (\,C \in Q\,)\,)\,) = k \approx 1$

(17) $P(\,\sim (\,P(\,(\,C \in Q\,)\,|\,N\,) \approx 1\,)\,) = m \approx 1 - 10^{-144}$

(18) $P(\,\sim (\,N \text{ and } (\,C \in Q\,)\,)\,) = i \geq (\,(\,k + m - 1\,)\,/\,k\,) \approx 1$

(19) $P(\,\sim N \text{ or } \sim (C \in Q)\,) \approx 1$

(20) $P(\,(\,C \in E\,) \text{ or } (\,Q \in E\,)\,) \approx 1$

(21) Given any member E_i of E, either E_i is the effect of a personal cause or E_i is not the effect of a personal cause.

(22) Examination of the explanatory options for E_i in the explanatory filtration procedure establishes that it is unlikely that E_i does not have a personal cause.

(23) It is likely that E_i has a personal cause.

(24) All members of E (including C or Q) are likely caused by a non-earthly person(s), where "God$_e$" is defined as that personal cause of the members of E.

(25) Since it is likely that E includes not only C or Q, but also all physical events described by all scientifically established physical laws not caused by earthly persons, God$_e$'s power and knowledge is evidently much greater than that of man, given the known inability of man to cause the members of E.

Here, (16), (17), and (18) exemplify the QLMT as discussed in Chapter 1. Premise (19) follows from (18), and immediately justifies rejection of any philosophical system (e.g., atheism) which entails (19) is likely false. The known human inability to cause any member of C or Q justifies (20), so long as C and Q are restricted to exclude human-caused physical phenomena. Premise (21) is clearly correct (even necessary). Premise (22) summarizes my contention regarding the implications of the nature of physical event causation. Premise (23) follows from (21) and (22), and may apply to any member of E; this consideration, taken together with (20), implies (24). Premise (25) identifies the great power and knowledge of God_e. Therefore we may conclude, with confidence, that theism is justified and atheism is false.

ACPO Metaphysics

The above fusion of my AFTLOP and fine-tuning arguments constitutes a case for agent-caused physical occasionalism (ACPO).[22] ACPO metaphysics consists of the following inductively supported key components:

(26)   Physical laws describe regular physical event patterns.
(27)   Fine-tuned physical events (e.g., C) are not described by physical laws.
(28)   Every physical event is agent-caused.
(29)   No non-agent possesses causal powers.
(30) God_e causes all physical events that are not caused by earthly agents.

Premise (26) simply follows from the definition of "physical laws". Premise (27) cites the improbability of a physical law-based description of conditions such as C, as shown in my fine-tuning teleological arguments above. Premise (28) is the critical component of the AFTLOP, where "agent" and "person" may be likewise defined as an entity with beliefs and desires. Premise (29) flatly opposes the widespread unjustified assumption (found in some writings of both theists and atheists) that impersonal, natural, physical causes exist. Premise (30) attributes all non-earthly causal activity in the physical world to God_e, thereby justifying theism.

A few objections to ACPO might conceivably be made. For example, since God_e is defined as the set of all non-earthly agents who cause all physical events that are not caused by earthly agents, God_e may be taken to include such possibly existing agents as angels, demons, and extra-terrestrials. God_e is not necessarily the traditional theistic God, since such is generally taken to be a worship-worthy personal agent whose power and knowledge are much greater than any possibly existing angels, demons, and extra-terrestrials. However, a considerably large subset of E consists of members that are caused by an agent(s) with power and knowledge *immensely* greater than human power and knowledge. It follows that evidence for a worship-worthy agent God$_w$ may be found within an appropriately identified subset of God$_c$, where God$_w$ is defined as the agent(s) whose power and knowledge are immensely greater than human power and knowledge. God$_w$ is taken to correspond much more closely to the personal agent generally associated with the traditional theistic God.

Granted, it has not been shown that God$_w$ possesses the omnipotent, omniscient, omnipresent, omnibenevolent properties often associated with theistic belief. This is no failure of my atheism-refuting ACPO metaphysics, however, as the further exploration of possible properties of God$_w$ may be reserved for investigations within the context of arguments for divinely revealed theology.

Recently, C. John Collins has argued against occasionalism primarily on Biblical exegetical grounds,[23] although he also argues philosophically (not exegetically) that "common sense" would require at least an initial disposition to reject a proposition such as (29).[24] However, since Biblical passages allegedly pertinent to questions regarding central tenets of an occasionalist metaphysics may be taken to be expressed in "ordinary language" (as even Collins concedes),[25] it follows that Collins' exegetical anti-occasionalist arguments fail to provide a Biblical basis for rejection of occasionalism. It is far from clear that we should interpret ancient common linguistic expressions as if they are intended to address the subtle nuanced considerations relevant to the occasionalist debate in modern philosophical theology. We may, therefore, dismiss his anti-occasionalist exegetical arguments, even if we are inclined to embrace (as I do) a "high view" of Biblical Scripture. Also, we may reject the claim that "common sense" justifies an initial disposition against (29), since such a disposition is grounded in nothing but the human observation of the perceived nature of physical event sequences which often occur in regular patterns (physical laws) as identified via scientific investigation. Human observation of physical laws does not disconfirm (29), as everything about the observed nature of those laws is happily consistent with (29). We observe physical changes; we do not observe any physical events exerting any causal powers. It follows that we may reject Collins' alleged "common sense" justification of an initial disposition against (29), especially given our inability to directly knowingly observe any counterexample to (29), even if one existed and were unknowingly observed.

Moreover, there is a Biblical passage that clearly provides a contrast between the divine causation of physical laws and the possession of causal powers by impersonal physical events described by physical laws. The passage is Jeremiah 14:22 from which we may infer that the skies do not cause physical law-based rain-producing events. Rather, it is God who causes such events. Thus, if Biblical exegetical arguments do not clearly address the contrast as in Jeremiah 14:22, then they may be considered to be an insufficiently clear basis for attempting to provide theological resolution of the debate regarding the occasionalist metaphysical thesis. On the other hand, the passage discussed here clearly addresses that contrast, and provides theological confirmation of the occasionalism I defend. Such confirmation may play a significant role in such noetic structures in which exegetical arguments of this nature are given significant epistemological value.

The objection could be raised that occasionalism is disconfirmed by its implausible implication that there exists no personal agency or identity through time.[26] In response, ACPO is immune to this objection, since (28) explicitly affirms the existence of agent-caused physical events, and since the key ACPO components do not imply personal identity through time is unlikely.

Graham Harman has argued that theistic occasionalism is less plausible than his non-theistic occasionalism.[27] Harman evidently rejects theistic occasionalism on the grounds that our ignorance of how God could "touch" other real objects renders such possible divine causes improbable.[28] In response, we can justify ACPO metaphysics, even if we do not have any detailed understanding of how divine causation of physical events actually operates. I can know the sun shines, regardless of whether I have any detailed understanding of how it is caused to shine. Also, since Harman does not account for the implications of the person-caused nature of physical events, his analysis does not even address the empirical-logical foundation upon which ACPO metaphysics is built. We may reject Harman's analysis, therefore, as it is not properly grounded in a correct understanding of the nature of physical event causation.

Summary

My AFTLOP and fine-tuning teleological arguments have been examined in the context of an explanatory filtration procedure designed to identify the *personal* nature of physical event causation in the physical world. These arguments have been fused into a case for ACPO metaphysics which constitutes a rational justification of natural theology.

NOTES

1. Stone, David Reuben (2007). *Atheism Is False: Richard Dawkins and the 'Improbability of God' Delusion.* Morrisville, NC: Lulu Press, Chapter 1.

2. Stone (2007), Chapter 2.

3. An explanatory filter (considerably different from mine presented here) is used in the ID arguments of William Dembski. See Dembski, William (1998). *The Design Inference: Eliminating Chance Through Small Probabilities.* Cambridge: Cambridge University Press, Chapter 2. See also Dembski, William (2002). *No Free Lunch: Why Specified Complexity Cannot Be Purchased Without Intelligence.* Lanham, MD: Rowman & Littlefield, Chapter 1.

4. Stone (2007), Chapter 1.

5. It follows that I reject the JTB (justified true belief) conception of knowledge, thereby avoiding the need to account for Gettier-type counterexamples in some sort of JTB+ conception.

6. Even atheist David Mills has discerned this point. See Mills, David (2006). *Atheist Universe.* Berkeley, CA: Ulysses Press, pp. 69-70, where Mills notes that physical laws describe the consistent behavior of the universe (p. 69:29-30), where it is absurd to presume those laws cause the outcomes they describe (p. 70:22-24).

7. Martin, Michael (1990). *Atheism: A Philosophical Justification.* Philadelphia: Temple University Press, pp. 322-324.

8. Loftus, John W. (2008). *Why I Became an Atheist: A Former Preacher Rejects Christianity.* Amherst, NY: Prometheus Books, p. 85:8-9.

9. Steele, David Ramsay (2008). *Atheism Explained: From Folly to Philosophy.* Chicago, IL: Open Court, p. 76. Steele evidently assumes that our ignorance of a deterministic physical law describing electron orbit shifts entails that such shifts are uncaused, but this assumption is unjustified, since it presupposes (without justification) that a person (e.g., God) is not the determining cause of such physical events. The fact that we may not presently know any physical law that determines all quantum phenomena does not entail the nonexistence of a physical law that determines all quantum phenomena, nor does it entail the nonexistence of a personal cause of the phenomena. I have the power to causally determine the occurrence of physical events such that no known physical law determines those caused physical events. Likewise, God could cause electron orbit shifts, even if we have no known deterministic physical law describing such shifts. Steele's inference to causeless physical events, therefore, is unjustified; so, too, is Loftus' unfortunate acceptance of this inference. As Bunge remarks, "Causality cannot consequently be defined in terms of predictability according to law....Ontological determinism is therefore consistent with epistemological probabilism..." See Bunge, Mario (2009). *Causality and Modern Science.* New Brunswick, NJ: Transaction Publishers, p. 330.

10. See Quentin Smith's comment regarding Bohm's interpretation of quantum mechanics in Martin, Michael, ed. (2007). *The Cambridge Companion to Atheism.* Cambridge: Cambridge University Press, p. 184. It is strange that Loftus does not refer to this idea, since he includes reference to this book in his bibliography on p. 423:48. Needless to say, Loftus has not justified acceptance of an interpretation of quantum mechanics in which uncaused physical events exist.

11. For details, please see Hawthorne, James, "Inductive Logic", *The Stanford Encyclopedia of Philosophy (Summer 2009 Edition)*, Edward N. Zalta (ed.), URL = <http://plato.stanford.edu/archives/sum2009/entries/logic-inductive/>, Section 4.

12. Stone (2007), Chapter 2.

13. See page 25 of the present volume.

14. Stone (2007), Chapter 1. See, also, the above support for (D).

15. For an argument for the superiority of a creation model of the origin of life and the origin of cellular chemistry, see Ross, Hugh and Rana, Fazale (2004). *Origins of Life: Biblical and Evolutionary Models Face Off.* Colorado Springs, CO: Navpress. See also Rana, Fazale (2008). *The Cell's Design: How Chemistry Reveals the Creator's Artistry.* Grand Rapids, MI: Baker.

16. Thus, it would not be prudent to say "God did it, so don't look for an explanation in terms of a physical law." Rather, we may say "God did it, so let's seek an explanation in terms of a physical law to better understand how God may have done it."

17. $k \approx 1 - 10^{-144}$. See Ross, Hugh (2001). *The Creator and the Cosmos: How the Latest Scientific Discoveries of the Century Reveal God.* Colorado Springs, CO: Navpress, 3rd edition, pp. 175-199.

18. Stenger, Victor (2006). *The Comprehensible Cosmos: Where Do The Laws of Physics Come From?* Amherst, NY: Prometheus Books.

19. Stone (2007), pp. 41-42.

20. Smith, Quentin in Martin (2007), pp. 191-192.

21. Ibid., p. 192:18-27.

22. During the past 1200 years, various forms of occasionalism (or occasionalism-confirming positions) have been defended. Noteworthy historical figures include Al-Ash'ari, Al-Ghazali, Louis de la Forge, Geraud de Cordemoy, Arnold Geulincx, Nicolas Malebranche, George Berkeley, Jonathan Edwards, Abraham Kuyper, and G.C. Berkouwer. For a discussion of some options within occasionalism, see Freddoso, Alfred J., "Medieval Aristotelianism and the Case Against Secondary Causation in Nature," in Morris, Thomas V. (1988). *Divine and Human Action: Essays in the Metaphysics of Theism.* Ithaca, NY: Cornell University Press, pp. 74-118. For an example of a recent critical introduction to an occasionalist position, see Edward Omar Moad's dissertation submitted to the University of Missouri in 2004 entitled "Prolegomena to an Occasionalist Metaphysics", accessible from the Internet at http://www.scribd.com/doc/7900343/Prolegomena-to-an-Occasionalist-Metaphysics, last accessed April 19, 2009. See also the occasionalist defense in McCann, H. J. and Kvanvig, J. L., "The Occasionalist Proselytizer: A Modified Catechism," in Tomberlin, James E. (1991). *Philosophical Perspectives, v. 5.* Atascadero, CA: Ridgeview Publishing Company, pp. 587-615.

23. Collins, C. John (2000). *The God of Miracles: An Exegetical Examination of God's Action in the World.* Wheaton, IL: Crossway Books.

24. Ibid., Chapter 4.

25. Ibid., p. 86.

26. Craig, William Lane and Moreland, J.P. (2003). *Philosophical Foundations for a Christian Worldview.* Downers Grove, IL: InterVarsity Press, p. 555.

27. Harman, Graham (2007). *On Vicarious Causation.* Collapse, v. 2, p. 187ff.

28. Ibid., p. 219.

CHAPTER 3

Evil and The Human Ignorance Principle

Abstract: *My AFTLOP and fine-tuning arguments establish the existence of an extremely powerful and knowledgeable person(s) whose moral nature is undetermined by those arguments. My theism is thus immune to a wide array of atheistic arguments grounded in the assumption that such a being would likely not permit the known nature of evil in the world. Even more importantly, given my theistic arguments, it follows that God's knowledge and power is immensely greater than that of man, and as such, we mere humans with such limited knowledge are simply in no position to determine, apart from divine revelation, what events God is likely to permit, even if God is maximally good and loving. Therefore, no amount of apparent or actual evil in the world renders improbable[1] the existence of a maximally good and loving God, since such a God must have good reasons for permitting the nature of existent evil, regardless of whether we may happen to grasp those reasons to some degree. Some possible reasons for God's permission of at least some evil are explored. Loftus' position on the problem of evil is critiqued in light of these considerations. Brief responses to Bart D. Ehrman and Graham R. Oppy are also provided.*

The relationship between our understanding of God and of the nature of evil hinges critically on the Human Ignorance Principle (HIP):

> HIP ≡ Humans are ignorant of the detailed nature of the decision procedures used by God to determine God's actions.

The HIP may be true, and is supported by the observation that God's power and knowledge is immensely greater than that of man, as entailed by my AFTLOP and fine-tuning arguments. Also, apart from law-based predictions grounded in knowledge of physics, we simply have no good reason to believe we can make predictions of actions God is likely to perform, unless divine revelation facilitates human knowledge of such predictions.[2]

Now, given the HIP, no instance of apparent or actual evil may be used by humans to formulate a compelling argument against the existence of a maximally good and loving God, since no basis exists for supposing human knowledge is sufficient to justify such an argument. Atheists often argue that the nature of existing evil renders the existence of a maximally good and loving God improbable, but the HIP entails that such arguments are unjustified, since atheists are incapable of establishing that their knowledge is sufficient to reject the HIP.

The objection may be raised that if God is maximally good and loving, then God would not permit the HIP to be true. In response to this objection, observe that it can be maintained only if the HIP is first assumed to be false. After all, if we do not know whether the HIP is true, then we surely do not know what actions God is likely to perform apart from any possible divine revelation or predictions based on physical laws. Also, we know no physical law that may be used to predict that a maximally good and loving God is unlikely to permit the HIP to be true. Therefore, even if we reject divine revelation claims that extend beyond the revelation acquired from physical laws, it follows that if we begin reasoning from the neutral position that it is unknown whether the HIP is true, then we may not object that a maximally good and loving God would not permit the HIP to be true, since this objection may be maintained only if we know the falsehood of the HIP enables us to acquire knowledge of the likelihood that God would permit the HIP to be false. The situation here is untenable, since those who claim "It is unlikely that God would permit the HIP to be true" seek to justify their rejection of the HIP by maintaining a claim which can be justified only by first assuming the HIP is false. It is a case of circular reasoning to seek to justify the rejection of a principle, where that rejection can be upheld only if the prior assumption is made that the principle is false. Therefore, we must not infer the HIP is unlikely on grounds which assume the HIP is unlikely. We must not reason: "I know the HIP is likely false, and this I know because the HIP is likely false."

I know that the nature of evil (as presently known by me) renders unlikely God's existence only if I know it is false that God's existence entails that such evil likely exists, and I know it is false that God's existence entails that such evil likely exists only if I know the HIP is false. But, since I don't know the HIP is false, I do not know it is false that God's existence entails that such evil likely exists. Since I do not know it is false that God's existence entails that such evil likely exists, I do not know that such evil renders unlikely God's existence.

My theistic arguments establish the existence of God independent of considerations (or implications) of the nature of existent evil.[3] Thus, no consideration of the nature of evil may be used to successfully argue against

God's existence. Furthermore, no amount of apparent or actual evil in the world renders improbable the existence of a maximally good and loving God, since such a God must have good reasons for permitting the nature of existent evil, regardless of whether the HIP precludes our ability to grasp those reasons to some degree.

In short: evil renders unlikely God's existence only if theism entails that the HIP is known to be likely false, but since theism does not entail that the HIP is known to be likely false, evil does not render unlikely God's existence.[4] This consideration is generally sufficient to refute atheistic arguments from evil, and this refutation stands firm even absent any known reason for which God may actually permit the nature of evil in the world. I have thus provided a defense of theism against the objection that the nature of evil renders theism unlikely.

I have not provided a theodicy (i.e., justification of God's permission of the existence of the nature of evil), and such justification is not necessary to maintain my defense of theism. Nevertheless, although the answer to the question "Why does God permit the nature of existing evil?" is not an essential component of a theistic defense, the exploration of possible answers may help shed light on the possible nature of divine action in this context.

Theists have offered many reasons as possibly significant considerations in the decision procedures used to determine God's actions.[5] Although such reasons may appear to provide at least a limited (and sometimes considerably large) degree of moral justification for God's permission of particular instances of evil, no such reason (so far as I know) appears to provide *indisputable* moral justification of all known instances of evil in general in the sense that I am capable of using my limited perception of the nature of moral reality to independently verify that God has acted morally appropriately in permitting all such evil instances. I do not know an indisputable detailed theodicy, but this fact in no way disconfirms theism, since the HIP is not known to be unlikely. Furthermore, since the HIP can evidently not (apart from divine revelation) be known to be unlikely, the fact that I do not know an indisputable theodicy can disconfirm neither theism nor the claim that such a theodicy exists.[6]

If a maximally good and loving God exists, then a successful theodicy exists, even if we don't know what it is. So, although our lack of knowledge of a successful theodicy may be taken as evidence against the existence of any possibly existing maximally good and loving god whose existence entails we would likely know a successful theodicy, this lack of knowledge is not evidence against the existence of any possibly existing maximally good and loving god whose existence does not entail we would likely know a successful theodicy.

Thus, the nature of evil is sufficient to trim down the set of possibly existing gods, but it is not sufficient to establish that that set is empty or likely empty.

Exploration of reasons which may be possibly significant considerations in divine decision procedures may help shed some light on the nature of any possibly existing successful theodicy. The first possible divine consideration I wish to examine here may be a significant moral consideration in God's decision procedures used to permit the truth of the HIP and to permit the nature of existing evil. Enter the Divine Revelation Principle (DRP):

> DRP ≡ God desires to maximize the measure of truth revealed to those who would choose good actions in response to that revelation, and God desires to minimize the measure of truth revealed to those who would choose bad actions in response to that revelation.

The DRP may be a significant factor in God's overall divine decision procedures used to determine God's actions in the world.[7] Also, the DRP carries with it, to me, a sense of just being morally right, given the existence of a maximally good and loving God. If I am capable of immediately perceiving morally right states of affairs independent of rigorous proof, then my direct perception that the DRP carries the ring of truth may be viewed as evidence that it is true, absent evidence to the contrary.

Consider also the MH principle:

> MH ≡ God desires to maximize the number of persons properly and freely related to God so as to maximally populate heaven, and God desires to minimize the number of persons improperly and freely related to God so as to minimally populate hell.

The MH principle may, in addition to the DRP, be a significant factor in God's overall divine decision procedures used to determine God's actions in the world.[8]

Let R represent the set of people inclined to reject divinely revealed truth such that they freely choose to ultimately resist acting so as to achieve a proper relationship to God. Then, it may be good that we know of no indisputable theodicy, since a maximally good and loving God's permission of the HIP may serve to prevent the members of R from acquiring knowledge of the specific details of the good reasons for which the nature of existing evil is permitted, thereby minimizing the eternal and just punishment in hell of the members of R. In fact, God's revelation of an excessive measure of truth (e.g., a detailed theodicy) to the members of R could serve to increase their liability for judgment, and God's loving hiddenness (via the DRP) with respect to them and their objections to theism could thus be justified.

The objection is oft raised that a maximally good and loving God would not permit the members of R to permanently reside in a place of hellish conscious torment. In response, this objection can be raised only if the HIP is assumed to be false, yet this assumption is not justified. Also, the permanent conscious torment of those members of R in hell may serve the good purpose of causing them to be so fully preoccupied with the horror of the torment itself that their capacity to further increase their measure of sin (and, thus, further increase their measure of torment) may be largely minimized or even eliminated. Thus, individual punishments in hell may be a function not only of the measure of divinely revealed truth that has been (and is continuously being) rejected, but also a function of the strength of the damned soul's desire to further sin in the presence of the torment designed to punish sin. Some self-destined permanent sinners may need greater torment than others so as to prevent their attainment of a still deeper measure of sin and consequent torment. Granted, the considerations in this paragraph are horrific and capable of generating intensely emotion-laden response, but this provides no justification for the assumption that horrific considerations are inherently or essentially implausible, nor does this provide justification for the assumption that horrific considerations are inherently incompatible with the existence of a maximally good and loving God.

The objection may be raised that a maximally good and loving God would not create a world in which R is nonempty. In response, again note that this objection can only be maintained if the HIP is known to be unlikely, yet the HIP is not known to be unlikely. Also, given the set W of possible worlds God could create, it is far from clear that no good member of W could exist with nonempty R. In fact, given the MH principle, God may need to create a world of type X (I define an X-type world as one in which R is nonempty) so as to maximize the number of persons not in R, and the fact that the HIP is not known to be unlikely entails that we are not able to argue (apart from divine revelation) that the probability of an X-type world is small.

Let W1 denote a world God could possibly create, where the number of persons not in R is maximized with R empty. Let W2 denote a world God could possibly create, where the number of persons not in R is maximized with R nonempty. The objection may be raised that a maximally good and loving God would favor W1 over W2, rendering improbable the existence of the Biblical God, since the Biblical God is taken to create W2. In response, again note that an objection such as this can be maintained only if the HIP is known to be unlikely, yet the HIP is not known to be unlikely. Also, there is no obvious reason why God should allow the number of persons not in R to be lessened due to a desire to minimize the number of persons in R. Why should the number of the citizens of heaven be lessened due to the rebellion of the citizens of hell? It may be good of God to pursue the maximization of the population of heaven, even if the population of hell must also be increased as an unfortunate but practically necessary consequence of this pursuit, and our lack of knowledge that the HIP is unlikely entails that we do not know that this possibility is improbable. Thus, the MH principle may play an important role in divine decision procedures.

My purpose in identifying the DRP and MH principles is not to suggest that we know the nature of existing evil is largely a consequence of God's operation in accordance with these principles. Rather, my purpose is to emphasize that we humans with such limited knowledge are simply in no position to determine whether God's existence entails that the nature of existing evil would largely be a consequence of God's operation in accordance with principles such as these. Thus, the nature of existing evil can not be used to render improbable God's existence, even if God is maximally good and loving. Also, identification of these possible reasons for which a maximally good and loving God would permit the nature of existing evil helps to focus not only on the good and loving nature of such a possible divine person, but also on the value of living one's life so as to participate in the pursuit of the accomplishment of the objectives such a divine being could also be pursuing. This value is especially great if conservative Biblical theology is true,[9] since the truth of conservative Biblical theology entails the truth of the HIP, of the DRP, of the MH principle, and of the eternally good value of our freely acting to achieve a proper loving relationship with the Biblical God by submitting to the work of the Holy Spirit of Jesus Christ in repentance from sin.

Response to John W. Loftus

My theistic arguments establish the existence of a person (i.e., God) whose power and knowledge are much greater than that of man, and whose moral nature is undetermined by those arguments. God may be omnibenevolent, but at this point I have not so argued. In fact, given my theistic arguments thus far, all we may expect of God is that He will likely continue to generally cause physical events to occur in accordance with physical laws, many of which have been discovered and well documented from research in the physical sciences. So, even if God is responsible for creating our world, and even given the nature of evil in our world, we find that evil is not evidence against the existence of

God, since we have no reason, at this stage, to presume God would prevent the known nature of evil in our world, if He could. We have little reason to expect much at all from God, given the theistic arguments I have provided, and such a being can be defended against atheistic arguments from evil, regardless of whether those atheistic arguments are deductively or inductively construed. So, unless Loftus can find some reason (other than the so-called "problem of evil"[10]) for rejecting my theistic arguments, we may presume that Loftus would be forced to agree with my theistic conclusions here. Indeed, Loftus confesses that God's actions are defensible, given limited expectations regarding divine action,[11] so his acceptance of the God established by my arguments thus far would presumably seem reasonable for him. This, in turn, would require his rejection of atheism.

Loftus uses the nature of evil to argue against the existence of a divine being who is understood to be omniscient, omnipotent, and omnibenevolent.[12] Even if we eventually discover that the God of my theistic arguments possesses these "omni" properties, Loftus' position fails to properly account for the implications of the HIP[13] in the context of "omni" theism. In what follows, I will respond to his views as they relate to this principle.

A fundamental mistake made by Loftus is his presumption that we know that God could have created a world better than the existing world.[14] In response, given the set G of possibly existing gods with the three "omni" properties, we may define the subsets G1 and G2 such that G1 consists of each member of G whose existence entails Loftus would know the HIP is false, and G2 consists of each member of G not in G1. Now, Loftus frequently claims that if God exists, then God could (or would, or should) perform some Loftus-specified action in some Loftus-specified context.[15] Observe carefully that this claim applies only to the members of G1, not G2, since the ways of the members of G2 are, by definition, beyond Loftus' ken. Therefore, Loftus may object all we wants that none of the members of G1 has acted the way Loftus would expect, but this does not establish that G2 is empty. So at most, Loftus effectively argues that G1 is empty, but since it is possible that G2 may be nonempty, and since the HIP entails Loftus can not establish G2 is empty, his argument fails to establish that G is empty. That is, his argument fails to show that an "omni" God probably doesn't exist.

Loftus may object that although it is possible that his argument from evil is wrong, it is still rather highly probable that it is right. In response, even if it is right, it shows only that G1 is empty, and it provides no reason to suppose G2 is empty. So note carefully: I am not resorting to a "merely possible" defense.[16] Rather, I am emphasizing that Loftus is unable to use the nature of evil in the world to establish that he knows the probability is high that no possibly existing members of G2 actually exist. In other words, I am using an "unknown probability of a logical possibility" defense. Of course, Loftus is correct that the mere identification of a logically possible theistic explanation does not entail the theistic explanation is a live option. However, the identification of a logically possible theistic explanation whose probability is unknown does entail that non-theistic explanations fail to establish that that theistic explanation is not a live option.

My position is rather similar, in certain respects, to the CORNEA defense.[17] Loftus claims that if such a defense is successful, it must still be shown that an "omni" God exists.[18] Of course, I agree that my central claim "The known nature of evil does not establish G2 is empty" does not, in turn, establish that an "omni" God exists, but the point worth emphasizing, here, is that Loftus fails to consider this central claim, and of critical note, Loftus fails to use the nature of evil to establish that the existence of each member of G2 is improbable. Thus, the "improbable possibilities" objection is without force.[19] Loftus also objects that a position such as mine could justify God-belief even if the preponderance of evidence were against the existence of God.[20] I disagree, and would argue that considerations relevant to the HIP are useful as a theistic defense, but do not, in and of themselves, justify theistic belief. Loftus considers that "God wants us to believe in him" entails we should know why God permits the nature of evil in the world.[21] In response, this objection presumes there is no existing member of G2 who wants us to believe in that member's existence, yet no reason is given for this dubious presumption other than a reference to arguments given by Theodore Drange and others,[22] all of which I have previously refuted in detail.[23] I do not understand why Loftus failed to respond to my detailed refutation.

After again audaciously claiming, without justification, that he knows what every possibly existing "omni" God should and could do,[24] Loftus goes on to claim that our ignorance of God's ways implies we are unlikely to know God's ways are good.[25] In response, this claim presumes it is unlikely that God's existence entails God would enable some persons to know that God's ways are good for reasons not fully understood by those persons, yet no reason is provided for that unjustified presumption. In other words, a theist could be in an epistemic state in which it is rational to accept a divine revelation which entails God's permission of the evil in the world is good (where that permission is good for reasons unknown by the theist), even if the theist is incapable of independently verifying God's goodness; Loftus has failed to show this possibility is improbable.

Loftus is puzzled by the allegation that an "omni" God could permit the nature of evil in the world, objecting that the "punishments do not fit the crimes."[26]

But again, Loftus is presuming that he knows the detailed nature of every possibly existing "omni" God's decision procedures such that the existence of each of those Gods would result in a world different from what he presently perceives, yet he fails to justify this presumption.

This point is worth repeating, since Loftus so frequently misses it: If an "omni" God exists, then it is reasonable to presume God would seek to maximize goodness in the world, and it's also reasonable to presume that the divine decision procedures required to calculate this maximal goodness are *wildly* beyond our ken as mere humans. For example, if the Biblical God exists, then something as simple as a seemingly inconsequential deviation from the nature of evil actually experienced by King David could, in fact, have lead him to alter slightly the wording of some of his psalms which, in turn, could have lead multitudes throughout subsequent Jewish and Christian history to have interpreted various Biblical passages differently, which could, in turn, ultimately have lead to the actualization of a considerably different human history H than has actually been actualized. The point is that neither Loftus (nor any other human on Earth, I could safely presume) is capable of evaluating the immensely massive quantity of data needed (but unavailable to us) to calculate the relative merits of histories such as H versus our actual human history, yet Loftus blindly assumes with wholly unjustified confidence that he knows the results of such calculations to the extent that he can state with assurance how God would have, could have, and should have done things differently, if God exists. It is indeed strange, nay inconsistent, for Loftus, an advocate of skeptical thinking, to fail to be skeptical of his own presumptions regarding the probable nature of all such possibly existing divine beings.

My position need not be construed as presuming that God's moral ways are "absolutely mysterious."[27] God may enable some persons to acquire a limited understanding of what is truly good and evil, yet not enable those persons to acquire the fully detailed understanding required to independently verify that God's decision procedures are, in fact, in full accordance with the maximal goodness God gives those persons good reason to presume God manifests. Again, we have identified a possibility which Loftus has failed to show is improbable. More generally, this rather simple apologetic strategy of identifying possibilities not shown (or known) to be improbable only serves to further emphasize the clearly erroneous nature of the widespread critical atheistic, skeptical, and agnostic presumption that such critics are capable of knowing what God would do, if God exists.

Having now refuted Loftus' attempted refutation of the "Ignorance Defense", it should be plainly obvious that his conclusion is unjustified,[28] and his final quotations[29] serve only to provide emotional impetus to his position, yet my refutation stands firm nonetheless. Thus, the "overwhelming" evidence from evil fails to establish that G2 is probably empty,[30] and unless Loftus finds new reasons to reject my use of the HIP in a theistic defense, we just might infer that Loftus is no longer able to find reasons to believe what he wants to believe.[31]

Response to Bart D. Ehrman

Bart D. Ehrman has recently written a book with the following subtitle: "How the Bible Fails to Answer Our Most Important Question—Why We Suffer".[32] This subtitle may be taken to imply that his primary thesis entails that exposition of Biblical texts fails to provide a detailed theodicy in which justification is provided for all instances of known suffering and evil. Even if this thesis is granted, it does not entail the nonexistence of such a theodicy. Ehrman even admits that the future divine revelation of such a theodicy is possible.[33] However, he considers this possibility unlikely, since he evidently takes the existence of (a maximally good and powerful) God and the nature of evil in the world to be "at odds with each other".[34]

In response, the nature of evil is known to be at odds with the existence of a maximally good and powerful God only if the HIP is known to be false. Since Ehrman has not established that the HIP is false, he has not shown that his knowledge is sufficient to justify the claim that God and the nature of evil in the world are at odds with each other.

We need not grant Ehrman his primary thesis, however, since he is apparently not even aware of the HIP, the Biblical basis for the HIP, or the implications of the HIP. For that matter, he neither considers the implications of the DRP and MH principles, both of which may be taken to have Biblical support as well. His thesis may be rejected, therefore, since it fails to account for Biblically grounded principles which, if taken to be true, entail the existence of a theodicy that is known by God, but may not be known in detail by us.

So, Ehrman may be taken to believe that since the Bible does not adequately explain why we suffer, that suffering constitutes evidence against the existence of the Biblical God.[35] But even Ehrman acknowledges that God could have reasons for permitting evil, where those reasons are simply beyond our ken.[36] And, if God's reasons are beyond our ability to understand, then our ignorance of such reasons does not constitute evidence for the nonexistence of God, but constitutes evidence of our own human ignorance of God's reasons. Ehrman should be aware of this consideration, sometimes described as *skeptical theism*, especially if he has truly examined the "highly sophisticated and nuanced reflections of serious philosophers and theologians" to which he refers.[37] Unfortunately, he does not respond to these ideas. If Ehrman's failure to respond to these ideas is due to his attempt to target "regular readers" rather than "specialists",[38] or due to his attempt to avoid "difficult intellectual concepts" and "esoteric vocabulary",[39] then we may conclude that the defense of his primary thesis fails due to oversimplification.

Ehrman appears to have recently experienced a genuine heartfelt desire to know the answer to the question, "Why do we suffer?"[40] He reasons that the suffering in the world is too intense to be consistent with the belief that the Biblical God has come into the darkness of the world to make a difference.[41] In response, we may agree with Ehrman that the measure of evil in the world is truly horrific; however, the subsequent inference to "therefore, God is unlikely to exist" simply does not follow. After all, God could have reasons unknown to us which justify His permission of the horrific evil in the world, and Ehrman is aware of this possibility. So, unless Ehrman can establish that God should reveal to Ehrman why we suffer as we do, then the fact (if it is a fact) that Ehrman has not perceived such a divine revelation would not constitute evidence that Ehrman is justified in believing that God (if God exists) has no good reasons for His permission of the nature of existing evil. Furthermore, Ehrman can establish that "God, if He exists, should reveal to Ehrman why we suffer as we do" only if he knows the falsehood of the HIP enables him to determine how God should act. However, Ehrman has not shown the HIP is false; therefore, he has not justified his belief that God's actions should result in any particular specific manifestation. Thus, we may infer that Ehrman has not established that "God, if He exists, should reveal to Ehrman why we suffer as we do". As genuine as Ehrman's frustration with the nature of existing evil appears to be, his unjustified philosophical presuppositions evidently lead him to erroneously suppose that he knows how the Biblical God should and would act, if the Biblical God exists.

In summary, Ehrman effectively asks: "If the Biblical God exists, then why do we suffer as we do?" We may reply: "If the Biblical God exists, then why should we suppose we should know why we suffer as we do, especially given principles such as the HIP, DRP, and MH, all of which find Biblical support and jointly entail our likely ignorance of God's detailed reasons?"

Response to Graham R. Oppy

My use of the HIP in response to evidential atheological arguments from evil may be understood to be within the "skeptical theist" category of theistic responses. Graham Oppy raises an objection to the kind of reasoning typically employed by skeptical theists. His position may be fairly interpreted to imply that my use of the HIP to block evidential atheological arguments from evil requires my acceptance of the claim that I am wholly incapable of justifying any moral judgment whatever (since any moral perception on my part could, for reasons beyond my ken, be incorrect).[42]

In response, I could take a strong position by claiming that all humans are utterly morally clueless, absent reasons for believing that some human-perceived moral truths are justifiably believed. In this case, it could be that some theists are justified in believing in the existence of a God of great knowledge and power whose moral nature is undetermined, where the nature of all moral truths is utterly beyond the ken of those theists.

Another (more plausible) option is to point out that the knowledge of moral truths by theists may be justified, yet limited to the extent that theists could be justified in seeking to minimize evil throughout the world, even though God may have reasons beyond their ken which entail that it is good of God to permit some evils which theists (given their limited understanding) ought to seek to prevent. Thus, a theist could be justified, given her limited understanding of moral reality, in seeking to prevent a particular instance E of evil, even if she does not know whether reasons beyond her ken entail it would be better for her to permit E, and even if God knows it would be better for God and her to permit E. Note carefully: even if a theist is not able to assess the probability of the existence of reasons beyond her ken which entail she should not prevent E, she may, nevertheless, perceive that the probability is high that she is morally obligated to seek to prevent E, given her limited knowledge of moral reality. It is wrong of Oppy to presume that a theist's ignorance of moral reasons beyond her ken entails she possesses no moral justification for the pursuit of elimination of evil, since a theist's knowledge of the rational basis for her perceived moral obligations need not be grounded in her possession of the knowledge which grounds God's moral justification.

So, if skeptical theists are utterly ignorant regarding all matters moral, then this is simply evidence that ordinary moral practice is unjustified for such theists. If skeptical theists possess a measure of knowledge of the nature of moral reality, then they may be justified in performing particular actions (e.g., preventing particular evils) even if they do not know whether such action may be best from the vantage point of the knowledge possessed by God. Since skeptical theists presumably typically do engage in ordinary moral practices, this merely shows that such theists presuppose that their moral practices are justified. This presupposition does not undermine the skeptical theist response to atheological evidential arguments from evil, however, since skeptical theists need not claim that their skepticism regarding *God's* moral obligations grounds the justification of *their* moral obligations. Rather, skeptical theists may take the position that the justification for their moral practices is grounded in reasoning independent of the claim of skepticism regarding God's moral obligations.

Theists may have limited moral knowledge which entails that their moral obligations include both acceptance of skeptical theistic responses to evidential arguments from evil, and also the pursuit of elimination of evil instances in the world, even if their pursuit of the eradication of particular evil instances may conflict with God's better informed perspective that is far beyond their ken. Thus, Oppy incorrectly concludes that skeptical theists can not derive reasonable views regarding whether they ought to prevent any instance of evil.[43]

Summary

The HIP, DRP and MH principles are shown to be both Biblical and an effective means by which atheistic arguments from evil may be refuted. John Loftus, Bart Ehrman, and Graham Oppy have failed to appreciate the implications of these principles.

NOTES

1. I have responded in detail to all of the atheistic inductive arguments from evil recently published in Martin, Michael and Monnier, Ricki, eds., (2006). *The Improbability of God*. Amherst, NY: Prometheus Books, Part 3. See Stone, David Reuben (2007). *Atheism Is False: Richard Dawkins and the 'Improbability of God' Delusion*. Morrisville, NC: Lulu Press, Chapter 5.

2. Biblical support for the HIP could include Romans 11:33-34, Isaiah 40:13-14, and Isaiah 55:8-9.

3. Stone (2007), Chapter 2. See, also, Chapters 1 and 2 of the present volume.

4. Note the QLMT argument form here. See Chapter 1 for QLMT details.

5. See, for example, Feinberg, John S. (2004). *The Many Faces of Evil: Theological Systems and the Problem of Evil.* Wheaton, IL: Crossway Books, Chapter 15.

6. Michael Martin attempts to infer inductive support for the impossibility of a theodicy from the failure of all known theodicies, but this inference is grounded in the erroneous assumption that it is likely that a successful theodicy would be known, if it existed. In fact, since the HIP implies that we are unlikely (apart from divine revelation) to know a fully successful theodicy (if it exists), our ignorance of a fully successful theodicy does not constitute evidence against the possibility of a fully successful theodicy. We are evidently unlikely to know a fully successful theodicy, even if one exists. See Martin, Michael (1990). *Atheism: A Philosophical Justification.* Philadelphia: Temple University Press, pp. 361, 412, 452.

7. Biblical support for a principle such as the DRP includes, for example, Matthew 13:12, Matthew 25:29-30, and Luke 8:18.

8. Biblical support for MH may include, for example, Matthew 23:33-39, 2 Peter 3:9, and 1 Timothy 2:3-5.

9. See Chapter 5 for my structuring of an argument for the truth of Biblical theology.

10. Loftus, John W. (2008). *Why I Became an Atheist: A Former Preacher Rejects Christianity.* Amherst, NY: Prometheus Books, Chapters 12 and 13.

11. Ibid., p. 240:22-23.

12. Ibid., p. 228:21-23.

13. Ibid., p. 256:22-259:44.

14. Ibid., p. 258:2-4.

15. For a few of the many such examples throughout his book, see Ibid., p. 236:31-32, 43-44; p. 237:20-29; p. 239:14-18; p. 240:1-21.

16. Ibid., p. 61:26-29.

17. Ibid., p. 257:22-30.

18. Ibid., p. 257:31-32.

19. Ibid., p. 257:32-37.

20. Ibid., p. 257:37-41.

21. Ibid., p. 257:41-43.

22. Ibid., p. 262:7-10.

23. Stone (2007), pp. 192-234.

24. Loftus (2008), p. 258:2-4.

25. Ibid., p. 258:9-10.

26. Ibid., p. 258:22-24.

27. Ibid., p. 258:35 36.

28. Ibid., p. 259:1-2.

29. Ibid., p. 259:25-44.

30. Ibid., p. 259:4-5.

31. Ibid., p. 259:6-9.

32. Ehrman, Bart D. (2008). *God's Problem: How the Bible Fails to Answer Our Most Important Question—Why We Suffer.* New York: HarperCollins Publishers.

33. Ibid., p. 270:17-22. See also p. 265:11-12.

34. Ibid., p. 270:22-27.

35. Ibid., p. 3:25-4:9.

36. Ibid., p. 201:17-18.

37. Ibid., p. 3:32-4:9.

38. Ibid., p. ix:2-4.
39. Ibid., p. 19:1-4.
40. Ibid., p. 4:10-6:20.
41. Ibid., p. 6:3-7.
42. Oppy, Graham Robert (2006). *Arguing About Gods*. Cambridge: Cambridge University Press, pp. 289-313.
43. Ibid., p. 313:26-29.

CHAPTER 4

Loftus on Rationality, Morality, and Control Beliefs

Abstract: *John W. Loftus' views on rationality and morality are briefly examined. The primary control beliefs that undergird Loftus' philosophy of religion are then explored. These beliefs, and the alleged justification for them, are critiqued in the context of their relationship to religious diversity, science, history, theistic arguments, religious experience, evil, miracles, the Bible, and prayer. It is argued that neutral agnosticism is a better starting point (in the theism-atheism debate) than Loftus' skeptical agnosticism.*

Loftus on Rational Superiority

Loftus claims that it is false that the case for Christian faith is rationally superior to alternative belief systems.[1] In its context, his claim is not persuasively defended,[2] but is rather expressed as a position statement which he hopes his book will support.[3] Nevertheless, some comments are in order.

A conservative Biblical belief system (of the kind advocated in Chapter 5 of this book) need not include the belief that all who reject that system are always irrational at all times in that rejection. It may be that all who ultimately choose to reject conservative Biblical beliefs are irrational at only a small number of moments (let M denote the set of all such moments) during the entire history of their rejection, where God permits the rejecter to persist in her state of rejection due to her exemplified irrational response (during the moments which comprise M) to divinely revealed elements of conservative Biblical truth, where that irrationality is a manifestation of her strong desire to ultimately choose to abstain from the attainment of a proper relationship to the Biblical God. This possibility P is virtually impossible to directly verify, but the near impossibility of direct verification of P does not entail that P is improbable, since other independent considerations may indirectly lend rational support for the claim that P is, in fact, probable.

Thus, the conservative Biblical theologian could take the position that ultimate rejecters of conservative Biblical beliefs are not only generally rational in their rejection, but also morally at fault for having persisted in that state of rational rejection throughout their lives. The light of divine revelation of elements of conservative Biblical truth may come only once, or only during brief periods, to some persons, and it could be good of God to abstain from continuous revelation of such knowledge to those predisposed to continuously reject it. This may help explain why Jesus cautioned us to carefully consider what we understand[4] lest it be taken from us.[5] This may also shed light on an instantiation of the proverb[6] in which a man genuinely perceives a measure of justification (except during any M-moments) for his erroneous belief system, yet is morally culpable for having failed to perceive its ultimate destructive end.

If the concept of rationality is defined in terms of the Biblical-God-influenced epistemic states of persons, then the conservative Bible-believer is arguably committed to accept that God sometimes intentionally permits some people (believers or not) to persist in a rational state of ignorance regarding truths divinely revealed to others.[7] Thus, even on the assumption that a conservative Biblical belief system is true, a rejecter of that system could be rational in the sense that God could enable that rejecter to perceive no good reason (except during the moments which comprise M) for accepting that system or components of that system. Lest we fault the God of such a possible system, observe that those who accept such a system are committed to also accept that many (if not all) who fail to ultimately discover whether essential teachings of Jesus are true may be at fault for that ultimate failure.[8] Loftus would presumably object to this position on the grounds that his book provides a rational basis for rejecting conservative Biblical theology, yet the conservative Bible-believer may consistently respond that conservative Biblical apologetics (e.g., my arguments) provide reasons for rejecting Loftus' atheism and anti-Biblical beliefs. In particular, Loftus may not presently perceive that conservative Biblical theology is true, in part, due to God's decision to not presently enable him to experience an M-moment, where God's reasons for that decision may not be presently known, and where we may have no good reason to suppose we are in a position to know what those reasons might be, if the Biblical God exists.

It should be evident that the Sennett quote[9] merely assumes what is claimed. Sennett is quoted as simply assuming that it is false that prominent figures such as Einstein, Russell, Freud, Hawking, and Marx failed to embrace the Lordship of Jesus due to irrationality or ignorance. It is safe to say that Sennett has not directly verified the accuracy of this assumption through observation of the full history of the epistemic states of these prominent figures. Pending further evidence, therefore, it would be prudent of Sennett, as well as the rest of us, to withhold judgment regarding the reasons why these figures did not apparently embrace the Lordship of Jesus during much of their lives.

Furthermore, the "historically prominent intellectual figures are not ignorant or irrational" thesis, of which some variation Sennett is evidently an advocate, also suffers from the fact that no reason is given to suppose that vices such as greed, lust, selfish ambition, pride, apathy, and rebellion did not (perhaps unknowingly) bias those figures to the extent that elements of irrationality were a contributing cause of their failure to accept the Lordship of Jesus. Also, no reason is given for accepting Sennett's definition of "movers and shakers".[10] In addition, no reason is given for supposing the "last two hundred years"[11] is an appropriate, adequate, or preferable reference period, nor are we given reasons for supposing that alternative reference periods would likely generate similar results (they presumably would not), nor are we told how to interpret the contradictory findings that would likely result from examination of varying reference periods on varying definitions of "movers and shakers". As well, no reason is given for supposing those figures do not now accept (or at least acknowledge) the Lordship of Jesus in a postmortem existence. We may also cite the Nagel quote[12] as an element of countering evidence that further exposes the limited value of Sennett's thesis. Also, if conservative Biblical theology is true, then we may as well expect that only a limited number of influential and prominent figures might be chosen to perceive such truth,[13] so Sennett's principle inductively begs the question against such divine revelation patterns in human knowledge.

Moreover, the "appeal to authority" feature of Sennett's argument is without merit, as I find no good reason to suppose the prominent figures Sennett references deserve recognition as philosophical, theological, or epistemological authorities. For example, Einstein may be regarded as a great mathematical physicist, but this does not guarantee or imply he was a great philosopher in general. Bertrand Russell's contribution to mathematics and logic may have been great, but his philosophy of religion was poor. Some persons may be famously influential in their field of expertise, yet woefully ignorant of issues of critical importance to their preferred worldview.[14]

The "appeal to authority" approach carries significant theory-confirming value only when adequately justified, and it is precisely such justification that is lacking in the careless appeal to influence and authority which appears on page 36 of Loftus' book. Although many scholars disagree on many issues, we have no choice but to draw conclusions based on the person-relative evidence available to each of us. Neither historical disagreements nor contemporary scholarly disagreements give any more reason to suppose excessive "chutzpa"[15] is required to claim "Conservative Biblical theology is true and all ultimate rejecters have exemplified irrationality" than to claim "Conservative Biblical theology is false and accepters irrationally presume that all ultimate rejecters have exemplified irrationality". Both claims are such that they ought to be accompanied by an appropriate measure of justification prior to acceptance by an informed inquirer.

This discussion regarding the rational superiority of competing theories is admittedly somewhat ambiguous, since an agreed upon conception of rationality has not even been more precisely explicated. I refer the reader to Chapter 7, where I explore my conception of rational superiority as it relates to a Minimalist Theistic position.

Loftus on Morality

Loftus claims that Christians do not have any "special access to moral truth" not also accessible to unbelievers.[16] This claim simply begs the question against a conservative Biblical theological belief system, however, since there is Biblical evidence that if such a system is true, then believers may have special access to divinely revealed knowledge (including moral truths) which may well be unavailable to unbelievers.[17] Either a conservative Biblical belief system (that entails meaning expressed in the Biblical passages I have referenced) is true or not. If such a system is true, then given that Loftus is evidently an unbeliever, we have no reason to expect that he should be aware of all moral truths perceived by believers. If, on the other hand, we presuppose that no such system is true, then Loftus might actually have as much access as any believer to any possible moral truths, but such a presupposition merely begs the question against such systems, and as such, is merely an exercise in circular reasoning. So, either Loftus is not privy to moral truths perceived by believers, or he must engage in circular reasoning to establish he may have equal access with believers to moral truths; neither option justifies his fundamental claim that he has equal access together with believers to any moral truths that may exist.

Of course, Loftus could cite the remainder of his book as evidence that conservative Biblical theology is false, opening up the possibility that he does, in fact, have equal access together with conservative Bible-believers to moral truths. However, in this case, his moral claim does not stand on its own, but requires that he assume his case against conservative Biblical theology is sound. I submit that the criticism throughout this chapter, and throughout the entire book, establishes that Loftus has failed to justify his case against conservative Biblical theology.

A conservative Bible-believer J could know that "God enables J to know that God's command C that J perform action X" entails "J is morally obligated to perform X", regardless of whether J understands God's relationship to moral truths. This possibility does not insure that unbelievers would have equal access to knowledge of such moral truths, since it does not necessarily follow that God would enable all unbelievers to perceive the commands God enables believers to perceive. Nevertheless, God's relationship to moral truths deserves a brief examination.

Let the position I wish to explore, here, be represented by SMT (Stone's Moral Theory). SMT consists of the following components:

> SMT1 $\equiv$ Objective moral truths exist and are not caused by God's will or action.

> SMT2 $\equiv$ "God performs action A" entails "A is good".

> SMT3 $\equiv$ Human perception of an objective moral truth T occurs only if God both commands T and enables the human perception of T.

SMT1 guarantees that moral truths are not grounded in arbitrary divine will or action.[18] SMT2 guarantees that God will not command an evil action, so we need not be concerned that God might command something evil.[19] SMT2 also guarantees that a human could never correctly accuse God of acting immorally. SMT3 guarantees that we will never actually perceive an objective moral truth that conflicts with God's commands. SMT3 also implies that our perception of objective moral truths is completely dependent upon God's divine enablement of that perception. SMT3 does not require, however, that God's divine enablement of human perception of objective moral truths entails human perception that it is God who divinely enables that human perception of objective moral truth.

Loftus claims, in effect, that SMT1 implies that the objective moral truth standard S would, if it exists, be "higher than God" and "is the real God".[20] In response, the "S is the real God" claim is a category mistake, since S is not a person, but may be understood as merely an impersonal abstract entity. The "S is higher than God" claim is misleading, since moral standards are not *higher* than persons, but are merely objective *descriptions* of the moral status of possible (or actual) personal actions.

SMT does not entail that human reason is a sufficient condition of human perception of objective moral truths. In fact, there is no good reason to suppose that human reason alone is such a condition. Therefore, the Pojman quotes beg the question against SMT3.[21] Granted, human reflection (for both conservative Bible-believers and nonbelievers) upon moral issues may result in the human perception of objective moral obligations, but such perception is possible only by virtue of God's divine enablement, assuming SMT is true.

Thus, SMT appears to withstand the criticism Loftus might be expected to bring against it. I take SMT to be a plausible working hypothesis regarding God's relationship to morality.

I have not actually established that SMT is true, but have merely emphasized that SMT is possibly both true and an effective way to resolve common objections. If a conservative Biblical belief system is true, then that system may lend support for the claim that SMT is actually true. Even absent such support, however, the nature of SMT is such that we are evidently incapable of using available evidence to directly confirm or disconfirm SMT. Nevertheless, so long as SMT is known to be a logically possible theory whose probability is undetermined, we may conclude that we have no good reason to suppose a theory such as SMT can not adequately account for the nature of the relationship between morality and a God who satisfies the three components of SMT.

Loftus claims that Christians can not be certain of their knowledge of objective moral standards.[22] In response, if conservative Biblical theology is true, then God could enable at least some conservative Bible-believers to be certain of at least some moral standards, and Loftus' presumption to the contrary merely begs the question. The fact that many conservative Bible-believers disagree on many issues does not entail that no conservative Bible-believer can ever have divinely enabled certainty regarding a moral standard or its application to a particular context.

Loftus objects that Biblical "cherry-picking" is inconsistent on the part of those conservative Bible-believers who embrace the entire Biblical canon.[23] This objection is vague and ambiguous, but appears to entail that Loftus thinks that such believers do not apply Biblical morality to their personal lives in the way that they should, given their epistemic state. In response, Loftus is evidently not privy to the epistemic state of the conservative Bible-believer's mind, and so is in no position to presume God does not guide such believers to apply Biblical morals to their lives in ways God prevents Loftus from understanding. After all, if conservative Biblical theology is true, then we should not expect unbelievers to understand all divinely revealed truth,[24] so the fact that Loftus appears confused regarding his "cherry-picking" concerns is not surprising, and may even be expected, given that he is an unbeliever. Moreover, even if we grant that some conservative Bible-believers do not consistently apply Biblical morality to their lives, this should only encourage believers to do a better job. We may thank Loftus, then, for encouraging the faithful to be even more faithfully consistent in their Scriptural obedience.

Loftus claims that moral truth perceived by both him and Christians is grounded in the pursuit of our happiness and the knowledge of our identity.[25] In response, conservative Bible-believers need not claim that their morals are all derived from the Bible, and SMT is consistent with God revealing any and every moral truth perceived by any believer or nonbeliever, regardless of whether it is perceived by those persons that it is God who is the revealing agent.

Loftus blames a Christian nation for the Holocaust.[26] The conservative Bible-believers may respond that the past abuse or misrepresentation of the conservative Biblical ethic is not the fault of that ethic, but of persons who failed to follow it.

Loftus quotes Nielsen's assertion that religious believers have subjective grounds for their morals.[27] This assertion begs the question against SMT, since SMT3 implies God could enable objective divine revelation of moral truth to religious believers in ways distinct from divine revelation of moral truth to secularists.

Loftus explains his motivation for accepting the moral code he embraces,[28] and claims that the motivation begins with an "overall life plan".[29] He does not explain, however, why that code should be presumed to be objectively true, and he evidently accepts his code for subjective reasons only. Atheists who embrace life plans for subjective reasons, therefore, should not be expected to agree with one another regarding the relative merits of different plans. Also, there appears to be no objective basis for an atheist to critique a fellow atheist who embraces an allegedly morally evil code, since there really is no objective moral evil on this construal, and since the atheist who embraces the allegedly morally evil code may perceive that her code is not evil at all. These problems with such subjective accounts of morality could be a recipe for moral societal degradation. The fact that many atheists may submit to a moral code that may be widely accepted as good at many levels does not eliminate the problem that such a code is unable to objectively justify a moral critique of another's moral code. Indeed, on the subjective account of morality, conservative Bible-believers may object that atheists have no objective basis upon which to critique Biblical morality, since conservative Bible-believers could embrace that morality for reasons which cohere with an overall life plan designed to maximize the conservative Bible-believer's pursuit of happiness and self-understanding in the context of a presumed conservative Biblical worldview. Moreover, on the subjective account of morality, there is no objective problem of evil! Thus, the linchpin of Loftus' positive case for atheism is pulled out from beneath his feet. The fact that Loftus critiques the morality of conservative Biblical belief systems, and the fact that Loftus treats the problem of evil as a problem of objectively existent evil, therefore, suggests that he really does seem to be invoking an objective account of morality in his epistemology, implying that Loftus is not even consistent in his own conception of morality.

Loftus' Primary Control Beliefs

For advocates of opposing positions, the goal of achieving mutual understanding of the relative merits of those positions may require not merely the acquisition of substantial quantities of evidence,[30] but the proper interpretation of evidence in the context of control beliefs (presuppositions) that are minimized in quantity and quality such that neither of the opposing positions is arbitrarily favored by a control belief that is not neutral with respect to the debate at hand. Thus, the pursuit of maximizing the degree to which one begins from a neutral position would seem to be the natural and preferred way to preclude philosophical self-deception and to resolve debates. Unfortunately, as will be shown throughout this chapter, Loftus embraces non-neutral control beliefs, and Loftus attempts to justify those beliefs through non-neutral reasoning.

Loftus identifies three key control beliefs which he claims play a significant role in his position:

> CB1 ≡ Evidential analysis of religious belief systems must begin with agnosticism/skepticism.[31]

> CB2 ≡ Probably, every event has a natural cause.[32]

> CB3 ≡ Probably, the scientific method is the only reliable guide for learning.[33]

It will be helpful to define a few terms to clarify the discussion that follows:

> Minimalist Theist ≡ A person whose maintains: (1) A person created the physical world and designed some of its features; and (2) A person sustains the existence of the physical world by causing physical events (except any physical events caused by humans) to continue to generally

occur in accordance with physical laws, including all such laws identified via the scientific method.

Neutral Agnostic ≡ A person who does not believe that any theistic or atheistic belief system is more probable than any other theistic or atheistic system.

Skeptical Agnostic ≡ A person who does not believe that any theistic belief system is highly probable, and who believes that all theistic belief systems are more likely false than true.

Loftus claims CB2 and CB3 may be derived from CB1,[34] but there is no clear deductive connection to which he may be appealing to justify that derivation, and any inductive connections he may have in mind are neither clearly identified nor justified. Loftus apparently believes CB2 may be derived from CB1, and this implies that the version of agnosticism envisioned in CB1 is skeptical agnosticism (not neutral agnosticism). This is confirmed by the characterization of his position as a "predisposition *against* the supernatural".[35]

Loftus contrasts starting "from above" with starting "from below".[36] Starting "from above" is understood to be the presupposition of some version of theism, and Loftus rejects this starting point because it "presupposes what needs to be shown".[37] Loftus' version of starting "from below" is understood to be the presupposition of his control beliefs.

Loftus seems to have in mind the idea that since we must either start "from above" or start "from below", and since starting "from above" inappropriately begs the question in favor of theism, we must start "from below" by beginning with acceptance of his control beliefs.[38] This idea is highly misleading, however, as other options are available. In particular, Loftus does not consider starting "from the middle", i.e., from the perspective of *neutral agnosticism*. Also, he views Geisler's approach as starting "from below",[39] when in fact, Geisler would not accept the control beliefs Loftus associates with starting "from below", and Geisler's approach would be better characterized as starting "from the middle".[40]

Clearly, a predisposition *against* the supernatural is not a neutral agnostic starting point. It should be apparent, then, that if Loftus rejects starting "from above" because it presupposes a non-neutral position in the theism-atheism debate, then Loftus should also reject CB1 because it presupposes a non-neutral position in the theism-atheism debate. Likewise, Loftus should reject CB2 because it presupposes that Minimalist Theism (MT) is probably false.

I find no difficulty in beginning with the presupposition CB3 so long as the scientific method is simply understood as summarized by the Moreland and Craig quote[41] and is very broadly interpreted so that terms such as *hypothesis testing* and *observational data* are permitted to include all possible forms of hypotheses and data that might exist, not merely physical hypotheses and physical data. Also, it should be noted that initial acceptance of CB3 may eventually lead to subsequent rejection of CB3, depending on whether we discover (later in our investigation) that the scientific method is limited in its ability to aid in the acquisition of all forms of knowledge.

Unfortunately, Loftus' interpretation of CB3 is not in accordance with a broad interpretation of the above-referenced Moreland and Craig quote, but is grounded in methodological naturalism, which narrowly restricts the range of possible metaphysical options to the presupposition that there is a natural explanation for every event.[42] So, even Loftus evidently has warrant for rejecting CB3 as he understands it, since it presupposes that MT is false.

Loftus opposes theistic presuppositions[43] presumably because they beg the question in favor of theism. It stands to reason that Loftus should also oppose his skeptical agnosticism, since skeptical agnosticism begs the question in favor of an anti-supernatural bias. When examining a debate between two opposing views, it would seem that the pursuit of the identification of a mutually agreed upon neutral starting point would be a reasonable goal. Granted, utterly pure and complete neutrality may be impossible to attain with respect to all possible belief system debates, since every form of neutrality is necessarily accompanied by a least one presupposition whose denial is entailed by a possible opposing system. Nevertheless, one might begin with neutrality with respect to the theism-atheism debate by starting an evidential analysis from the position of neutral agnosticism. Since neutral agnosticism presupposes neither any theistic nor any atheistic belief system, beginning with neutral agnosticism appears to be a reasonable approach to beginning one's analysis of the theism-atheism debate. One might expect that Loftus' opposition to presuppositions which beg the question should incline him to favor neutral agnosticism over skeptical agnosticism.

Loftus does not claim to arbitrarily choose to accept his favored control beliefs, but provides reasons he believes justify acceptance of those beliefs. In what follows, I will show in greater detail why the reasons offered by Loftus fail to justify acceptance of those control beliefs.

Control Beliefs, Religious Diversity and the Outsider Test

Loftus proposes an "Outsider Test" as a solution to the problem of determining which religious faith, if any, deserves rational acceptance. This test includes the assumption A that one's "culturally inherited religious faith is probably false".[44] In response, a neutral examination of confirming/disconfirming evidence relevant to the case for/against a religious faith may be performed without presupposing A. STONE (Stone's Test Of Neutral Evidence)[45] is a test of neutral evidence which starts from a position of neutral agnosticism (not skeptical agnosticism), where A is rejected in favor of a neutral starting point in which no faith is presumed to be either likely or unlikely. STONE is motivated by a desire to engage in a neutral analysis in which one begins with no presupposition for (or against) any faith. Thus, Loftus' struggle to determine whether to begin analysis from the "inside" versus the "outside"[46] may be properly resolved by neutrally beginning from "the middle" as in STONE, not by arbitrarily initially presuming all faiths are improbable.

STONE is characterized by many of the positive features of the Outsider Test, yet is not characterized by the negative features of the Outsider Test.[47] For example, STONE encourages skeptical testing of one's belief system, but from the perspective of neutral agnosticism (not skeptical agnosticism). Thus, STONE does not arbitrarily presume all religious faiths are probably false, but begins from a neutral position in which no religious faith is known to be either likely or unlikely. STONE carries with it the intention of performing a disinterested investigation: follow the evidence wherever it leads. STONE may be used to determine which faith is correct, independent of any prior religious affiliation. STONE need not pretend to presume nothing is at stake in the investigation; clearly, examination of the evidential support for religious faith carries with it implications of profound significance, regardless of the outcome of that examination. STONE need not presume hell is not to be feared, but may begin with an agnostic presumption that hell is not known to be likely fear-worthy or likely not fear-worthy, pending evidence to the contrary.

Loftus suggests that religious believers are inconsistent when embracing their own faith and presuming that incompatible faiths are unlikely.[48] In response, STONE may be used to establish the rational superiority of a religious faith by consistently evaluating neutral evidence in accordance with justified standards of analysis. We need not presume religious believers are inconsistent, since such believers may generally presume other faiths are unlikely by grounding that presumption in a justified response to STONE-based reasoning.

In the context of urging acceptance of his Outsider Test, Loftus claims that Christians should be willing to read Loftus' book.[49]   In response, either conservative Bible-believers are objectively morally obligated to act as Loftus urges, or they are not. If they are, then consistency would appear to require that Loftus' subjective account of morality deserves conversion into an objective account.[50]   If they are not, then conservative Bible-believers need not feel obligated to respond to Loftus' subjective moral assertions.   Furthermore, if conservative Biblical theology is true, then God may enable some conservative Bible-believers to know that they should not read Loftus' book until some future better time (or not at all), and Loftus is begging the question against this possibility by presuming all conservative Bible-believers should be willing to read his book. Advertising can be appropriate, but illegitimate advertising need not be highly regarded.

Loftus also asserts that he knows that a loving God (as specified in his book[51]) should enable us to verify that a true religious belief system should pass the Outsider Test. In response, a loving God may have good reasons (unknown to Loftus) for not enabling all people to verify that a true religious belief system passes the Outsider Test. Loftus' assertion, thus, begs the question against this possibility. It would be better of Loftus to remain agnostic regarding what the members of the set of all possibly existing loving gods would do, pending additional evidence. Indeed, Loftus is a champion of skeptical thinking, so why not be skeptical of Loftus' presumptions regarding the reasons a loving God might have for acting in ways we don't understand?   Moreover, if Loftus' subjective account of morality is correct, then there is no objective moral basis for supposing anyone should pay attention to Loftus' moral reasoning.

Loftus casts doubt upon the human ability to make independent rational judgments.[52]   We may agree that no rational analysis may be divorced from presuppositions, but this does not entail that all human reason is hopelessly mired in rational darkness. STONE[53] is designed to resolve debates between proponents of competing theories, where theory-presupposing assumptions are set aside, and where mutually agreed upon neutral evidence is analyzed to see where the evidence leads.   STONE, of course, does not eliminate all presuppositions from rational analysis (no evidential test can do this), but it does provide a methodology which may be used to resolve disputes between advocates of opposing theories.   One advantage of STONE over the Outsider Test is that STONE begins with the neutral assumption that supernaturalism is known to be neither likely nor unlikely, whereas the Outsider Test is a positively anti-supernatural bias.[54] On this point, STONE is clearly superior.

Although mutually agreed upon neutral evidence and arguments play an important role in debate resolution using STONE, the existence of mutually agreed upon tests is not a necessary condition of rational belief acceptance.[55] An individual's perception of truth is not necessarily contingent upon the epistemic state of other individuals. Thus, the nonexistence of universally agreed upon tests for rational belief acceptance is not evidence against the human ability to make rational judgments.

I can make rational judgments independent of all presuppositions not necessary or justified, and I may use STONE to show the superiority of my judgments over the opposing judgments of those willing to productively engage my judgments in STONE. People may often exemplify reasoning which is, technically, irrational by virtue of failing to properly question presuppositions, but this does not constitute evidence that STONE can not be used to help minimize one's irrationality by eliminating unjustified presuppositions. Indeed, the admirable pursuit of neutrally minimizing unnecessary presuppositions should incline one to favor STONE over the Outsider Test. Loftus' failure to perceive the superiority of STONE over the Outsider Test, therefore, may help explain why it may be hard for Loftus to "shake" his unjustified skeptical agnosticism.[56]

Religious neutral agnosticism (i.e., I don't know whether any faith is likely or unlikely) is distinct from religious skeptical agnosticism (i.e., I don't know any faith is likely, and I know all faiths are probably unlikely). Loftus quotes Moreland and Craig, suggesting there may be some merit to the presumption of agnosticism,[57] but the form of agnosticism Moreland and Craig may have in mind is arguably religious neutral agnosticism, not religious skeptical agnosticism. Loftus does not explain the distinction between these forms of agnosticism, and it is misleading to suppose all references to religious agnosticism are references to religious skeptical agnosticism.

Loftus argues in favor of religious skeptical agnosticism by asserting that it is likely that any particular faith under investigation is probably wrong.[58] Something is wrong, however, with Loftus' assertion. After all, if conservative Biblical theology is true, then it may be likely that God enables many believers to know conservative Biblical theology is true independent of having performed an evidential analysis of conservative Biblical theology. Loftus' assertion begs the question against this possibility by presuming that conservative Bible-believers who begin an evidential analysis of the case for conservative Biblical theology must presuppose God has not already enabled them to know conservative Biblical theology is true. Yes, if conservative Bible-believers possess any divinely enabled perception of the truth of conservative Biblical theology, then they may hypothetically suppress that knowledge as in STONE for the purpose of performing a neutral analysis (not a skeptical analysis[59]) to see where the evidence leads from that religiously neutral agnostic starting point. When such believers use STONE to confirm the faith they were already divinely enabled to know, however, this may simply strengthen the believer's conviction regarding the truth of the presuppositions (favorable to conservative Biblical theology) she already knew were justified. Thus, Loftus engages in circular reasoning by skeptically insisting all investigators must presume the faith under investigation is probably wrong. We may urge Loftus to be skeptical of his own skeptical presumptions, leading to religious neutral agnosticism which entails that all investigators must initially presume the faith under investigation is not known to be either right or wrong.

More may be said in response to Loftus' assertion that any particular faith under investigation is probably wrong.[60] Let F represent the set of all possible religious belief systems, where no two members of F are identical. Let F_i represent the number of religious belief systems being examined by an investigator at some time T_i. Let F_t represent the total number of members of F. Now, Loftus' intuition, in context, may be interpreted to entail that evidential analysis of religious faith properly begins with the assumption that acceptance of any religious faith is initially unjustified, since the ratio F_i/F_t is small at T_i. That is, Loftus' position appears to require that since $F_i = 1$ (when a particular single faith is being examined) and F_t is very large (the number of possibly true religious belief systems is very large), religious skeptical agnosticism is justified.

In response, observe that although no two members of F are identical, many members of F may have much in common. So, if a particular feature of a religious belief system is under investigation, and if that feature is shared by many members of F, then F_i may be much larger than 1 when that feature is under investigation, in which case it may not follow that F_i/F_t is small (at T_i) with respect to that feature.

In addition, we may identify a subset FV (the "universalism" subset) of F, where each member of FV includes the belief B that we are objectively morally obligated to accept the set C of beliefs that comprise either the religious faith we first accepted in life or the religious faith we presently accept, with the exception of any member of C that entails B is false (or likely false). If any member of FV is true, then even if F_i/F_t is small, acceptance of religious faith is morally obligatory for all (including Loftus) who have ever accepted a faith at some point in their lives. Thus, Loftus incorrectly identifies the smallness of F_i/F_t as proper justifying grounds for the assertion that any particular faith under investigation is probably wrong. Granted, the truth of any member of FV would imply many traditional conservative Biblical belief systems are not entirely true, but the point, here, is that we must not arbitrarily presuppose (as Loftusian methodology evidently requires) that no member of FV is true.

Furthermore, how can Loftus know that the smallness of Fi/Ft justifies a religious skeptical agnostic approach to evidential analysis of religious faith unless he has already performed an evidential analysis A of the members of F and their relationship to rational belief acceptance? It seems that A must be performed by Loftus *prior* to establishing the rational implications of the smallness of Fi/Ft. Herein lies a dilemma: If Loftus uses the Outsider Test in A to establish that the Outsider Test should be accepted, then he begs the question. However, if Loftus does not use the Outsider Test in A, then he must use some *other* approach to evidential analysis of religious faith when performing A, in which case the Outsider Test is not properly accepted in one's initial evidential analysis of religious faith after all. In either case, the Outsider Test is unwarranted as a starting point in evidential analysis of religious belief systems.

Loftus appears to imply that if analysis of empirical evidence is not able to establish which religious faith might be true, then religious skeptical agnosticism is warranted.[61] However, Loftus does not explain why religious neutral agnosticism would not be better justified in this case.

An important point in favor of STONE (and against the Outsider Test) relates to presuppositions regarding religious belief origination. Either (A) religious beliefs originate due merely to social and cultural conditions, or (B) religious beliefs originate for reasons that may include divinely enabled perception of the truth of that faith. Evidential analysis of religious belief systems must begin with the presupposition P1 that (A) is known, or the presupposition P2 that (B) is known, or the presupposition P3 that neither (A) nor (B) is known. An analysis that begins with acceptance of P1 (as in the Outsider Test, see, for example, p. 70:4-5) arbitrarily rejects P2. An analysis that begins with acceptance of P2 (which presupposition, incidentally, may be implied by the truth of conservative Biblical theology) arbitrarily rejects P1. An analysis that begins with acceptance of P3 (as in STONE) does not arbitrarily favor undue skepticism (P1), and blocks the possible arbitrary favoring of religious faith via divine revelation presuppositions (P2). STONE, therefore, carries with it the advantage of beginning from a neutral standpoint with respect to religious belief formation presuppositions, and this neutrality paves the way for us to more wisely follow the evidence wherever it leads us, while removing unnecessary blinders.[62] Some blinders may be necessary or justified, but P1 is neither.

Loftus disagrees, though he may do well to change his mind after reading this book! He asserts that the RDVT leads to the RDPT.[63] We may interpret the RDPT to mean that cultural/sociological conditions are, predominantly, the exclusive cause of religious faith. P1 would appear to be an appropriate claim to accept in one's evidential analysis of religious faith, but only if the RDPT is established. The case for the RDPT, then, is critical to Loftus' case for the Outsider Test.

Now, we may grant Loftus' RDVT,[64] but he needs to soften his overly confident assertions to read as follows: "If you were born in India, then you would likely (but not certainly) be a Hindu right now…"[65] The Voltaire quote[66] also implies that Loftus' assertions should be considered not certain, but at most, likely.

A persuasive case for the RDPT, however, must be more compelling than the mere assertion that the RDVT leads to the RDPT.[67] After all, the RDPT is a *causal* theory,[68] and as such, it deserves interpretation in the context of an overall theory of causation, including consideration of such issues as: (1) definition of a causal relation, (2) the nature of causal relata, (3) conditions sufficient for identification of a causal relation, (4) the relationship between causal relations and physical events, and (5) the scope of causal explanations. I would expect Loftus to carefully consider issues such as these so that he would be able to more meaningfully establish the rational basis for his assertion that the RDPT instantiates a causal relation, especially given his inclusion of Graham Oppy's book in his bibliography[69] which includes a brief mention of the richness of the philosophy of causation terrain.

Unfortunately, Loftus does not develop anything close to a justified interpretation of the concept of "causation", but merely appeals to the strong influence (i.e., correlation) between religious faith and the correlated social/cultural/geographical/psychological conditions C,[70] as if that is all we need in order to prove the causal RDPT thesis (recall that RDPT is the thesis that C is the predominant cause of religious faith). In response, correlation does not imply causation, and this fact is no "slender reed",[71] but is a fundamental supportive foundation for invoking a skeptical reaction to Loftus' erroneous presumption that a correlation between A and B requires that we acknowledge a causal relationship between A and B. If Loftus' mere appeal to a correlation is a sufficient condition of establishing proof of causation, then the correlation between American disasters and American anti-Zionist governmental activity[72] might practically lead Loftus to support Zionist politics for the sake of America's safety! Moreover, the "correlation implies causation" inference may lead Loftus to accept that the correlation between my waking each morning and the Weather Channel's weather broadcasts each morning would be a sufficient condition of establishing proof that there is a likely causal relationship between my waking each morning and the Weather Channel's morning weather broadcasts! Of course, I suspect Loftus would reject (as do I) that there is such a causal relationship.

The point, here, is that something is missing in Loftus' inference from "A is correlated with B" to "A is caused by B". Specifically, he has failed to define "cause", and he has failed to show how the RDPT satisfies the definition of "cause" he has in mind. Also, he has failed to consider the concept of "cause" used in my natural theology,[73] and he has failed to consider the implications of the critical fact that the RDPT fails to instantiate a causal relation on my definition of "cause".

For example, if my philosophy of causation is correct, then "A causes B" only if A is likely a person, where "cause" is interpreted to mean "bring about, produce, or make happen". Since C is not a person, it follows that C is likely not a cause, even though it correlates with caused religious beliefs. In other words, theory T may be true, where T is the theory that God, humans, and possibly other non-human persons, may all be contributing causes of the correlation between C and religious faith. In this context, Loftus' arbitrarily restricts the scope of metaphysical possibilities by naïvely assuming the RDVT correlation entails the RDPT causal thesis.

Note carefully: I do not claim religious faith does not strongly depend on, for example, social and geographical conditions.[74] The mere acknowledgement of a dependence relation, however, is not synonymous with the acknowledgement of a causal relation. It is clear that "A depends on B" need not entail "A is causally related to B".

Note also: I do not claim that a person's time and location of birth is largely unrelated to a person's religious beliefs.[75] I simply point out that since not all relationships are causal, the mere identification of a relationship is an insufficient condition of identifying that that relationship is causal.

Loftus concludes: "That's all anyone can ask me to show."[76] In response, I have clearly demonstrated that much more must be shown to establish the RDPT thesis, especially since my natural theology constitutes considerable evidence against that thesis. Thus, it does not help Loftus' case to establish the existence of an "overwhelming role",[77] unless that role is shown to be a causal role, since the RDPT thesis is a *causal* thesis, not a thesis about strong correlations.

Loftus, in effect, claims "C causes religious beliefs" entails "we should all become agnostics."[78] In response, if C causes religious beliefs, then presumably we have no free will to choose alternative beliefs! Thus, if C causes religious beliefs, then we are presumably hopelessly bound to persist in our acceptance of what C causes us to believe, and that may well be something other than the agnosticism Loftus urges us to accept. On the other hand, if we have free will to perform actions that lead to our acceptance of beliefs not caused by C, then C may not be the cause of our religious beliefs after all. Thus, we've found another dilemma for Loftus: either C alone causes all our beliefs, or it does not. If C alone causes all our beliefs, then we have no choice but to believe whatever C continues to cause us to believe, in which case we may well be incapable of becoming agnostic, as Loftus urges. On the other hand, if C alone does not cause all our beliefs, then the door is opened wide to reject the RDPT, since a multitude of other causal factors may be at play.

Loftus evidently accepts that it is fallacious to reason that "C causes religious faith" entails "religious faith is false".[79] He claims, however, that his position is actually that "C causes religious faith" entails "skepticism of faith is warranted".[80] Here again, as often elsewhere,[81] Loftus favors religious skeptical agnosticism over religious neutral agnosticism, yet fails to justify that preference, and in fact, fails to even identify religious neutral agnosticism as an option.

Both T and RDPT predict the observed distribution patterns in religious faith, however, RDPT (but not T) is grounded in an unjustified philosophy of causation. T is, therefore, a better explanation.

I conclude that the Outsider Test manifests an arbitrary, unjustified skeptical stance towards religious belief, whereas STONE minimizes unnecessary, unjustified presuppositions by seeking a maximally neutral mutually agreed upon starting point in debate resolution. We may, therefore, reject both the control belief CB1 and the Outsider Test (which is now shown to fail to support CB1).

Control Beliefs and Science

Loftus presents evidence in support of his control beliefs CB2 and CB3 in his sixth chapter.[82] Loftus claims that by the time of the Copernican revolution, it was established that the universe uniformly changes in accordance with physical laws.[83] In response, this was not established then, nor is it established now. We do not even have good reason to believe that all physical processes in the universe have been discovered, and if unknown physical processes may well exist, then there is surely no means by which we may directly verify that those processes occur uniformly in accordance with physical laws. Furthermore, most physical processes in the past are beyond our capacity to investigate, so again, we are unable to directly verify that all past physical processes have occurred uniformly in accordance with physical laws. Also, future physical events have not yet occurred, so we can not directly verify that all future physical events will occur in accordance with physical laws. The inference from "many physical processes occur in accordance with physical laws" to "all known and unknown physical processes uniformly occur in accordance with physical laws" is clearly deductively invalid. If, instead, Loftus has some inductive inference in mind, then it deserves elucidation, but his proof by mere assertion is not persuasive. Inconsistently, Loftus later appears to contradict himself, shying away from the assertion that nature operates uniformly.[84] So, it is far from clear what position Loftus actually takes on the question of whether physical laws uniformly describe physical processes.

I do not wish to imply that we may not accrue inductive support for a uniformitarian principle which may justify the claim that physical laws generally describe physical event patterns; indeed, I accept a version of just such a principle. The point, here, is that support for such a principle is inductive, and the certain confidence presumed by Loftus is wholly unjustified.[85] In fact, even if a uniformitarian principle as I have described is true, it only follows that known and unknown physical events generally (but not with exception-less uniformity) occur in accordance with physical laws. Loftus has expressed unjustified faith in a uniformly law-described universe.

Loftus refers to the "God of the Gaps" idea that a physical event (or event pattern) thought to be evidence of the existence of God (by virtue of its not being explained in terms of a known physical law) may become explained in terms of a newly discovered physical law, thereby eliminating the need for appeal to divine existence/action to explain the physical event (or event pattern).[86] In response, the description of a physical event (or physical event pattern) in terms of a physical law does not explain the causal origin of the physical event or event pattern, since the law is merely a description (not a causal explanation). Furthermore, my AFTLOP[87] establishes that physical events described by physical laws are generally God-caused. Therefore, contrary to Loftus' supposition, a physical law-based description of a physical event provides evidence for the existence of God. It is wholly unjustified to presume that identification of a physical law-based description of an event entails that the description explains the causal origin of the event. Physical laws describe patterns of caused physical events; they do not cause the events they describe. It is rather absurd to suppose that a description causes what it describes. Thus, scientific advancement evidenced by increased knowledge of physical laws only serves to provide further evidence for the existence and action of God. It is the atheologians who need to retreat in the face of science, for every discovery of every new physical law only further establishes the existence and action of God as the cause of the obtaining of that law. In short, physical science focuses upon the study of how God acts in the physical world.

Loftus implies that religious beliefs are inferior to scientific beliefs, since there are universally accepted reliable tests for the latter, but not the former.[88] In response, if "science" is interpreted broadly to apply to acquisition of knowledge of all kinds, then the science/religion distinction is superfluous. If science is interpreted narrowly to refer only to acquisition of knowledge of physical processes in the physical universe we inhabit, then a difference in the degree to which tests are universally accepted in science (as compared to the corresponding degree in religion) may merely result from the distinct nature of analyses often required in those respective domains. There is no good reason to suppose a universally accepted religious test is a necessary condition of acquisition of religious knowledge. Moreover, there is doubtfully even universal acceptance of any test for acquisition of scientific knowledge. After all, it would take only one person somewhere in the jungles of Africa to disagree with conventional scientific methodology to refute the claim that there exists universal acceptance of appropriate testing of scientific hypotheses. The "universal acceptance" requirement, or for that matter, the "mutually agreed upon" requirement may be rejected in both the scientific and religious domains, since one's personal perception of truth need not be dependent on the epistemic state of other persons. Yes, STONE (see Chapter 7) may be used to resolve debates in a context in which there is mutual agreement, but note that STONE may be applied to either a scientific or religious context.

Unfortunately, Loftus resorts to the unjustified "proof by assertion" tactic.[89] These mere assertions do not even deserve a response.

Loftus presumes "we are insignificant".[90] In response, I presume we *are* significant! The significance of God's interest in humanity (evidenced via the truth of conservative Biblical theology) is only strengthened by our discovery of the vastness of God's great power and knowledge evidenced by the vastness of the cosmos God created and sustains.[91]

Loftus presumes a multiverse eliminates need for God as an explanation.[92] In response, a multiverse increases the need for God as an explanation, since a multiverse would require the existence of a creator of many universes, not just one![93]

Loftus attempts to justify methodological naturalism (MN) so that he may use it to support his control beliefs CB2 and CB3. He evidently takes MN to be the assumption that every physical event has a natural cause.[94] In response, MN, so defined, is not particularly meaningful unless "natural cause" is defined. Unfortunately, Loftus provides no clear definition of "natural cause". I will assume A is a natural cause of B if and only if A causes B, where A and B are both physical events. On this definition, it is far from obvious that any natural cause exists. Yes, we have ample empirical evidence for the existence of physical laws (i.e., physical event patterns), but there is no good reason to suppose an identified pattern actually causes the physical events described by that pattern, nor does the identification of a physical event pattern, in and of itself, adequately ground the assumption that the pattern consists of only (or any) natural causes.

The De Vries quote[95] would, if true, imply that MN is a neutral method with respect to the existence of God. In response, MN technically presupposes the nonexistence of a God who causes physical event patterns to occur in accordance with physical laws God causes to obtain. Thus, MN is technically not neutral with respect to the existence of God. As such, it begs the question against the possibility of the existence of any divine cause of the obtaining of physical laws, and it deserves to be rejected on that basis, since it is a non-neutral unnecessary presupposition. It follows that MN is *not* compatible with this form of belief in God.[96]

Loftus might respond that MN is not intended to be an actual denial of supernaturalism, but merely a practical assumption for the purpose of facilitating productive inquiry.[97] In response, the productive inquiry achieved by making the (technically question-begging) MN assumption may be better achieved by embracing non-question-begging LP (Lawful Physicalism). LP may be understood as the search for a description of all physical events in terms of physical laws. Thus, both MN and LP lead to the search for a description of all physical events in terms of physical laws, but MN (and not LP) presupposes the additional unjustified view that all physical events have natural causes. We may search diligently and everywhere for physical law-based descriptions of physical events (as in LP) without arbitrarily presupposing that this search must be grounded in the unjustified assertion that all physical events have natural causes. Clearly, it is possible that all physical events might someday conceivably be described in terms of physical laws, even if no natural cause ever exists. After all, it is possible that the obtaining of all physical laws is God-caused, where all physical events are caused either by God or other persons, implying the nonexistence of any physical event having its occurrence grounded in the causal action of another physical event. Also, some physical events may never become described in terms of any known physical law, and such events need not be presumed to have a natural cause as a necessary condition of the diligent pursuit of any possible physical law that might describe those events. LP does not demand that all physical events have physical causes, but it insures that we actively seek any physical law that may describe any physical event. MN arbitrarily blinds us to the possibility that some physical events may not be caused by physical events; LP carries with it no such blinding influence, but leaves open the question of whether some physical events may (or may not) be caused by other physical events.

MN thwarts the advancement of religious knowledge by its religiously non-neutral presuppositions. LP facilitates the advancement of both scientific and religious knowledge by urging "If God didn't do it, then search for a physical law-based description of it; If God did do it, then search for a physical law-based description of how God did it!" LP does not thwart scientific progress by claiming "God did it, so don't look for an explanation in terms of a physical law!" Thus, we refute the common claim that a methodology that is not anti-supernaturalistic may be prone to thwarting scientific progress.[98]

MN carries with it, therefore, excessive and unnecessary presuppositional baggage which arbitrarily limits the scope of metaphysically possible operative principles, whereas LP neatly preserves the diligent, testable, evidence-based, logic-grounded, prediction-lending, research-directing, truth-pursuing approach to discovery of the physical world without unjustifiably presuming an anti-supernatural bias against any possible nonphysical features of reality. LP has all the benefits of MN, yet none of the arbitrary naturalistic presuppositions of MN. LP is neutral with respect to the possibility of any supernatural agency, whereas MN positively (and needlessly) presupposes the inaction of any supernatural agency in the physical realm. After all, even if we all knew that God causes physical events to occur in accordance with physical laws, MN would force us to reject this knowledge. Such rejection is needless, since religiously non-neutral MN may be replaced by religiously neutral LP, regardless of whether we know that God causes physical events to occur in accordance with physical laws, and regardless of whether we know God exists.

Granted, MN has resulted in the productive discovery of many new features of physical reality. "MN is productive", however, does not entail "MN is the best methodology". As I have argued, LP brings with it all the productivity of scientific discovery often associated with MN,[99] yet LP is religiously neutral (unlike MN). Clearly, LP is better than MN. Thus, modern educated people may derive their deductions from LP, not MN,[100] and they have nothing to lose but the needless blinding influence of MN in so doing.

If I hear a noise N in the night,[101] then, following LP, I presume there is likely a physical law-based description of N, unless I know (or eventually discover) that N happens to be caused by some person to be not physically law-based. MN is completely unnecessary in this experience.

Loftus speaks of natural (physical) laws, as if they provide an alternative to explanations in terms of divine agency.[102] This reveals the blinding influence of

MN in Loftus' thought…he fails to recognize that natural (physical) laws may be descriptions of regular physical event patterns caused by God. If Loftus rejected MN in favor of LP, he would be in a better position to perceive this possibility and evaluate its probability. Blinded by MN, however, it is evident that he fails, unfortunately, to perceive the viability of alternative metaphysical possibilities.

LP-acceptance could help enable Loftus to see that my AFTLOP (see Chapter 2, and my previous book) is not merely a logical possibility,[103] but a rational response to available evidence. It could also enable him to see that since physical laws are a manifestation of supernatural divine agency, physical laws lead to successful predictions of probable future divinely-caused physical events, thereby refuting the charge that there is no method for knowing the supernatural.[104] Also, my AFTLOP could help enable Loftus to see the error of MN and its evidence-contradicting assumption, by exposing that most (if not all) physical events are caused by persons.

The Shotwell quote[105] expresses some important concerns that proponents of MN may typically share. In particular, since LP permits (though does not require or presuppose) the possibility of supernatural explanations, there is concern that LP-acceptance may lead to an "anything goes" mentality. In response, there is no reason to suppose LP must (or probably would) lead to such erroneous thinking. LP is fully compatible with conventional, logical reasoning principles, including considerations related to simplicity, scope, explanatory power, evidential support, and minimization of presuppositions that are neither necessary nor justified. Thus, the unjustified "ghostly little gremlin" theory may be rejected in favor of a more conventional, justified theistic explanatory hypothesis by virtue of the application of these accepted principles of reasoning via such arguments as my AFTLOP and fine-tuning arguments.[106] Research may be directed in LP just as in MN, in the sense that they both share the active pursuit of the discovery of possibly existing physical law-based descriptions of physical events. Hypotheses may be tested in both LP and MN; granted, a free agent can not be tested by presuming that the agent will always act regularly, but this problem afflicts MN just as much as LP, and so is not evidence against the superiority of LP. In addition, LP's pursuit of physical law-based explanations manifests the expectation that observations and experiments will occur in accordance with physical laws, even though exceptions to such laws may occasionally be identified. Thus, LP is not only *not* useless to scientists, but it is a needed antidote to the unjustified naturalistic mindset often erroneously assumed to be an essential component of a successful scientific research program.

The Martin quote[107] focuses on the truly important component of MN: the value of not blocking further inquiry. We may agree with Martin that inquiry should not be blocked, and LP captures precisely this essential feature of MN without the accompanying metaphysical presupposition that God is not the cause of any physical events. The noble pursuit of not blocking inquiry, therefore, favors LP over MN, given that MN is accompanied by unnecessary and unjustified presuppositions which do not plague LP. Thus, even if we think God caused some physical event P, LP nevertheless insures that we will continue to pursue the discovery of a physical law-based description of how God caused P, regardless of whether we ever eventually discover such a description. The pursuit of such a description is not motivated by a desire to disprove that God is the causal agent, but is motivated by a desire to learn the nature of God's causal agency, provided our reasons for supposing that God's causal agency were in operation are not subsequently disproven by future analysis. It follows that the Sharp quote[108] is incorrect, since appropriately justified supernatural explanations do not block further inquiry, and may even be discovered to be unjustified at some future time.

Loftus has failed to justify MN and he has failed to evaluate LP as an alternative to MN. I have argued that LP is superior to MN. It follows that we may reject both MN and the control beliefs CB2 and CB3 which MN is now seen to fail to support.

Control Beliefs and History

Loftus' control belief CB2 is, in effect, assumed and used in his explanation of his philosophy of history.[109] CB2 is shown to be unjustified in the previous section of this chapter.[110] Clearly, CB2 is not a neutral approach to historical analysis, as it simply begs the question against the possibility or high probability of non-natural causes of historical events. Acceptance of CB2 is even further unjustified, given my AFTLOP and fine-tuning arguments,[111] which entail the existence of a rational basis for supposing both the nonexistence of impersonal natural causes, and the abundant evidence of theism-confirming non-naturalistic personal causes.

Granted, pure and utter objectivity may be practically difficult or impossible to achieve, but it hardly follows that we must embrace a blatantly question-begging anti-supernaturalistic presupposition in historical analysis. Also, we may grant that the naturalistic presupposition of methodological naturalism (MN) in scientific or historical analysis does not lead to an entirely useless approach to one's quest for truth, but the limited measure of effectiveness of MN-acceptance throughout history does not guarantee that MN is the only (or best) presupposition for maximizing practical efficiency in one's scientific and historical investigations.

Moreover, the claim "Historical analysis should begin with the MN assumption, since MN-acceptance has been historically successful in scientific progress" is unjustified. Loftus claims that we must begin historical analysis with MN-acceptance, yet appeals to already-performed historical analysis A in support of this claim. Here, A represents the historical analysis that consists of the conclusion that MN-acceptance has been historically successful in scientific progress. So, either A is grounded in the MN assumption, or it is not. If it is, then Loftus manifests circular (and unjustified) reasoning. If it is not, then he presupposes the soundness of a historical analysis (A) that is not grounded in MN after all, in which case historical analysis need not begin with the MN assumption; if MN may be rejected in A, then the door is open to reject MN in other historical analyses as well. Thus, the MN assumption in historical analysis is not justified by the appeal to its alleged effectiveness in the historical growth and development of scientific knowledge.

The context in which the Price quote[112] is given appears to imply that the options available to the historian are either MN-based skepticism or unbridled acceptance of any wild tale whatever. In response, there is no good reason provided for the supposition that a position between these two extremes can not be justified. To be sure, good historical analysis includes critical evaluation of available evidence, but (1) there is no good reason to insist that such critical analysis must be grounded in MN-acceptance, (2) there is good reason to suppose MN should be rejected, (3) there is no good reason to suppose MN-rejection requires that the critical historian accept all alleged miraculous instances as being actual miraculous instances, and (4) the logical impossibility of all alleged miraculous instances being actual miraculous instances entails that the critical historian can not consistently accept that all alleged miraculous instances are actual miraculous instances, even if MN is rejected. Thus, we see that the threat "MN-rejection leads to acceptance of any miraculous allegation whatever" is an empty threat.

Loftus mentions three considerations which lead some historians to claim that miraculous/supernatural events are not within the proper domain of their investigation as historians.[113] The first is directly related to the assumption that religious propaganda is not history.[114] In response, the assumption "religious propaganda is not history" is, technically, ambiguous, since a definition of the key terms is not given. Nevertheless, we may state the obvious fact that although religious propaganda (on a common understanding of this term) is possibly historically inaccurate, it is also possibly historically accurate; the mere fact that religious propaganda is possibly historically inaccurate does not justify the conclusion that it is historically inaccurate. So, even if the Biblical Gospels (i.e., the Gospels of Matthew, Mark, Luke, and John) are religious propaganda, it does not follow that their content is necessarily (or probably) generally historically inaccurate, and it does not follow that any specific miraculous/supernatural content within the Gospels is necessarily (or probably) historically inaccurate. Thus, this first consideration does not lend support for the claim that miraculous/supernatural events are not within the proper domain of investigation by historians.

A second consideration, mentioned by Loftus, is grounded in the claim that evidential support for the set AMBS of ancient miraculous Biblical stories is apparently the same as the evidential support for the set AMNS of ancient miraculous non-Biblical stories.[115] In response, Loftus has not clearly specified the set CE of common elements of evidential support shared by the members of both AMBS and AMNS, nor has he explained why that alleged shared similarity in evidential support justifies the conclusion that it is irrational for conservative Bible-believers to accept the historicity of AMBS, yet reject the historicity of AMNS. Also, it is doubtful that all elements of evidential support for the members of AMBS are identical, in every respect, to all elements of evidential support for the members of AMNS; Loftus does not explore these differences, nor does he consider their rational implications.

Furthermore, Loftus' claim that CE is a nonempty set of shared evidentially supportive conditions for the members of both AMBS and AMNS is a historical claim justified by a historical analysis B. Either B is grounded in MN-acceptance, or it is not. If it is, then B is an instance of unjustified circular reasoning. If it is not, then Loftus is seen to accept the legitimacy of historical analysis not grounded in MN-acceptance after all, thereby opening the door to the proper acceptance of historical analyses not grounded in MN-acceptance. Either way, B does not lend support for the conclusion that the miraculous is outside the proper domain of the historian's investigation.

Loftus implies that the early Christians may have exaggerated the true nature of Jesus' deeds.[116] In response, we may simply grant this theoretical possibility, yet deny that the possibility has been shown by him to carry with it a significant probability. The mere possibility of exaggeration in miraculous Biblical stories does not lend support for the claim that supernatural/miraculous events are outside the proper domain of the historian's investigation. Also, even if every miraculous/supernatural element of AMBS is a false exaggeration, it would not follow that every miraculous/supernatural element of AMNS is necessarily (or probably) a false exaggeration. Furthermore, the claim "historical proponents of miraculous/supernatural events are prone to exaggeration" is, itself, a historical claim derived from a historical analysis C. Either C is grounded in MN-acceptance, or it is not. If it is, then use of C to justify MN-acceptance exemplifies circular reasoning. If it is not, then MN-acceptance is not a necessary component of historical analysis after all, thereby opening the door to historical analyses not grounded in MN. Either way, consideration of the possibility of exaggerated miraculous/supernatural claims does not justify MN-acceptance in historical analysis.

Loftus provides a third reason which allegedly supports the claim that miraculous/supernatural events are not within the proper domain of historical investigation. The reason is the mere assertion that "miracles and supernatural events simply don't take place".[117] In response, proof by assertion is not particularly compelling. Furthermore, my Chapters 1 and 2, as well as my previous book, support the claim that natural physical miracles[118] routinely occur throughout the physical history of the universe, and also support the claim that the inadequacy of known physical laws as a complete explanation of physical reality points to the miraculous nature of physical events known to occur in ways unlikely to be described by any known (or unknown) physical laws.

Loftus then softens his position, merely claiming that neither he nor modern historians have experienced miracles.[119] In response, it is quite obvious that Loftus has not surveyed all existing modern historians to verify his assertion. Also, he provides no inductive support for the claim that all modern historians have probably not experienced miracles. In addition, some religious historians would likely flatly reject the assertion that they have never experienced a miracle. Furthermore, if "modern historian" is defined to include all modern people, then Loftus' position here amounts to the claim that no modern person has experienced a miracle, and Loftus has surely not surveyed all modern persons to acquire verification, nor has he clearly provided any inductive support for the claim that probably no modern person has experienced a miracle. On the other hand, if "modern historian" has some narrower definition in Loftus' mind, then he owes us the identification of that narrower definition so that we may scrutinize his intended position. Since Loftus has not even established that no modern historian has experienced a miracle, it hardly follows that no ancient person has experienced a miracle.[120] Thus, Loftus' considerations here do not provide support for the claim that miraculous/supernatural events are outside the proper domain of investigation by modern historians, especially since my AFLTOP and fine-tuning arguments[121] provide significant evidence to the contrary.

Even if Loftus' three lines of evidence (considered above) established that miraculous/supernatural events are outside the proper domain of historical investigation, there would still remain the potential for establishing that miraculous/supernatural historical events have occurred. After all, history is not our only source of knowledge. Indeed, my philosophical/scientific theistic arguments provide a rational basis for the inference to the actual routine occurrence of natural physical miracles[122] throughout the history of the universe. Also, God could reveal (by direct and immediate divinely-initiated experience) to some persons that miraculous events are historical.[123]

The situation for Loftus is even worse, however, for if he has established that miraculous/supernatural events are outside the proper domain of historical investigation, then he would be incapable of using historical analysis to shed any light at all upon whether any alleged miraculous/supernatural event is historical. That is, if Loftus were correct, then he could not use history to discount miracles, for if Loftus were to use history to discredit miracles, then we could object that Loftus had used history inappropriately by assuming it can inform us regarding the nature of possibly existing miraculous/supernatural events, whereas such historical informing is not possible on the thesis that miraculous/supernatural events are outside the proper domain of historical investigation.

Loftus' position is problematic for another reason. Suppose Bob presently knows that Bob observes miracle M at a time T minutes before present. In this case, Bob could not even use historical reasoning to justify Bob's ongoing acceptance of the fact that Bob observed M, since historical reasoning (according to Loftus) is not an appropriate miraculous/supernatural investigative tool. The absurdity of this conclusion becomes especially evident as T approaches zero. Again, we have reason to reject the claim that miraculous/supernatural events are outside the proper domain of historical investigation.

We may grant that it is theoretically possible that an individual with limited knowledge and insight could perform a historical analysis of limited available evidence and ultimately conclude that miraculous/supernatural events have not occurred. There is no good reason, however, to suppose that even such an individual must accept MN in the performance of that historical analysis.

Loftus appeals to physical laws when arguing that ancient people experienced what modern people experience.[124] This move undermines Loftus' own position, however, since my AFTLOP establishes that physical laws ground the inference to routine divine action as manifested by the general obtaining of those laws throughout the history of the physical universe. So, when the modern historian (and Loftus) experience physical laws not caused by humans, they experience evidence of divine action in the physical world. Since Loftus accepts that physical laws also obtained during ancient times, it follows that Loftus may proceed to accept that ancient people also experienced evidence of divine action in the physical world. Far from refuting historical miraculous claims, the appeal to the historical obtaining of physical laws only further confirms theism and the prevalence of the natural physical miracles those laws have historically manifested.

Loftus quotes Geisler to the effect that one's knowledge of the resolution of the theism-atheism debate is a necessary condition of one's knowing objective historical meaning.[125] In response, this is simply not true. I could know that I ate eggs for breakfast many times last year (a historical fact), regardless of whether I happen to know that the theism-atheism debate has been resolved in my mind. The door is thus opened to acquisition of historical knowledge independent of the resolution of the theism-atheism debate.

Loftus then interprets the Geisler quote to the effect that one's knowledge of the resolution of the Biblical worldview debate is a necessary condition of one's knowing that Biblical miracles are objective historical facts.[126] In response, I could know that I ate eggs for breakfast many times last year (a historical fact), regardless of whether I happen to know that the Biblical worldview debate has been resolved in my mind. The door is thus opened to acquisition of historical knowledge independent of the resolution of the Biblical worldview debate, and such an open door could enable the knowledge of the miraculous/supernatural nature of Biblical miracles, even if the Biblical worldview debate is not resolved in one's mind. It is possible to admit the miraculous nature of Jesus' ministry, yet deny the historically traditional conservative Biblical worldview;[127] although this possibility does not represent my position, it is sufficient to refute Loftus' position.

Loftus claims that some Biblical miracles must be justified (if at all) by historical analysis, not philosophical analysis.[128] In response, historical and philosophical analyses are intimately intertwined, and the supposition that good historical analysis can exist independent of good philosophical analysis is simply incorrect. Presumably Loftus knows this, but then his comments are in need of clarification so that we may understand his intended thought.

Let PCH represent the probability that the conservative Biblical theologian's view of history describes actual past events. Historical analysis could begin with the neutral presupposition that the value of PCH is unknown. Thus, the fact that conservative Bible-believers view history from a perspective in which PCH is assumed to be high does not entail that conservative Bible-believers can provide no noncircular justification of that perspective. For example, a person could perform historical analysis from the perspective of many different frameworks, and then determine which analysis is good and best, without blindly presupposing one's finally accepted analysis and framework. Conservative Biblical theology need not be blindly presupposed as a prerequisite for perceiving such theology is true. Loftus' conundrum is, thus, without force,[129] as he has not shown faulty this option available to the historian.

The Marshall quote[130] emphasizes the impossibility of presupposition-less historical analysis, but this fact does not entail the nonexistence of a maximally neutral historical analysis in which religious beliefs may be confirmed by past events without arbitrarily presupposing those beliefs in that analysis. A conservative Bible-believer could theoretically consider the option of rejecting the conservative Bible-believer's view of history, and then use subsequent religiously neutral analysis to infer that rejection of that rejection is warranted. The charge of circular reasoning in the justification of the conservative Bible-believer's view of history is unjustified.[131] Yes, some conservative Biblical apologists engage in circular (and, in my opinion, unjustified) reasoning at different levels, but it does not follow that a non-circular historical conservative Biblical apologetic probably does not exist.

Loftus objects that it is inappropriate of God to use a person's historical beliefs to determine a person's eternal destiny.[132] In response, if God has knowledge K that one's eternal destiny-determining historical beliefs are, themselves, properly determined by factors which include one's free choices, then Loftus' objection does not follow. After all, it is possible that God providentially arranges human history to evolve such that each person's historical beliefs ultimately lead to God's morally proper determination of each person's eternal destiny, and our inability to empirically establish the improbability of this possibility defuses Loftus' objection. Pending support for the claim that God does not know K (assuming God exists), we may identify Loftus' objection as unwarranted.

In dealing with some possible objections to his position, Loftus reveals an important unjustified component of his philosophy. He discusses what God (if God exists) would or could do.[133] In response, let G represent the set of possibly existing gods. Let GS represent the subset of G, where the ways of a member of GS would, if that member actually existed, be fully scrutable for Loftus. Let GI represent each member of G not in GS. Thus, the ways of a member of GI would, if that member actually existed, be at least partially (if not fully) inscrutable (indiscernible) for Loftus. Now, Loftus may claim "If the Christian God exists, then the Christian God would or could or should do such and such" only if Loftus knows that the Christian God is a member of GS (or a member of GI, where the Christian God enables, or does not prevent, Loftus' limited knowledge of the ways of the Christian God, thereby leading to Loftus' justified claim regarding the ways of the Christian God). However, it is likely that if the Christian God exists, then the Christian God is a member of GI[134] such that we may doubt that Loftus possesses sufficient knowledge of the ways of the possibly existing partially inscrutable Christian God to the extent that Loftus may justifiably assert that he knows what the Christian God would/could/should do, if the Christian God exists. To be more precise, we may grant that all of Loftus' comments (throughout all of his writings) regarding what God would/could/should do in some circumstance may apply to at least some members of GS or GI, but it does not follow that Loftus knows what a possibly existing member of GI would/could/should do in some circumstance, unless that member enables, or does not prevent, knowledge of what that member would/could/should do. Therefore, since we may reject the claim that Loftus' comments are known to apply to the Christian God, those comments may not be used to disconfirm the existence of the Christian God. Loftus has failed to show that his knowledge of the ways of the Christian God is such that Loftus knows that "the Christian God exists" entails "Loftus' observations of reality (assuming the Christian God exists) would differ from Loftus' actual observations".

Considerations in the preceding paragraph may be posed in the form of another dilemma for Loftus. Are the ways of the possibly existing Biblical God at least partially inscrutable? If Loftus answers "no", then the full and detailed ways of the possibly existing Biblical God have not been sufficiently identified and explained by Loftus to the extent that his anti-Biblical writings demonstrably justify his rejection of conservative Biblical theology. If "yes", then Loftus is not in a position to claim that the Biblical God does not permit his anti-Biblical beliefs for reasons he doesn't understand, in which case his epistemic state (as described in all of his writings) does not constitute evidence that the existence of the Biblical God is unlikely. It is possible that the Biblical God permits Loftus to persist in his anti-Biblical beliefs for reasons unknown to Loftus, and Loftus is in no position to establish that the probability of this possibility is small. It follows that Loftus' anti-Biblical writings do not constitute evidence that the Biblical God is unlikely to exist.

Loftus claims that the existence of a large number of sincere nonbelievers confirms that insufficient evidence exists to justify our acceptance of distinctively Christian beliefs, even if the Christian God exists.[135] In response, since a person can know truths unknown by billions of others, the mere existence of billions of non-Christian believers would not disconfirm a Christian's belief, and it would not confirm a non-Christian's non-Christian belief. Furthermore, the global distribution of Christian belief is a function of many variables, and Loftus has not shown that the variables that determine the non-Christian belief of others justify our own non-Christian belief. In fact, he has not even persuasively identified all such variables.

Loftus claims that God chose the poor medium of historical evidence as a form of divine revelation.[136] In response, if Loftus accepts this claim, then Loftus is a theist! After all, God makes choices only if God exists. Presumably Loftus means "Historical evidence is a poor form of divine revelation by any possibly existing God". In response, Loftus is not in a position to critique the ways of the members of GI, and since the Biblical God is likely a member of GI (see above), Loftus' objection to the efficacy of divine revelation via history is not justifiably applicable to the Biblical God.

Furthermore, we need not suppose that history is the only means by which possibly existing gods facilitate divine revelation. So, even if historical evidence alone is insufficient to justify a person's religious belief, it does not follow that rejection of religious belief is justified. Religious beliefs (including religious historical beliefs) could be justified by arguments that are not merely historical in nature.

Loftus provides some historical arguments which he believes support the claim that Christianity is disconfirmed by the fact that God has failed to communicate his will effectively to believers.[137] In response, if Loftus maintains this claim, then he is a theist! After all, God can fail only if God exists. Presumably Loftus means "If Christianity were true, then God would effectively communicate the way Loftus would expect." In response, the fact that the Biblical God has evidently not communicated the way Loftus would expect (if the Biblical God exists) is evidence against conservative Biblical theology only if the Biblical God is a member of GS (see above), but since the Biblical God is not shown to be a member of GS (and is likely a member of GI), Loftus is unable to use his historical arguments as evidence against the existence of the Biblical God.

Loftus also claims that the Holy Spirit fails to "do his job".[138] Again, this claim is not properly made by atheists, since atheists are taken to generally reject the existence of the Holy Spirit! Presumably Loftus means "If the Holy Spirit exists, then Loftus would expect Him to cause reality to be different than it is." In response, the nature of reality can be used to disconfirm the existence of the Holy Spirit only if the ways of the Spirit are not inscrutable. Since Loftus has not shown that the ways of the Spirit are not inscrutable, he may not use the nature of reality as evidence against the existence of the Holy Spirit.

We may conclude that Loftus has failed to justify his approach to historical analysis. Rejection of his MN-grounded historical methodology is in order, especially since that methodology is, itself, grounded in Loftus' unjustified control belief CB2.

Control Beliefs and Theistic Arguments

Loftus includes a critique of common theistic arguments[139] in an attempt to establish that they are "inconclusive".[140] This section of his chapter does not directly support a fundamental control belief that he accepts, although it may help to confirm in his mind, to some degree, that God-belief that is grounded in theistic arguments would be an unacceptable control belief for theists to accept. Unfortunately, Loftus does not interact with my own theistic arguments.[141] This leads him to incorrectly infer that theistic arguments do not imply the existence of a personal God,[142] when in fact, my AFTLOP and fine-tuning arguments do imply the existence of a personal God.[143]

Ontological arguments play little role in my noetic structure, so I have nothing important to say about either them or Loftus' critique of them. Regarding cosmological arguments, my AFTLOP[144] might be construed as a cosmological argument of sorts, but Loftus' critique of cosmological arguments does not really interact with my AFTLOP. A few comments are in order, though.

The Hick quote[145] refers to the possibility that the physical universe is unexplained. In response, my AFTLOP establishes that we have no evidence of any uncaused physical events, and we have evidence that physical events are caused by persons. Therefore, the possibility that the physical universe is unexplained is improbable, given the known nature of physical event causation. Even Loftus would be expected to discourage a resort to a "merely possible" defense, given his resistance to such reasoning.[146]

Loftus does not establish the existence of uncaused physical events with a single-sentence reference[147] to two non-referencing sentences.[148] I refer the reader to my fuller response to Steele's mistaken thinking which Loftus erroneously accepts.[149]

Loftus raises the "fallacy of composition" objection to establish that an inductive inference from part to whole is not always justified.[150] He does not, however, consider the details of the inductive reasoning contained in my theistic arguments.[151] I have no reason to suppose my theistic arguments are fallacious in the sense Loftus considers. So long as my arguments use acceptable inductive reasoning to infer from part to whole in all cases where we have no good reasoning to challenge that inductive support, the fallacy of composition may be presumed inapplicable to my arguments. Loftus' reference to this fallacy, therefore, does not establish that it applies to my arguments.

The Stenger quote refers to an objection not applicable to my fine-tuning arguments.[152] Loftus likewise raises this objection, inapplicable though it is to my fine-tuning arguments.[153] My fine-tuning arguments include an examination of the implications of the consequences of the improbability of a physical law-based explanation of physical conditions necessary, but insufficient, for the existence of the kind of life that happens to exist on Earth. I argue that the implications of these consequences are theistic. There is nothing in my arguments that requires a commitment to the incorrect assumption that the form of life on Earth is the only possible form of life that could conceivably exist in our physical universe. Also, my arguments do not require commitment to the claim that existing life could not have been different than it is. Indeed, even if we knew that multiple exotic and radically non-Earthlike forms of life were discovered to exist throughout the universe, my fine-tuning arguments would stand.

In an attempt to account for the probabilistic resources required to provide a physical law-based description of the origin of life in our universe, Dawkins is quoted as appealing to the large number of planets which probably exist in our universe.[154] In response, Dawkins, as quoted, is woefully simplistic in his conclusion, and fails to interact with the full scope of relevant scientific considerations.[155] We have good reason to doubt, therefore, that Dawkins' probabilistic estimate accurately accounts for the relevant scientific considerations needed to justify his conclusion. I made this same point in my previous book,[156] but Loftus has failed to respond to this point.

Loftus quotes Stenger as claiming that physical laws help explain the origin of DNA.[157] In response, my AFTLOP establishes that such physical laws are caused by God to obtain. Thus, far from avoiding intelligent design implications, Stenger actually confirms intelligent design of DNA by acknowledging its causal origin in physical event patterns which my AFLTOP establishes are caused by God to obtain.

Loftus briefly (and incompletely) refers to the possibility of poorly designed physical entities.[158] He also lists of a few of the theological considerations that may be relevant to such possibilities.[159] And that's it! We are left hanging, wondering whether Loftus considers those theological options to be adequate or not, and if not, then why not. Needless to say, a poor design is a design nonetheless, and if Loftus acknowledges that a physical system is poorly designed by a non-human designer, then Loftus may well be on his way towards theistic belief after all. In fact, he appears to acknowledge the validity of the design inference in cases where impersonal scientific explanations are implausible.[160] It is unclear, therefore, why he thinks the Biblical God is not a member of the set of all plausible designers of not-humanly-designed physical systems,[161] given these considerations.

Loftus refers to Dawkins' "Ultimate Boeing 747 gambit".[162] Unfortunately, Loftus fails to respond to my critique of it.[163] It is worth noting that my critique does not rely on the assumption that God is a simple being. Loftus' conclusions[164] are, therefore, preliminary, and especially unjustified, given my sharp and detailed critique of his views throughout this book.

Loftus considers the question of who (or what) made God.[165] In response, we may note that either God is made or God is not made. In either case, my arguments show God exists.[166] Knowledge of who (or what) made God is not a necessary condition of our knowing God exists. Also, the conservative Bible-believer need not define God as "not made" to avoid otherwise insurmountable difficulties associated with establishing the existence of God; perhaps Copan prefers to resort to such definitional tactics,[167] but it does not follow that all conservative Bible-believers do so,[168] and it should be clear that I do not.

The personal causal principle (i.e., all physical events are caused by persons) that I advocate in my AFTLOP does not require that God's existence is caused, since we have no good reason to suppose God's existence (assuming God exists) is a physical event. So, it is not question-begging to claim that God and the universe are in different categories.[169] The universe is comprised of physical events. God is not reasonably presumed to be a physical event.

Loftus mentions multiverse theory, as if it is a viable alternative to theistic inference in natural theological arguments. In fact, my AFTLOP stands firm, even if multiverse theory is true, and a multiverse would even further magnify the need for theistic inference, since a multiverse would require a creator and sustainer of each universe that ever exists in the multiverse.

Furthermore, multiverse theory is, perhaps, the ultimate "anything goes" theory, and Loftus' resistance to such a theoretical property[170] may lead us to expect his rejection of multiverse theory for that reason. In fact, hell (defined, here, as a place of unfathomably immense and long-term suffering resulting from resistance to, and rejection of, conservative Biblical truth) is not merely possible in a multiverse, but is virtually inevitable in not one, but in a multitude of universes.[171] Loftus' disdain for a place such as hell[172] and his rejection of its reality[173] implies he rejects multiverse theory, unless he accepts some specialized version of a multiverse theory that entails nothing like hell exists in any universe, in which case we'd need evidence for such a specialized version, but Loftus provides no justification for such an arbitrary position.

Loftus makes a passing comment regarding "Occam's razor".[174] In response, the simplest explanation is not always best. However, the simplest explanation that best explains (and is best supported by) available evidence E may be considered more strongly confirmed than a less simple explanation that explains (and is supported by) E, all other things being roughly equal. It follows that the best explanation may not be very simple at all, in general.

Loftus considers that the creator of the universe may no longer exist.[175] In response, my AFTLOP entails that God's ongoing existence may be inferred by the continuing existence and evolution of the universe in general accordance with physical laws, including all such laws discovered through scientific investigation.

Loftus considers a multi-personal source of creation.[176] In fact, conservative Biblical theism includes a trinitarian conception of the divine nature, in which God may be understood to instantiate three centers of consciousness.

Loftus considers that God's power and knowledge may not be large.[177] In response, my AFTLOP and fine-tuning arguments establish the existence of a God whose power and knowledge are *immensely* (and this is an understatement!) greater than that of man.

The conservative Biblical apologist may agree that it is generally true that natural theology is not sufficient to establish the existence of the Biblical God. Loftus goes further than this, though, and briefly argues, in effect, for the probable nonexistence of the Biblical God on the grounds that Biblical theism is morally unacceptable (barbaric).[178] In response, if objective morality does not exist, then the conservative Bible-believer need not mind Loftus' moral concerns, since the conservative Bible-believer need not embrace any anti-Biblical subjective moral standards embraced by Loftus. If objective morality does exist, then the conservative Bible-believer need not suppose Loftus is in a position to properly perceive the nature of that morality, thereby defeating the grounds upon which Loftus may seek to pronounce moral judgments upon Biblical morality. Thus, Loftus has not established that he has accurately perceived objective morality such that those perceptions justify rejection of Biblical morality.

Furthermore, even if all of Loftus' moral perceptions of objective morality are flawless (a dubious assumption, especially from Loftus' perspective, given his subjective account of morality),[179] Loftus has not established that his Biblical interpretations are entailed by a conservative Biblical system of Biblical ethics. Moreover, even if Loftus' Biblical interpretations are entailed by a conservative Biblical system of Biblical ethics, Loftus' disdain for that system does not entail it is incorrect, since Biblical ethics could be indirectly inferred via an overall Biblical apologetic, the point being that evaluation of the apparent degree to which Biblical morality coheres with one's sense of immediately perceived objective morality is insufficient to justify rejection of Biblical morality, since the larger context in which one's moral system is developed and justified must be accounted for when evaluating the probability that a particular ethical system is objectively best, even if the resultant justified system consists of some moral elements inconsistent with what one might otherwise presume corresponds to objective morality. Of particular note, one must account for the problem of God's immense knowledge (assuming God exists) of essential factors critical to moral judgments, where human understanding of such factors may be generally ignorant and, consequently, insufficient to justify critiques of the kind Loftus makes. Unfortunately, Loftus does not engage such issues as have been raised here, but proceeds to confidently pronounce moral judgments,[180] as if he were actually capable of justifiably doing so.

Control Beliefs and Religious Experience

Loftus includes a chapter on a form of religious experience known as the "Self-authenticating witness of the Holy Spirit".[181] That chapter does not contain an argument in support of a particular control belief embraced by Loftus, but it may be viewed as an attempt to confirm in Loftus' mind that religious beliefs grounded in the "witness of the Spirit" are not valid control beliefs.

Let P represent a person who has a religious experience E in which P perceives that it is apparently God who enables P to know that God enables P to know that P experiences God in E. Indeed, conservative Biblical theology evidently entails not only that such experiences occur,[182] but also that such experiences are genuine (and not merely apparent) experiences of God.

Loftus claims, in effect, that P can not be certain that P experiences God in E, since it is possible that P could subsequently acquire "incontrovertible evidence" that Christianity is false.[183] In response, if the Biblical God enables P to be certain that P experiences God in E, then it is not possible that P could subsequently acquire "incontrovertible evidence" that Christianity is false. Thus, Loftus' presumption that it is possible that P could subsequently acquire "incontrovertible evidence" that Christianity is false presupposes that it is not the case that the God of Biblical Christianity enables P to be certain that P experiences God in E. But, P need not be concerned that Loftus might embrace such a presupposition, since P need not be subject to Loftus' anti-Christian presuppositions. Therefore, the only threat, here, to P's recognition that P experiences certain awareness of the God of Biblical Christianity in E is the possibility that the Biblical Christian God (if such God exists) does not actually enable persons such as P to be certain of an experience of that God in an experience such as E. However, the Biblical evidence referenced above implies that the existence of the Biblical God entails, with high probability, that God routinely enables Christian believers to know they experience God-enabled knowledge of God's existence and action in their lives. Therefore, Loftus' "incontrovertible evidence" objection fails, for even if God merely enables P to be certain that God enables P to be certain that it is highly likely that P experiences God in E, P may confidently assert that P knows that "incontrovertible evidence" against Christianity does not exist, and this assertion may be confidently embraced even if P's certainty extends not to P's first-order Christian beliefs themselves, but to P's awareness of God-enabled certainty that God enables P to possess certain second-order beliefs that P's first-order Christian beliefs are highly likely.

Loftus asserts that the witness of the Spirit is never more reliable than visual sense perception.[184] In response, sensory data lead to beliefs about the external world via presupposition-laced inductive reasoning, whereas the witness of the Spirit is direct, divinely enabled, certain knowledge. Therefore, Loftus is simply wrong. If the witness of the Spirit ever exists, then it is necessarily maximally certainty-generating. Conceivably, the nature of that certainty-generation could be such that the Spirit may sometimes will that truths be divinely enabled to be perceived by some individual P to be highly likely, in which case P may be maximally certain that P perceives that those perceived truths are precisely as likely as the Spirit enables P to perceive. Regardless of whether Spirit-enabled certainty applies to a certain or uncertain belief, we have no good reason to suppose the witness of the Spirit (if it exists) is never more reliable than visual sense perception.

The Martin quote[185] implies billions of people claimed to never experience the witness of the Spirit. In response, I have no good reason to suppose billions of people ever claimed any such thing. Furthermore, even if billions of people did make such a claim, it would not follow that the claim is correct or justified. Moreover, even if the claim was correct and justified when made, it does not follow that the claim is still made by those people later in their lives (or in their afterlives). Thus, the existence of unbelievers is not evidence against the witness of the Spirit. In fact, conservative Biblical theology predicts large numbers of wayward persons.[186]

Loftus may object that there is no hard objective evidence that P experiences God in E,[187] but this objection merely begs the question against the possibility that P actually experiences God in E. In fact, if P's perception of God is actually a perception of actually existing God, then P's experience of God in E is maximally hard and objective evidence. Loftus may not be privy to P's certainty, and thus, Loftus may not be obligated to believe P's certainty is certain, but this only entails that P's certainty does not necessarily guarantee that Loftus has certainty of P's certainty. It does not follow that P is delusional.[188]

The Feinberg quote may be interpreted as an objection to the practical apologetic value of "Holy Spirit Epistemology".[189] In response, first-person religious experiences can support third-person conservative Biblical apologetic arguments. So, the fact that I claim to personally experience the Spirit's witness may, to some degree, confirm to other people that I actually experience that witness.[190]

Loftus implies that intellectual honesty requires that those who believe they experience the witness of the Spirit should acknowledge the possibility that they do not *certainly* experience that witness.[191] In response, if P certainly experiences that witness, then intellectual honesty would require that P *reject* the possibility that P does not certainly experience that witness! Thus, Loftus' presumption that intellectual honesty requires acknowledging the possibility of incorrect perceptions presupposes (without justification) the absence of certain perceptions.

Loftus claims, in effect, that P's experience of the witness of the Spirit should be accompanied by P's acquisition of propositional knowledge in that experience.[192] In response, Loftus does not explain or justify, precisely, what propositional knowledge he thinks persons such as P should acquire in the experience of the Spirit, so it is not established that Biblical theological disagreements are evidence against the existence of that experience.

The Holy Spirit might also lead people to perceive propositions in varying degrees of confidence, not always with certainty. For example, conservative Biblical theology entails that the Holy Spirit leads, guides, directs, teaches, helps, comforts, convicts, etc., and these actions need not be presumed to be always accompanied by certainty on the part of the individuals experiencing those divine actions. For example, I could, at times, be lead by the Spirit, even when I am less than certain that the Spirit is leading me. In addition, I could be certain that the Spirit is leading me to accept that some uncertain belief is highly probable. Also, certainty is not a necessary condition of knowledge, so I could know the Spirit interacts in my life in various ways, yet not always have certainty regarding that interaction.

The Schellenberg quote considers the "wish fulfillment" objection.[193] In response, P's experience of God in E, if actual, is not merely an experience, but is an experience that is accompanied by P's divinely enabled certainty that P experiences God in E. Therefore, we may note that wish fulfillment may lead to some experiences (veridical or not) of some kinds in some people, yet also note that it does not follow that wish fulfillment is a better alternative explanation of P's claim to experience God in E, especially if P actually experiences God in E. In fact, if P actually experiences God in E, then P is certain that P experiences God in E, regardless of what wishes P may happen to have.

The Guiness quote does not block perception of Spirit-enabled certainty.[194] Let C represent "Every belief is uncertain." Now, either (1) we are not certain C is true, or (2) we are certain C is true. If (1), then a belief could be certain, contradicting C. On the other hand, if (2), then a self-contradictory epistemic state ensues. In either case, not-uncertain beliefs are possible, and may be actual. The fact that some beliefs may well be uncertain does not entail that no beliefs are certain, and if some beliefs may be certain, then the Spirit could be the cause of some of those certain beliefs.

On a different interpretation of the Guiness quote, let D represent "Every belief system is uncertain." Now, either (1) we are not certain D is true, or (2) we are certain D is true. If (1), then a not-uncertain belief system is possible, and the Spirit may even cause some beliefs systems to be not-uncertain. On the other hand, if (2) is true, then even though every belief system would be uncertain, individual beliefs in uncertain belief systems could still be certain, including beliefs caused by the Spirit to be certain. In either case, considerations relevant to the finitude of human knowledge do not preclude the viability of not-uncertain Spirit-enabled perceptions.

We need not suppose that Spirit-enabled knowledge is perceived via the physical senses.[195] Therefore, the fact that physical sense perception of the external world may be less than certain does not entail the Spirit could not (or probably would not) enable not-uncertain knowledge in the noetic structures of some persons at some times.

Loftus presumes to know why Craig developed his "Holy Spirit epistemology".[196] In response, Craig may have developed this epistemology as a natural expression of the Spirit-led development of his personal understanding of the nature of his Biblically informed experience of Spirit-enabled truth perception which he may have perceived even long before codifying its propositional expression. Regardless of Craig's actual motivations, the witness of the Spirit is Biblical, and is claimed by many conservative Bible-believers (including myself) to be experienced. As such, it constitutes evidence of the existence of God and of other Biblical truths variously caused by the Spirit to be variously perceived, even if Loftus has not ever had such an experience. Thus, Loftus' presumption that Christianity can never be known[197] merely begs the question against the possibility that Spirit-enabled knowledge of Biblical truth occurs in the epistemic states of some persons.

Control Beliefs and Evil

Loftus' chapters on the problem of evil[198] are not taken to provide direct positive support for his primary control beliefs, but are interpreted as an attempt to block theistic control beliefs by providing evidence against the Biblical theistic conception of God.[199] Indeed, if conservative Biblical theism were established, then Loftus' control beliefs would need to be rejected. Loftus' acceptance of his control beliefs is such that it is in his interest, therefore, to attempt to disconfirm conservative Biblical theism.

I have addressed Loftus' analysis of the problem of evil in detail in Chapter 3. It may be helpful to add, here, that Loftus' analysis of the problem of evil is not even necessary for him. After all, if he begins with a control belief that requires the assumption that any examined religious belief system is probably false (CB1), then Loftus already "knows" God-belief is unjustified, regardless of the nature of evil in the world. Such a procedure for rejecting God-belief, however, is merely an exercise in circular reasoning, and as such, may be rightly rejected.

Loftus often resorts to the claim that God could/would/should perform such and such action.[200] In response, Loftus' position is apparently incoherent. Either God does not exist, or God does exist. If God does not exist, then it is not true that God could/would/should perform any action; a nonexistent being can perform no action. On the other hand, if God does exist, then God exists regardless of the apparent nature of evil in the world, in which case the problem of evil is not a problem after all. Either way, Loftus' position is unclear and apparently incoherent.

Loftus might object that I have misconstrued the nature of the evidential atheistic argument from evil. He might rather simply take the position that the existence of the Biblical God is apparently inconsistent with the nature of evil in the world. In response, even if such an inconsistent state were apparent to Loftus, it does not follow that the apparent inconsistency is an actually inconsistency. Other possibilities exist. For example, the apparent inconsistency may be due to Loftus' misunderstanding of the nature of the Biblical God, or due to his misunderstanding of the nature of evil, or both. Also, even if the apparent inconsistency were an actual inconsistency, it need not necessarily follow that belief in the Biblical God be rejected. "A is inconsistent with B" need not entail that A is false. Perhaps B is false, yet A is true. So, even if Loftus provided (and he has not provided) a formal (or even informal) proof that Biblical God-belief is inconsistent with the nature of evil in the world, there remains the challenge (not met by Loftus) of showing that rejection of belief in the Biblical God would be warranted.

Most importantly, Loftus' position may be rejected for reasons expounded in Chapter 3, and for the reason that Loftus' control beliefs prevent acceptance of a theistic belief system (regardless of the nature of evil in the world). Loftus has not properly evaluated the logical options available to us.[201] Skepticism regarding Loftus' conclusion is in order.

Control Beliefs and Miracles

Loftus chapter on miracles[202] may be viewed as an indirect argument in favor of his control belief CB2. That is, since miracles (on Loftus' definition of this term) are highly improbable, given the laws of physics,[203] it stands to reason (in Loftus' mind) that every physical event probably has a natural cause (CB2). Loftus may favor, too, the idea that physical laws describe cause-effect patterns of physical event relations in a closed system in which subsequent physical events are caused exclusively by prior physical events.[204]

In response, it is evident from the previous paragraph that one's understanding of physical laws and physical event causation is highly relevant to one's understanding of the concept of miracles. So, given a particular philosophy of physical laws and physical event causation, the term "miracle" may be subsequently defined and understood. Much confusion may easily result from failure to separate and justify the distinct conceptual elements required in an analysis of the miraculous. We must exercise caution, therefore, in our definitions and conceptual analysis of metaphysical options.

My AFTLOP[205] and theistic filtration procedure includes an examination of the nature of physical event causation. That examination establishes that we have no good reason to believe any physical event is a cause of any physical event. It also establishes that it is highly probable that all physical events are caused by persons. Given this understanding of physical event causation, and given that physical laws are regular patterns of physical events, we may infer that since most physical laws are not human-caused, it follows that most physical laws are caused by a non-human person(s). It also follows that any physical event that is both not human-caused and not described by a known physical law is caused by a non-human person(s). In addition, it is inferred that it is highly improbable that any physical event has an impersonal cause.

We may now proceed to define a number of important terms. An event E is a miracle if and only if E is caused by neither a physical event nor an Earthly person. Two categories of miracles may be further identified: physical miracles and nonphysical miracles. E is a nonphysical miracle if and only if E is both a miracle and a nonphysical event. E is a physical miracle if and only if E is both a miracle and a physical event. Two categories of physical miracles may be further identified: natural physical miracles and supernatural physical miracles. E is a natural physical miracle if and only if E is a physical miracle that instantiates a physical law. E is a supernatural physical miracle if and only if E is a physical miracle that does not instantiate a physical law. A law is a physical law if and only if it is a regular physical event pattern. E is a nonphysical event if and only if it is not a physical event. E is a physical event if and only if it is an element of the space, time, and matter which comprise the external world which our human senses are generally corporately presumed to mutually perceive, where that mutually agreed upon perception facilitates a shared scientific analysis of that world. Physical science may thus be defined as the theoretical formulation and testing of models of that external world in pursuit of the model that best approximates that world. More generally, metaphysical science may be defined as the theoretical formulation and testing of models of all of metaphysical reality in pursuit of the model that best approximates that reality. Physical science is, therefore, a form (or "branch") of metaphysical science. The pursuit of truth may be defined as the pursuit of the best model of metaphysical reality. Truth may be defined as the nature of all of metaphysical reality.

Definitions have now been carefully associated with important and distinct metaphysical possibilities in the context of my philosophy of physical event causation. It is worth emphasizing that the definitions I have set forth in this analysis may not correspond, precisely, to definitions used by other analysts. The relationship between my definitions and those of others must be kept in mind. Now I will proceed to further elucidate the nature of miracles and the implications of that nature in the context of a response to Loftus' position on miracles.

It is evident that Hume's definition of "miracle", as described by Loftus,[206] would correspond well to my definition of "supernatural physical miracle". So, even if we agree with Hume's position as interpreted by Loftus,[207] it follows merely that we know no reason to believe any supernatural physical miracle has occurred. This, in no way, entails that it is necessarily (or probably) the case that we know no reason to believe any miracle has occurred. In fact, my AFTLOP establishes that we have reason to believe natural physical miracles generally describe the physical history of the universe, even if we deny the existence of any known rational basis for believing supernatural physical miracles have occurred.

Loftus' analysis of miracles, therefore, is incomplete, as it focuses on the identification of the appropriate theoretical rational basis R required for inferring that a given physical event is a supernatural physical miracle. His analysis does not account for the fact that the existence of miracles, even physical miracles, may be inferred independent of one's identification of R. Also, if one identifies R, a physical event could be established to be a physical miracle, even if one's knowledge of R entails it is not rationally established that the physical miracle is a supernatural physical miracle.

The nature of R is surely of theoretical interest for those interested in determining whether supernatural physical miracles have occurred. However, neither the knowledge of R nor its pertinence to specific miraculous (or allegedly miraculous) instances is a necessary condition of identification of either (1) the occurrence of a physical miracle, or (2) the implications of an occurrence of a physical miracle. Thus, the implications of the identification of physical miracles, even distinctively Biblical miracles, may be explored independent of the determination that those miracles are supernatural physical miracles.

For example, in the ministry of Jesus, the events JM commonly referred to as "the miracles of Jesus" may carry significant theory-confirming evidential value, even if we have no idea whether any member of JM is a supernatural physical miracle. Even if each member of JM was known to be a natural physical miracle, the evidential value of the coincidence of the occurrence of such a large number of "unusual" natural physical miracles in the religious/historical context of the ministry of Jesus would carry significant evidential value in the analysis of the implications of the nature of Jesus' ministry. Thus, even if, somehow, it could be shown that each member of JM instantiates a physical law, the evidential and apologetic significance of the members of JM would remain.

Suppose that the evidential value of some member x of JM is historically investigated. First, observe that we need not establish that x is a supernatural physical miracle as a necessary condition of evaluating its historical significance. For all we know, a physical law may exist that accounts for the occurrence of x, and regardless of whether we know any such physical law, historical analysis of x may proceed. We then need merely note that if x is historical, then x is either caused by Jesus or it is not caused by Jesus. If x is caused by Jesus, then it may carry positive apologetic significance even though it does not even satisfy my definition of "miracle" (since x may be taken to be caused by Earthly person Jesus). If x is not caused by Jesus, then x is a physical miracle and may carry positive apologetic significance, regardless of whether we ever determine that x is a supernatural physical miracle. These considerations are critical to a complete analysis of the nature of the evidential value of miracles in conservative Biblical apologetics, and Loftus does not account for such considerations in his analysis.

The "catch-22" problem[208] is, consequently, not a problem for the conservative Biblical apologist. We need not believe the Biblical God exists as a necessary condition of identifying "foundational Christian miracles" that confirm conservative Biblical theology (let CM represent the set of such miracles). Rather, members of CM may be variously established to possess, in varying degrees, a measure of evidential value in the confirmation of conservative Biblical theology, regardless of whether any (or all) of those members happens to be a natural physical miracle by virtue of instantiating some physical law we may or may not know. Knowledge of the existence of the Biblical God is not a necessary condition of knowing the evidential value of members of CM. In fact, even if we know the Biblical God exists, it does not necessarily follow that we know that the members of CM are supernatural physical miracles! For all a conservative Bible-believer may know, God may cause physical events to occur in accordance with physical laws that account for all foundational Biblical miracle instances! Clearly, then, the apologetic significance of those physical miracles is not dependent upon our resolution of the debate regarding whether those miracles are natural physical miracles or supernatural physical miracles. If the laws of physics "coincidentally" result in the historical occurrence of the members of CM, then a conservative Bible-confirming apologetic may nevertheless be formulated. It follows that the explanatory power (likelihood) of conservative Biblical belief systems must be analyzed independent of the unjustified assertion that the members of CM are historical only if they are supernatural physical miracles.

Several additional critical remarks are in order. Loftus claims that scientific progress is grounded in the assumption that "miracles don't occur in the laboratory".[209] In response, my AFTLOP entails that physical science is fundamentally motivated by the pursuit of the knowledge of the nature of physical laws, where those laws are general descriptions of regular physical event patterns properly identified as natural physical miracles. Granted, supernatural physical miracles, if they exist, may not "testably" occur "in the laboratory", but this is hardly evidence against the existence of supernatural physical miracles, since we have no reason to suppose that supernatural physical miracles would be caused by a person (God or otherwise) to occur in regular testable patterns, even if such miracles exist. In fact, if God (or some other person or persons) chose to cause physical miracles to "testably" occur in the laboratory in ways distinct from any previously humanly-known physical law, then we would simply proceed to identify such tested physical miracles as natural physical miracles which occur in accordance with a newly discovered physical law per the laboratory testing. Clearly, then, the inability to test for supernatural physical miracles in a laboratory is not evidence against the existence of supernatural physical miracles. Laboratory testing is not the only means by which we may acquire knowledge of metaphysical reality.

In my fine-tuning arguments I establish that the improbability of a physical law-based explanation of particular physical conditions known to be necessary for the existence of a physical law-based explanation of Earth-like life implies those conditions are probably not explained in terms of a physical law. It is incorrect to infer that those particular conditions, therefore, probably do not exist! Likewise, the improbability of a physical law-based explanation of the members of CM would not require the subsequent inference that those members are probably not historical. Again, such an inference would be incorrect.

Either new physical laws can be discovered or they can not. If new physical laws can be discovered, then the members of CM could be discovered to be described in terms of presently unknown physical laws, in which case they may still carry positive conservative Bible-confirming evidential value. On the other hand, if the members of CM are denied on the basis that they do not occur in accordance with presently known physical laws, then a foundational premise in physical science is denied, namely, it is denied that new physical laws can be discovered. So, if the critic of conservative Biblical theology denies the historical occurrence of the members of CM on the grounds that they accord with no known physical law, then the critic is seen to embrace an unjustified inquiry-blocking anti-scientific position. On the other hand, if the critic of conservative Biblical theology admits that the members of CM may occur in accordance with physical laws not presently known, then the critic can not use the general uniformity of physical laws to deny the possibility of the occurrence of those physical miracles. In neither case is the conservative Bible-confirming evidential value of miracles rationally denied, for even if it is ultimately established that the members of CM do not occur in accordance with physical laws, then their conservative Bible-confirming historical significance may persist as instances of supernatural physical miracles.

Of course, the mere possibility that the members of CM occurred is not sufficient to establish that the members of CM probably occurred. The actual probability, given available evidence, that the members of CM occurred may be evaluated in the context of the development of a neutral philosophy of history that does not presuppose either the existence of supernatural physical miracles or the absolute uniformity of natural physical miracles. However, it should now be evident that the denial of the historicity of CM-members merely on the grounds that those members are, if actual, not instances of presently known physical laws, is both unscientific (inquiry-blocking), irrelevant (a new physical law not previously known could be operative), and unjustified (historical events need not have explanations in terms of presently known physical laws).

The evidential value of physical miracles (whether they be natural physical miracles or supernatural physical miracles) in conservative Biblical apologetics is that they are unusual physical events in a religious context. Whether such physical miracles happen to be known to be described by some known or unknown physical law is quite beside the point. Thus, when Jesus urged religious belief in response to the evidential value of "miracles",[210] we need not presume that the religious belief is intended to be justified by virtue of using extensive knowledge of the physical laws required to infer that the "miracles" are probably not properly described in terms of any known (or unknown) physical law. Rather, the idea may be that the unusual nature of the "miracles" in the religious context in which they occurred contributes to a rational basis for the inference to the religious belief urged by Jesus.

Loftus favorably quotes Craig's definition of miracle.[211] Loftus apparently believes quantum events are uncaused.[212] It follows that even for Loftus, all quantum events are miraculous by virtue of their uncaused nature, on Craig's definition. Presumably this implication has escaped Loftus' notice. If Loftus rejects the claim that quantum events are miraculous, then he must either reject his favorable acceptance of Craig's definition, or he must reject the view that quantum events are uncaused (in which case we may request that Loftus identify who causes quantum events). This apparently incoherent feature of Loftus' thought is in need of reformulation.

Loftus apparently has a conception of causation in mind which requires acceptance of a contiguity condition[213] such that C is a cause of E only if C has a "point of contact" with E. However, there is no good reason to believe this contiguity condition is a necessary component of the definition of causation I use (i.e., C causes E if and only if C brings about E, or produces E, or makes E happen). So, pending evidence that my definition of cause requires acceptance of the contiguity condition, we may reject the assumption that that condition must be satisfied in all (or even any) instances of causation.

Loftus apparently believes that it is reasonable to believe God causes physical events only if we understand how God causes physical events.[214] In response, I can know the sun shines, yet not understand how or why it shines. Likewise, I can know God acts, yet not know how or why God acts. Thus, skeptics may not reject the historicity of an allegedly miraculous event merely on the grounds that it is unknown how that event, if actually miraculous, took place.[215]

Loftus makes a common error by presuming that a natural physical miracle is not God-caused.[216] In response, it does no good for atheists to identify a physical law-based descriptive explanation of some event E claimed by theists to be miraculous, since the mere identification of a descriptive explanation of E fails to account for the cause of E. Descriptions are not causes. Physical laws describe physical event patterns. Physical laws do not cause physical events. Thus, E may be God-caused, even if atheists and theists mutually agree and understand that E instantiates a physical law.

Generally speaking, atheists may think that they have satisfied their explanatory requirements by identifying a descriptive physical law that accounts for E; in fact, they have not satisfied their explanatory requirements in so doing. When asked "What is the cause of E?", I do not want to know that E is an instance of a more general descriptive physical event pattern. Rather, I want to know the *cause* of E. Atheists routinely fail to identify physical causes, and typically merely identify patterns of physically caused events. Theists simply identify the personal cause (God) of the physical events atheists merely describe.

As evidence of miraculous events, Loftus apparently wants to see a supernatural physical miracle.[217] This is not required. God's power and knowledge is evident (via natural physical miracles) from what has been seen.[218] Loftus sees this evidence every day…via physical laws.

Control Beliefs and the Bible

If people during Biblical times had good reasons for their beliefs as recorded in the Bible, then this could lead to a significant disconfirming effect upon the claim that Loftus' primary control beliefs are justified. Chapter 7 of Loftus' book[219] is taken to be an attempt to show that we need not be concerned about this possible disconfirming effect by virtue of the alleged fact that we do not have good reason to suppose that people during Biblical times had good reasons for their beliefs as recorded in the Bible.[220] That is, Loftus is taken to believe that since people's beliefs in Biblical times were superstitious (i.e., erroneous and contradicted by a better informed perspective),[221] we have no good reason to accept superstitious Biblical beliefs, just as we have no good reason to accept superstitious non-Biblical beliefs.[222]

In response, my interpretation of Loftus' purpose in his Chapter 7, as described above, is that he is not focused upon arguing in support of one of his three primary control beliefs. Rather, he is focused upon the negative argumentative task of showing that his primary control beliefs are not disconfirmed by Biblically informed reasoning. However, I have already mounted considerable evidence against his primary control beliefs, where that evidence is not dependent upon refuting the claim that Biblical people were "barbaric and superstitious".[223]

It follows that I may take the position that even if Biblical people were barbaric and superstitious, Loftus' control beliefs remain unjustified. Furthermore, since Loftus' noetic structure is pivotally built upon those control beliefs, I need not refute his position in detail in Chapter 7, since I have already accomplished my primary task of challenging his core control beliefs.

Of course, the conservative Biblical worldview (including its many miraculous/supernatural elements) makes no sense to a person such as Loftus who embraces control beliefs which flatly presuppose that the conservative Biblical worldview is false (or probably false). Loftus' control belief CB1 presupposes that a religious belief system under investigation is probably false. Given this presupposition, it is no surprise that Loftus rejects Biblically grounded belief systems, but this only shows that if we begin with an unjustified measure of religious skepticism, then we may be likely to persist as a religious skeptic. Loftus' control belief CB2 presupposes the probable nonexistence of theistic causal activity in the physical world, so it is no surprise that he rejects the existence of Biblically grounded theistic causal activity; again, this simply shows that if we begin with an unjustified measure of anti-theistic bias, we may be likely to persist as a non-theist. Loftus' control belief CB3 is grounded in MN (methodological naturalism), which presupposes, among other things, the probable nonexistence of a God who causes physical events; it is no surprise, therefore, to discover that Loftus rejects that the God of the Bible actually causes physical events as described in the Bible, but again, this simply manifests the principle that those who begin with unjustified anti-Biblical presuppositions are likely to persist in anti-Biblical beliefs. Of course the world of the Bible is "strange and superstitious" to Loftus[224]…his unjustified control beliefs naturally lead to such a conclusion. Even Loftus recognizes that it is no surprise that his skeptical presuppositions lead to his rejection of conservative Biblical theology.[225] Hopefully Loftus will also come to recognize that his skeptical presuppositions are unjustified, as I have now clearly shown.

Loftus' examination of the extent to which pseudonymity may exist in the Biblical texts[226] may help to minimize the probability (in Loftus' mind) that a Biblically informed viewpoint justifies rejection of his control beliefs. However, my rejection of Loftus' control beliefs has been justified by reasoning independent of the degree to which pseudonymity may exist in the Biblical texts, so the issue of Biblical pseudonymity is not an essential focus in my critique.

Likewise, Loftus' examination of the nature of Biblical archaeology[227] may help to minimize the probability (in Loftus' mind) that a Biblically informed viewpoint justifies rejection of his control beliefs. However, my rejection of his control beliefs is justified by reasoning not grounded in consideration of the nature of Biblical archaeology. It follows that Biblical archeology is not an essential focus in my critique.

We may vividly bring into focus a foundational point of contention, here, by noting that we may doubt Loftus would ever embrace theism, even if he actually suffered the horror of eternity in hell, since he could rationalize away his apparent experience of God's wrath via conscious torment there as some kind of strange physical law-based dream or hallucination which modern science has simply not yet explained. After all, if Loftus "knows" (by virtue of his control beliefs) that every investigated religious belief system is false due to the high probability that every event probably has a physical cause (as entailed by the MN-laced approach to science he presupposes), then Loftus could not perform a rational investigation that leads to the inference that he apparently suffers the fiery judgment of God that consumes those who reject God, even if Loftus actually suffers that very judgment.

The point of the preceding paragraph is to show the absurd results that can obtain from arbitrarily accepting unjustified claims that are grounded in circular reasoning derived from unwarranted presuppositions. In seeking to persuade a critic to accept the conservative Biblical worldview, therefore, we need not attempt to argue that conservative Biblical theology is likely on presuppositions that entail it is false (or most likely false). Rather, we may expose the circular (and unjustified) nature of those anti-Biblical presuppositions and urge their replacement with Bible-neutral presuppositions to better see where the evidence properly leads us. Consequently, I urge Loftus to reject his primary control beliefs, since they beg the question in favor of the anti-Biblical atheism he incorrectly espouses. Until Loftus rejects those control beliefs, he would even apparently agree that he is blinded.[228] If you fail to remove your sunglasses, then you may never see the Son. The choice is yours.

Control Beliefs and Prayer

The existence of the Biblical God is a significant control belief in the belief systems of many persons. Loftus' chapter on prayer is taken to be an attempt to challenge the rational basis of such a control belief.

Loftus apparently considers unanswered prayer to be a version of the problem of evil.[229] In response, we know unanswered prayer is evidence against the existence of the Biblical God only if we know that our knowledge is sufficient to justify the claim "If the Biblical God exists, then I know the nature of unanswered prayer would not be as it is." However, this claim is dubious, given Biblical evidence that the ways of the Biblical God are unlikely to be understood[230] apart from divine revelation.[231] Also, if a person experiences divinely enabled knowledge regarding the probable nature of unanswered prayer (assuming there is divine existence), then that person is no longer in the position to deny divine existence, since that knowledge is a sufficient condition of knowledge of divine existence in that case.

Unanswered prayer is, therefore, not problematic for conservative Biblical apologetics, since the Biblical God may choose to respond to prayer in ways we don't understand. Yes, any inconsistency between the nature of prayer and human expectations regarding prayer may be taken as evidence against the existence of any God whose existence entails the probable nonexistence of that inconsistency. It does not follow, however, that the existence of the Biblical God is improbable, since there is no good reason to suppose the existence of the Biblical God entails the probable nonexistence of a known inconsistency between the nature of prayer and human expectations regarding prayer. Erroneous human expectations are not evidence against the existence of a God who permits erroneous human expectations. Loftus has not established that unanswered prayer is a problem not exclusively grounded in erroneous human expectations. The fact that the ways of the Biblical God are inscrutable to some degree, therefore, renders unproblematic Loftus' human expectation that the existence of the Biblical God (or any omniscient, omnipotent, and omnipresent God) entails that the nature of prayer would be different than it is, since he has not shown that his expectation is not erroneously grounded in presumptions contradicted by inscrutable facts inaccessible to him.

Scientific tests of the efficacy of prayer are interesting,[232] but an efficacy-confirming scientific prayer test is not a necessary condition of justified belief in the efficacy of prayer. Also, the nonexistence of such a test is not evidence against the efficacy of prayer, since God could choose to answer all scientifically tested prayers such that the test does not clearly confirm that prayer is efficacious. That is, scientifically inconclusive prayer tests may be inconclusive simply because God providentially arranged that such tests are inconclusive. In addition, it is not even apparent that Loftus has thoroughly searched the scientific prayer literature, so his conclusions regarding the degree to which prayer is scientifically tested (or testable) are not obviously informed by modern science.

Moreover, consider the belief B that prayer is either (1) efficacious, or (2) unanswered for good unknown reasons. B may be justified in one's overall belief system by virtue of being entailed by that system, where that system is known to be justified for reasons independent of the consideration of the degree to which direct empirical confirmation of the efficacy of prayer has been provided. In this case, B may be justified regardless of whether any scientific test of the efficacy of prayer is known.

In addition, scientific tests of the efficacy of prayer may be typically grounded in the assumption that efficacious prayers are, by definition, prayers of type P that are correlated with effects of type E such that no known physical law explains that correlation. There is a problem here. Even if P is shown to be correlated with E such that no known physical law explains that correlation, then this may simply result in the inference to the existence of a new physical law identified as the descriptive explanation of the correlation. The identification of such a new law, however, does not thereby constitute evidence for the existence of God, since the atheist might take that newly discovered physical law as simply another member of the set of known impersonal physical laws which describe physical reality. In this case, the theist may punt to the AFTLOP[233] to show the theistic implications of all such physical laws.

But there is another problem. The existence of a newly discovered correlation between P and E would not, in and of itself, imply that there exists a causal relationship between P and E. Correlation does not imply causation. So, a scientific test of this type would not even be particularly useful in the attempt to acquire empirical confirmation of the efficacy of prayer. Again, what is needed is recognition of the personal nature of physical event causation as emphasized in my natural theology.[234] In particular, since humans are unlikely to be the cause of any correlation between P and E, then such a correlation would be evidence of the physical causal activity of a non-human person. Once more, considerations from my AFTLOP are helpful in filling in the details which justify such an inference. Scientific prayer tests, alone, would not appear to accomplish the task.

God may influence human belief systems and answer prayers in ways which lead many people to become justified in the belief that specific prayers have been (and are) efficacious in some circumstances. Pending support for the improbability of this possibility, incomplete human understanding of the nature of prayer is not evidence against the efficacy of prayer, and specific instances of apparent prayer-efficacy may be justifiably held to be actual instances of prayer-efficacy in the noetic structures of many persons. Indeed, one need not search hard at all to find anecdotal evidence amongst groups of conservative Bible-believers of the alleged efficacy of prayer, and the limited faith-confirming effect of such testimonies may serve to properly enhance the faith of the faithful who may know that prayer-efficacy is justified for reasons independent of that anecdotal evidence. This may be taken to be one of the benefits of the regular gathering together of believers.[235] Those who choose to abstain from social interaction with believers, therefore, may be guilty of choosing to limit the probability that undesired religion-confirming evidence may be acquired. Indeed, my experience is that I know many instances in which religious experiences including apparent prayer-efficacy (confirming the existence of God and the truth of Biblical principles) is a better explanation than any known alternative explanation available to me. My acquisition of such knowledge is, to some extent, a function of my choice to be available to circumstances in which that knowledge is more likely to be acquired (if at all) by me. The evidently widespread atheistic rejection of participation in activities that manifest submission to presently understood truth and genuine openness to spiritual realities, therefore, may often manifest a willingness to avoid inconvenient truths inconsistent with that atheism. A person's failure to find religion-confirming evidence, then, may be at fault for that failure.[236]

We may conclude that B may be justified within a larger belief system, regardless of whether we fully understand the observed nature of prayer, and regardless of whether any scientific test enhances the theistic implications of the AFTLOP in my explanatory filtration procedure. Loftus does a sufficient job of establishing there is much that he does not understand about the nature of prayer, but this is very much beside the point that our lack of full understanding of the nature of prayer is not evidence against the existence of the Biblical God.

Summary

It should now be clear that I disagree with the false dichotomy stated by Loftus[237] in which we either (1) start "from above" by presupposing some version of theism, or (2) start "from below" by presupposing skeptical agnosticism. In fact, there is a third option: we may neutrally evaluate both the "from above" and "from below" alternatives from the neutral agnosticism starting point. Also, I disagree with the Strauss quote regarding theistic presuppositions,[238] since I find no basis for supposing why a neutral agnostic starting point could not also lead to theistic belief. We might start from neutral agnosticism and get to God.

Neutral agnosticism is clearly an alternative to the skeptical agnosticism advocated by Loftus, and my refutation of Loftus' control beliefs and the alleged justification for them illuminates the many faults of skeptical agnosticism. Moreover, Loftus does not explain why starting "from the middle" is unjustified, whereas the evidently high value of the noble pursuit of the maximization of neutral objectivity constitutes considerable evidence in favor of starting "from the middle" via neutral agnosticism.

I have now presented my case for rejecting Loftus' skeptical agnosticism in favor of neutral agnosticism. The soundness of my position rightly requires the rejection of both the basis for Loftus' control beliefs as outlined in his Part 1 of his book[239] and the rejection of Loftus' examination of Biblical evidence in the context of those control beliefs in Part 2 of his book.[240] At this point, I would hope that it is apparent that Loftus may wish to convert to acceptance of neutral agnosticism as his starting point, thereby avoiding the problem of merely presupposing what needs to be shown. Such a conversion would require a substantial reformulation of his position, and I look forward to seeing either this conversion or a justification for not so converting.

NOTES

1. Loftus, John W. (2008). *Why I Became an Atheist: A Former Preacher Rejects Christianity*. Amherst, NY: Prometheus Books, p. 37:1-3.
2. Ibid., p. 35:1-37:4.
3. Ibid., p. 37:3-4.
4. Mark 4:24.

5. Matthew 13:12.

6. Proverbs 14:12.

7. Exodus 7:3-4; Daniel 4:34-5:21; Daniel 12:4; Matthew 11:25; Matthew 13:11-17; 1 Corinthians 1:18-31; 1 Corinthians 8:7.

8. John 7:17.

9. Loftus (2008), p. 36:20-25.

10. Ibid.

11. Ibid.

12. Ibid., p. 36:27-29.

13. 1 Corinthians 1:26.

14. Stone, David Reuben (2007). *Atheism Is False: Richard Dawkins and the 'Improbability of God' Delusion.* Morrisville, NC: Lulu Press. See Chapter 7 for a sharp critique of Dawkins' atheism, revealing an embarrassing and poor quality of philosophical analysis on the part of a widely known and influential scientist.

15. Loftus (2008), p. 36:42-44.

16. Ibid., p. 38:21-23; p. 40:32-34.

17. John 14:15-26; 1 Corinthians 2:12-14.

18. Loftus (2008), p. 38:36-38.

19. Ibid., p. 38:38-40.

20. Ibid., p. 39:26-28.

21. Ibid., p. 40:6-9, 16-18.

22. Ibid., p. 41:15-17.

23. Ibid., p. 41:24-35.

24. 1 Corinthians 2:13-14.

25. Loftus (2008), p. 41:38-41.

26. Ibid., p. 42:3-8.

27. Ibid., p. 42:21-24.

28. Ibid., p. 42:25-44:4.

29. Ibid., p. 43:28-44:4.

30. Ibid., p. 59:10.

31. Ibid., p. 59:16-19.

32. Ibid., p. 59:23-27.

33. Ibid.

34. Ibid.

35. Ibid., p. 59:33-35, italics mine.

36. Ibid., pp. 59-60.

37. Ibid., p. 60:3-4.

38. Ibid., p. 60:2-5.

39. Ibid., p. 60:6.

40. Loftus' comment expressing doubt regarding the knowability of truth about reality (Ibid., p. 60:19) is perplexing, if not self-refuting. In fact, the self-refuting assertion "Truth about reality is not knowable" entails that truth about reality *is* knowable, and it is quite unclear why Loftus apparently has reservations regarding this entailment. Moreover, to the extent that we join Loftus in his doubts regarding this entailment, we may in turn doubt every knowledge claim made by him throughout his writings, further emphasizing the self-refuting tendency of that very doubt.

41. Ibid., p. 65:3-7.

42. Ibid., p. 60:44-61:1.

43. Ibid., p. 60:3-4.

44. Ibid., p. 67:5-6.

45. See Chapter 7 of this book for more details on STONE.

46. Loftus (2008), p. 66:12-25.

47. The remainder of this paragraph responds to a number of issues raised on pages 66-67 of Loftus' book.

48. Loftus (2008), p. 67:21-27.

49. Ibid., p. 69:38-39.

50. Ibid., pp. 42-44.

51. Ibid., p. 71:36-39.

52. Ibid., p. 70:10-71:5.

53. See Chapter 7 for details.

54. Loftus (2008), p. 59:33-35.

55. Ibid., p. 70:31-34.

56. Ibid., p. 70:39-71:5.

57. Ibid., p. 71:7-10.

58. Ibid., p. 71:10-12.

59. Ibid., p. 69:35-36.

60. Ibid., p. 71:10-15.

61. Ibid., p. 71:15-17.

62. Ibid., p. 70:10-14.

63. Ibid., p. 69:26-27.

64. Ibid., p. 69:21-23.

65. Ibid., p. 68:15-16.

66. Ibid., p. 69:7-9.

67. Ibid., p. 69:26-27.

68. Ibid., p. 69:23-26.

69. Ibid., p. 425:15. See also, Oppy, Graham (2006). *Arguing About Gods.* Cambridge: Cambridge University Press, pp. 170-171.

70. Loftus (2008), p. 74:41-75:2.

71. Ibid., p. 74:41-75:1.

72. For interesting information on just such a correlation, see McTernan, John P. (2006). *As America Has Done to Israel.* Longwood, FL: Xulon Press. See also, Koenig, William R. (2004). *Eye to Eye: Facing the Consequences of Dividing Israel.* Alexandria, VA: About Him.

73. See, for example, Chapters 1 and 2, as well as Stone (2007).

74. Loftus (2008), p. 74:31-33.

75. Ibid., p. 74:38-40.

76. Ibid., p. 75:3.

77. Ibid., p. 75:10-11.

78. Ibid., p. 73:15-17.

79. Ibid., p. 73:38-74:7.

80. Ibid.

81. See, for example, Ibid., p. 72:35.

82. Ibid., p. 106:1-123:13.

83. Ibid., p. 109:7-9.

84. Ibid., p. 114:37-38.

85. Ibid., p. 109:7-9.

86. Ibid., p. 111:22-28.

87. See Chapter 2, and also Stone (2007).

88. Loftus (2008), p. 112:3-10.

89. Ibid., p. 112:11-33.

90. Ibid., p. 113:5.

91. If Loftus can presume at will, then so can I.

92. Loftus (2008), p. 113:6-7.

93. Again, if Loftus can resort to proof by assertion, then so can I. It would be better, of course, to pursue resolution of our debate via STONE, but this would require Loftus' rejection of his theory-favoring presuppositions.

94. Loftus (2008), p. 117:4-14.

95. Ibid., p. 116:41-117:3.

96. Ibid., p. 119:29-30.

97. Ibid., p. 119:13-15.

98. Ibid., p. 79:5-7.

99. Ibid., p. 118:10-11.

100. Ibid., p. 117:23-26.

101. Ibid., p. 117:40-41.

102. Ibid., p. 118:3-9.

103. Ibid., p. 118:22-23.

104. Ibid., p. 118:20-21.

105. Ibid., p. 118:38-119:4.

106. See Chapters 1 and 2, and Stone (2007).

107. Loftus (2008), p. 120:11-26.

108. Ibid., p. 120:29-32.

109. Ibid., p. 185:38-39.

110. See the above section on Control Beliefs and Science.

111. See Chapters 1 and 2, and Stone (2007).

112. Loftus (2008), p. 186:3-5.

113. Ibid., p. 186:6-187:37.

114. Ibid., p. 186:31-32.

115. Ibid., p. 187:15-17.

116. Ibid., p. 187:17-23.

117. Ibid., p. 187:24-25.

118. See my discussion of Control Beliefs and Miracles, below, for further exploration of the significance of the term "natural physical miracles".

119. Loftus (2008), p. 187:25-26.

120. Ibid., p. 187:27-28.

121. See Chapters 1 and 2, and Stone (2007).

122. See my discussion of Control Beliefs and Miracles, below, for further exploration of the significance of the term "natural physical miracles".

123. See the below discussion of Control Beliefs and Religious Experience for more details on the nature of religious experience.

124. Loftus (2008), p. 187:30-34.

125. Ibid., p. 188:18-24.

126. Ibid., p. 188:25-32.

127. Mark 3:22.

128. Loftus (2008), p. 188:30-32.

129. Ibid., p. 189:1-6.

130. Ibid., p. 189:7-18.

131. Ibid., p. 190:11.

132. Ibid., p. 189:23-190:15.

133. Ibid., p. 193:5-195:2.

134. Psalm 145:3; Psalm 147:5; Isaiah 40:28; Isaiah 55:8-9; Romans 11:33.

135. Loftus (2008), p. 195:3-5.

136. Ibid., p. 195:8-10.

137. Ibid., p. 195:6-196:35.

138. Ibid., p. 196:34-35.

139. Ibid., p. 78:1-93:37.

140. Ibid, p. 60:34.

141. See Chapters 1 and 2, and Stone (2007).

142. Loftus (2008), p. 102:31-33.

143. See Chapters 1 and 2, and Stone (2007).

144. See Chapter 2 and Stone (2007).

145. Loftus (2008), p. 83:35-36.

146. Ibid., p. 61:23-41.

147. Ibid., p. 85:8-9.

148. Steele, David Ramsay (2008). *Atheism Explained: From Folly to Philosophy*. Chicago, IL: Open Court, p. 76:12-13.

149. See Chapter 2, note 9.

150. Loftus (2008), p. 88:10-25.

151. See Chapters 1 and 2, and Stone (2007).

152. Loftus (2008), p. 89:28-33.

153. Ibid., p. 92:37-38.

154. Ibid., p. 89:34-90:2.

155. Consider, especially, the probabilistic estimate in Ross, Hugh (2001). *Creator and the Cosmos: How the Greatest Scientific Discoveries of the Century Reveal God*. Colorado Springs, CO: Navpress, 3rd edition, p. 198.

156. Stone (2007), p. 251.

157. Loftus (2008), p. 91:43-44.

158. Ibid., p. 93:18-31.

159. Ibid., p. 93:29-31.

160. Ibid., p. 93:32-36.

161. Ibid., p. 93:36-37.

162. Ibid., p. 94:4-9.

163. Stone (2007), Chapter 7.

164. Loftus (2008), p. 94:20, p. 96:26-27.

165. Ibid., p. 96:38-98:2.

166. I believe I have good reasons which establish God is not made, but this is beside the point here.

167. Loftus (2008), p. 97:7-9.

168. Ibid., p. 97:41.

169. Ibid., p. 97:12-15.

170. Ibid., p. 118:44-119:4.

171. D'Souza, Dinesh (2007). *What's So Great About Christianity*. Washington, DC: Regnery Publishing, p. 134:24-29.

172. Loftus (2008), p. 394:6.

173. Ibid., p. 394:5.

174. Ibid., p. 98:1-2.

175. Ibid., p. 98:7-8.

176. Ibid., p. 98:8-9.

177. Ibid., p. 98:9-10.

178. Ibid., p. 99:7-100:4.

179. Ibid., pp. 42-44.

180. See, for example, Ibid., p. 99:7.

181. Ibid., pp. 213-219.

182. Ibid., p. 213:8-13.

183. Ibid., p. 215:4-10.

184. Ibid., p. 215:10-12.

185. Ibid., p. 215:37-40.

186. Matthew 7:14.

187. Loftus (2008), p. 216:16-27.

188. Ibid., p. 216:26-27.

189. Ibid., p. 216:28-36.

190. The measure of confirmation may actually be a function of many variables, but these need not be explored here.

191. Loftus (2008), p. 216:44-217:4.

192. Ibid., p. 217:24-26.

193. Ibid., p. 218:27-35.

194. Ibid., p. 219:1-4.

195. Ibid., p. 219:6-9.

196. Ibid., p. 219:18-19.

197. Ibid., p. 219:20-22.

198. Ibid., p. 228:1-262:17.

199. Ibid., p. 61:18-21, p. 259:1-2.

200. For example, see Ibid., pp. 236-240, p. 258:2-4.

201. Loftus (2008), p. 240:22-25.

202. Ibid., pp. 199-212.

203. Ibid., p. 60:38-40.

204. Ibid., p. 199:8-9.

205. See Chapter 2 and Stone (2007).

206. Loftus (2008), p. 201:15-202:12.

207. Ibid., p. 203:20-22.

208. Ibid., p. 205:40-206:8.

209. Ibid., p. 208:8-9.

210. John 14:11.

211. Loftus (2008), p. 201:27-29.

212. Ibid., p. 85:8-9.

213. Ibid., p. 209:18-21.

214. Ibid., p. 210:3-7.

215. Ibid., p. 210:28-29.

216. Ibid., p. 210:29-31.

217. Ibid., p. 210:39-41.

218. Romans 1:20. See, also, my AFTLOP in Chapter 2 and Stone (2007).

219. Loftus (2008), p. 124:1-166:46.
220. Ibid., p. 61:6-9.
221. Ibid., p. 164:10-13.
222. Ibid., p. 164:30-33.
223. Ibid., p. 61:8-9.
224. Ibid., p. 124:2-3.
225. Ibid., p. 62:7-8.
226. Ibid., p. 167:1-176:37.
227. Ibid., p. 177:1-180:31.
228. Ibid., p. 70:10-14.
229. Ibid., p. 61:18-21.
230. Romans 11:33-34; Psalm 145:3; Psalm 147:5; Isaiah 40:13-14; Isaiah 55:8-9.
231. 1 Corinthians 2:13-14.
232. Loftus (2008), p. 225:34-227:21.
233. See Chapter 2 and Stone (2007).
234. See, especially, my explanatory filtration procedure described in Chapter 2.
235. Hebrews 10:25.
236. John 7:17.
237. Loftus (2008), p. 60:2-5.
238. Ibid., p. 58:5-6, p. 58:11.
239. Ibid., p. 19:1-262:17.
240. Ibid., p. 265:1-395:36.

CHAPTER 5

The Justification of Biblical Religious Belief

Abstract: *A procedure for justifying key components of Biblical religious belief is briefly outlined. First, atheistic belief systems are rejected, being unsound instances of the Standard Objection. A plausible rational basis for acceptance of the key components is then outlined. Biblical religious belief is further confirmed by emphasizing the inadequacy of competing unbiblical theistic systems.*

Thus far, I have reasoned that God exists (Chapters 1 and 2), that evil is not problematic for theism (Chapter 3), and that the control beliefs embraced by Loftus are unjustified (Chapter 4). I now outline a procedure which may be used to justify a rational basis for conservative Biblical religious belief.

Preliminary Considerations

The following definitions will help clarify the critical terms needed in my argument:

> Christian Bible (CB) ≡ The set of writings which may be identified as the joint intersection of (1) the set of books included in the Biblical canon presently widely accepted by Orthodox Christians, (2) the set of books included in the Biblical canon presently widely accepted by Catholic Christians, and (3) the set of books included in the Biblical canon presently widely accepted by Protestant/Evangelical Christians.

> Biblical God (GB) ≡ The God described in the CB.

> Biblical Theology (BT) ≡ The belief system entailed by "GB exists as described in the CB".

Gospel of Jesus (JG) ≡ A synthesis of the words and works of Jesus Christ as described in the Biblical books of Matthew, Mark, Luke, John, and the first chapter of Acts.

Biblical Gospel (BG) ≡ The belief system entailed by "Jesus Christ exists as described in the CB".

Christ Followers (CF) ≡ The set of human persons whose love of God and others matures in obedience to Jesus Christ and in submission to the work of the Holy Spirit who is described in the CB.

Rejecters of Christ (RC) ≡ The set of human persons, where each member of RC is not a member of CF.

Presumed CB Inerrancy (PCBI) ≡ The belief that for each CB-derived informational unit i, it is a moral obligation to presume i is without error, unless there is compelling evidence that i is not without error.

The members of CB are taken to be defined as those reconstructions which are the product of textual criticism techniques used to approximate (1) the content of the Old Testament manuscripts during the time of the earthly ministry of Jesus Christ, and (2) the content of the originally autographed New Testament manuscripts.

Note that the content of the JG does not include all Biblical information relevant to the person of Jesus Christ, but is derived from material found in the four Gospels and in Acts 1.[1] The content of the BG, however, is derived from the complete Biblical understanding of Jesus Christ as derived from material throughout the entire CB.

The Standard Objection to BT

Prior to examination of positive reasons for accepting Biblical religious belief, it is useful to consider, at once, the argument form assumed by atheistic members of RC who maintain that there exists a rational basis for their rejection of BT. Such members of RC may desire to justify their RC-membership by providing BT-disconfirming philosophical, historical, scientific, and experiential evidence (of course, the domains of these categories overlap). Loftus' book[2] would be a fine contemporary example of atheistic arguments used by an apparent member of RC in an attempted (yet failed) rational justification of BT-rejection. All such anti-BT arguments may be construed as atheistic instances of the Standard Objection to Biblical Religious Belief (SOBRB):

(1) If BT is true, then it is likely that K = KBT.
(2) It is likely that K ≠ KBT.
(3) Therefore, it is likely that BT is false.

Here, K represents the knowledge possessed by the member of RC who raises the SOBRB. KBT represents the knowledge that member would possess, if BT. The SOBRB is a form of the QLMT argument structure justified in Chapter 1, and it yields a sound conclusion so long as premises (1) and (2) are true.

The problem with the SOBRB is premise (2). BT entails GB has good reasons for permitting the epistemic state of each member of RC. For example, everything GB does is good,[3] so God's permission of the epistemic states of each member of RC is good, implying those states can not be used to justify BT-rejection, since BT entails that any such states are consistent with BT. Also, BT predicts the existence of those who reject truths entailed by BT,[4] so BT is not disconfirmed by anti-BT arguments embraced by RC-members.

The epistemic state of a member of RC can not be used to justify the SOBRB, since BT is not disconfirmed by that state, even if that member of RC is unaware of GB's detailed good reasons for permitting that state. To see this, note that if a member of RC has no good reason R to believe that his epistemic state would be different conditional upon BT, then his epistemic state can not be used as evidence against BT. A member of RC could have reason R only if it is not the case that BT entails GB has good reasons for permitting his epistemic state. Since BT does entail GB has such good reasons, a member of RC can not have reason R. Therefore, since RC-members can not have reason R, the epistemic state of RC-members can not be used as evidence against BT.

The failure of the SOBRB as an atheistic argument against BT is not sufficient to establish the truth of BT, but is sufficient to draw the noteworthy conclusion that all such anti-BT arguments may be rejected, even without consideration of all the details of those arguments. In addition, so long as we know of good positive reasons for accepting BT, we may persist in acceptance of BT, the existence of an uncounted number of uninvestigated SOBRB-formulated atheistic anti-BT arguments notwithstanding.

The Case for BT

How, then, shall we establish BT? After all, competing theistic religious belief systems might equally well reject the respective atheistic SOBRB-formulated anti-religious arguments against those systems, yet no such religious system decisively emerges as best based merely on the consideration that those objections to those systems are atheistic SOBRB-type arguments. BT, therefore, may be established through BT-confirming philosophical, historical, scientific, and experiential evidence. BT may be further confirmed as an inference to the best explanation, when competing arguments for alternative systems inconsistent with BT are disconfirmed by available arguments that are structured independent of the purely pro-BT arguments. For example, I could confirm that anti-BT religious belief system X is false not only via consideration of directly BT-confirming evidence, but also by additional evidence that is directly X-disconfirming.

The task of establishing BT is clearly defined. BT is the belief system entailed by "GB exists as described in the CB".

Some key components of BT include:

(A)   God exists.
(B)   Jesus Christ existed.
(C)   Jesus Christ exists.
(D)   JG is true.
(E)   CF-membership is a moral obligation for truth-seekers.
(F)   BG-acceptance is a moral obligation for truth-seekers.
(G)   PCBI-acceptance is a moral obligation for truth-seekers.
(H)   Acceptance of conservative Biblical systematic theology is a moral obligation for truth-seekers.
(I)   Full integration of the above components into one's personal life is a moral obligation for truth-seekers.

These nine components do not merely identify the core essence of BT, but suggest the outline of a sequentially structured rationale which may be used to justify BT, although one's coming to accept BT may, in fact, typically follow an epistemological evolution that is not identical to a rigid sequential acceptance of the components. In fact, the interrelationship between the components is such that they need not actually be established sequentially (consecutively), since many of them have significant effects on one's noetic structure such that a simultaneous perception of several of them in varying degrees may carry greater epistemological consequences than would the mere sequential acceptance of them. What follows is but one member of a large set of possible approaches to justifying acceptance of the components. The complete space of possibilities is immense and the full extent of the relevant literature here is vast. I will outline (only very briefly) a few critical considerations in this possible approach.

Component (A) is established in Chapters 1 and 2. Also, (A) is further confirmed by considerations in Chapters 3 and 4. To the extent that one finds support for the non-(A) components of BT that is independent of the assumption that component (A) is true, (A) may be even further confirmed.

Support for (B) may come from historical analysis.[5] In addition, to the degree that one finds support for the non-(B) components of BT that is independent of the assumption that component (B) is true, (B) may be further confirmed.

Support for (C) includes arguments for the resurrection[6] and Biblical miracles,[7] and also (C)-confirming evidence of such experiences as answered prayers, modern miraculous events, "coincidental" instances of divine providence, visions, direct perception of the presence of Jesus, the witness of the Holy Spirit, angelic appearances, demonic manifestations, exorcisms, Biblical and extra-Biblical prophetic revelation and fulfillment, near-death experiences, out-of-body experiences, heaven/hell experiences, physical healings, and other supernatural experiences. In addition, to the degree that one finds support for the non-(C) components of BT that is independent of the assumption that component (C) is true, (C) may be further confirmed.

Support for (D) is derived from (A), (B), and (C). In particular, the miracles and resurrection of Jesus Christ, in conjunction with the distinctive religious-historical context of that resurrection, lends validating support for the authenticity of the teachings of Jesus, thereby establishing (D). In addition, to the degree that one finds support for the non-(D) components of BT that is independent of the assumption that component (D) is true, (D) may be further confirmed.

Since the concept of moral obligation is central to the support for (E), as well as to the points that follow, a brief analysis of moral obligation is in order. Let "Person J is morally obligated to perform action A" mean that J has the strong desire D to perform action A. I use the term "strong desire D" such that a person instantiates D if and only if that person has no D-conflicting desire which is of sufficient strength to override D. In common language, then, we could say that persons are morally obligated to perform precisely whatever actions they strongly desire to perform. If person J strongly desires to perform "good" actions (given J's definition of "good"), then J is morally obligated to perform such actions. If J strongly desires to perform "bad" actions (given J's definition of "bad"), then J is morally obligated to perform such actions.

My conception of moral obligation is likely distinct from widespread usage and analysis of the concept. Nevertheless, it functions well as an adequate device for urging the person-relative response to the truths of points (A), (B), (C), and (D). In particular, one's decision to accept (or reject) an element of perceived truth will closely hinge upon the strength of one's desire to modify one's actions in accordance with obedience to one's perception of the true nature of reality. Those who strongly desire to live in accordance with the truth (whatever they perceive that might be) will seek to modify their lifestyle accordingly. Those who strongly desire to persist in some lifestyle pattern, regardless of whether they perceive that such a pattern should be modified so as to accord with the truth, will discard the truth in favor of preservation of their truth-rejecting lifestyle.[8] As it is written, light has gone out into the world, and although some live by the truth, others hate the light because their evil works are revealed by it.[9]

To the extent that one perceives that (A), (B), (C), and (D) are true (or likely true), there ensues the moral obligation to accept (E), if one strongly desires to live in obedience to one's perception of that truth.[10] On the other hand, those who strongly desire to preserve some element of their lifestyle, regardless of the degree to which they perceive that (A), (B), (C), and (D) are true, will be morally obligated to reject (E). So, the "good" thing for a person to do (i.e., the thing that a person "should" do) is precisely whatever corresponds to that person's strong desires, conditional upon the measure of truth perceived by that person.[11] It follows that not all who perceive such truths as (D) should embrace (E). Even the Lord has hardened (or even commanded) people with truth-rejecting desires to disobediently perform evil actions,[12] although such evil actions unfortunately result in their self-imposed entrance into divine judgment.[13] Be careful, therefore, that you strongly desire to properly modify your life in accordance with God-revealed truth, for such a desire shall result in truly good actions[14] as you obey your moral obligations.

Those who choose to obey God will learn the truth that the JG is truly from God,[15] and this truth entails (E). The JG entails that the pursuit of a life of love requires obedience to Jesus' commands.[16] Those who strongly desire love will strongly desire CF-membership. Also, those who desire to accept truth desire to become members of CF, since JG entails that it is true that CF-membership is desirable for truth-seekers. In addition, to the degree that one finds support for the non-(E) components of BT that is independent of the assumption that component (E) is true, (E) may be further confirmed. Therefore, CF-membership is a moral obligation for truth-seekers.

Support for (F) may be found, for example, in the observation that Jesus' confidence in the authority of Scripture, taken in conjunction with confidence that CF-members will be guided into authoritative knowledge of Jesus,[17] implies that the identification of the set W of writings widely accepted by CF-members as authoritative constitutes a basis for the supposition that the members of W are authoritative insofar as they describe Jesus and his teachings. Since BG is a subset of W, it follows that (F) is thereby supported. In addition, to the degree that one finds support for the non-(F) components of BT that is independent of the assumption that component (F) is true, (F) may be further confirmed. It follows that BG-acceptance is a moral obligation for truth-seekers.

Support for (G) may come from the observation that God's guidance of theologically informed people of God into proper recognition of an authoritative Biblical canon (as confirmed, for example, by Jesus' use of material from the Biblical canon CY of that time) implies that the eventual acceptance (by theologically informed people of God) of a canon that is expanded to include material in addition to CY confirms that CB is properly recognized as an authoritative Biblical canon. Given the truthful nature of God,[18] we may then presume that the canon CB consists of only accurate information, in the absence of compelling evidence to the contrary. This is especially true in light of the detailed nature of Jesus-attested divinely inspired Biblical revelation.[19] Thus, we find justification for acceptance of PCBI. In addition, to the degree that one finds support for the non-(G) components of BT that is independent of the assumption that component (G) is true, (G) may be further confirmed. PCBI-acceptance is, therefore, a moral obligation for truth-seekers.

Support for (H) is derived from the observation that a PCBI-grounded Scriptural canon, generally interpreted along the lines of the ICBI statement on inerrancy,[20] affords the theologian a wealth of information which may be systematically organized to provide insight (much greater than that available from natural theology) regarding such theological categories as Christology, pneumatology, anthropology, angelology-demonology, hamartiology, soteriology, ecclesiology, Israelology, and eschatology.[21] In addition, to the degree that one finds support for the non-(H) components of BT that is independent of the assumption that component (H) is true, (H) may be further confirmed. Acceptance of conservative Biblical systematic theology is, therefore, a moral obligation for truth-seekers.

Component (I) serves to emphasize that theology is not purely academic, but leads to the practical application of theological truth to one's personal life. The pursuit of the development, defense, and demonstration of a theologically informed worldview, personally tailored to one's unique giftings and abilities, motivates the quest of the Bible-believer to know and love God in eager and joyous expectation of promised inheritance. For those who vigorously accept that it is strongly desirable to follow the truth wherever it leads,[22] the truth of components (A) through (H) entails that it is a moral obligation to fully integrate those components into one's personal life.

The 'Holy Spirit Epistemology' Justification of BT

CF-members can justify acceptance of the nine components of BT as outlined in the previous section, although this is surely not the only way to know that BT-acceptance is justified. For example, GB could enable me to know that it is GB who enables me to know that GB causes (or GB and I together jointly cause) my acceptance of BT to be justified. Such religious experience may constitute direct perception of the reality of the Biblical God by individuals who understand, only to a limited degree, the full and detailed nature of that God or the fullness of the implications, in detail, of propositions divinely caused to be self-evident in that very experience, such as: "I directly and immediately perceive that God strongly desires that I persevere in my ongoing pursuit of the attainment of full BT-integration into my personal life, not because that pursuit is guaranteed to ensure my inerrant perception at all times of the implications of BT in all its details, but because that pursuit is, itself, the outward manifestation of my openness and submission to the Holy Spirit who continues to teach (and lead, guide, direct, convict, draw, and love, etc.) me in all truth."[23]

BT and the Disconfirmation of Non-BT Systems

I have shown that we may immediately dismiss *atheistic* anti-BT arguments used by members of RC, since we have seen that such arguments are unsound instances of the SOBRB. Also, I have shown how BT may come to be properly accepted through the witness of the Holy Spirit, or through examination (with or without one's conscious awareness of the role of the Holy Spirit in that examination) of the evidential considerations relevant to the nine key components of BT. Now I also wish to emphasize that although BT-acceptance may be justified, even if one has achieved no substantive ability to provide detailed refutations of competing atheistic *or theistic* SOBRB-formulated anti-BT arguments, our confidence in BT may, nevertheless, be further strengthened by exposing the detailed failings of such anti-BT arguments, and such analyses may play a helpful role in the further confirmation of the justification of BT-belief.

For example, recent atheism literature may be examined[24] and found to contain no substantive or successful refutation of ideas justified in my theistic arguments. Claims that Jesus never existed[25] may be shown to be grounded in incorrect assumptions about the nature of historical analysis, and in the mishandling of the available historical data.[26] Alleged counterexamples to the claim that PCBI is justified[27] may be shown to be grounded, typically, in improper hermeneutics and, in any case, may be used as a smokescreen in an illegitimate attempt to avoid the real issue of primary significance: CF-membership. Even if PCBI is not yet accepted, observe that CF-membership is rationally justified and morally obligatory (for strong-willed truth seekers), given components (A) through (E), and given the evidential support for components (A) through (E).

Evidential considerations pertinent to the following noteworthy religious non-BT systems further confirm BT: Islam,[28] anti-BT Judaism,[29] Buddhism and Hinduism,[30] Mormonism,[31] and Jehovah's Witnesses.[32]

Have You Decided To Follow Jesus?

It is worth emphasizing that acceptance of PCBI is not a prerequisite for CF-membership, even though CF-membership may naturally lead to PCBI. So, objections to CB-inerrancy are not relevant to the pivotal point that since becoming a follower of Jesus is strongly desirable (given one's knowledge of BT-components (A) through (E), and given that one strongly desires to follow truth), failure to follow Jesus is strictly irrational.

It is also important to note that acceptance of a particular systematic theology in every detail is not a prerequisite for CF-membership, even though CF-membership may naturally lead to one's development of a systematic theology that one ultimately accepts in every detail. So, objections to specific theological systems may be largely irrelevant to the fundamental question of whether you choose to follow Jesus.

Fear of full BT-integration into one's life may be a deterring consideration for some people considering CF-membership, especially if that integration may require the personal, emotionally painful acknowledgement that previously cherished (and now known to be false) beliefs must now be exchanged for true beliefs. Briefly, I would respond that it is better to seek and accept truth (even if it might be painful to do so) rather than flee and reject truth, since truth rejection is fundamentally incoherent.

To see the incoherent nature of truth rejection, consider person J with desire D, where D is defined as J's strong desire to know that each of J's strong desires is satisfied.[33] Now, if J chooses to reject some measure M of truth in a context in which M-rejection is not necessary for J, then J behaves inconsistently, since J's choice to reject M serves to reduce the probability that D is satisfied. To see this, consider that J knows D is satisfied in the actual world only if J knows that (1) the possible world PW represented by J's personal worldview includes D-satisfaction, and (2) PW is more likely to be the actual world than any other possible world known by J. Also, J's rejection of M serves to reduce the probability that J knows condition (2) is true. It follows that J's M-rejection reduces the probability that J knows D is satisfied in the actual world. M-rejection, therefore, overrides D in every context in which that rejection is not logically (or practically) necessary for J, and such overriding is logically inconsistent with D and represents a fundamentally incoherent rational state.[34] Since everyone with desires also has a D-type desire, each person who rejects known truth (or does not appropriately maximize one's degree of truth acquisition) acts irrationally by acting contrary to the pursuit of D-fulfillment.[35] So, in short, it's better to follow the truth wherever it leads (rare though genuine truth-seeking persons may be[36]), since anything else is prone to drowning in incoherence, as has now been shown.

It may be helpful to remind the reader, here, that my theistic arguments do not require understanding of why God permits the nature of evil in the world, even if God is maximally good and loving. Likewise, my arguments in support of BT need not include the moral justification of why GB permits the epistemic state of those who claim the nature of evil renders BT unlikely, since BT entails not only that God is maximally good and loving, but also that we should not expect to know, *in detail*, why God may act in any particular specific circumstance. We may know God acts, yet not always know why.

As a matter of practical evangelistic expediency, it may be prudent to explore ways to justify CF-membership even when all the details of BT (and its implications) are not yet fully known. In fact, knowledge of doctrines such as PCBI, knowledge of detailed systematic theologies, and presumably knowledge of truths implied by other essential BT components as well, may not be GB's immediate and primary focal objective at all times in each person's noetic structure, critical though they are to the development of an informed conservative Biblical worldview. Recall that during his very crucifixion, Jesus assured a criminal of his imminent experience of paradise in the afterlife, yet we have reason to suppose that the criminal knew little of BT in all its constituent interrelated intricacies. A minimalist approach to justifying the urgency of CF-membership may, therefore, provide proper emphasis on the issue of fundamental and primary significance: global evangelism and discipleship via the presentation, defense, and demonstration of the BG. Such an approach may consist of merely the epistemic content corresponding to a person-relative context-appropriate summary statement of BT components (A), (B), (C), (D), and (E). The faith confessions widely promulgated in the early centuries following Jesus' earthly ministry would appear to be an instance of just such an approach.

Thus, something as simple as a basic Gospel message, intelligibly expressed and sensitively targeted to an audience, can justify the strong desire for CF-membership, especially if taken in conjunction with a perceived spiritual conviction in regards to one's sin, with an awareness of God's righteous requirement of sin's judgment in the form of death and hell, and with the critical need for repentance and personal acceptance of Jesus as one's Lord, Savior, and Messiah, guaranteeing the gracious free gift of righteousness by faith and the glorious destiny of eternal life which far outweighs the relatively light and momentary troubles of this world.

Summary

To summarize why I have become no atheist, I note that Chapters 1 and 2 seem, to me, to provide compelling support for (A). In addition, nothing I know is inconsistent with what I would expect to know, if BT. Thus, nothing I know is evidence against BT. My perception of the available evidence from science, history, philosophy, and religious experience is that BT is both the best explanation and much better than any competing system. So, I accept BT and intend to persist in that acceptance so long as no other system becomes evidently rationally superior. I further note that my degree of confidence that BT is true is sufficiently high that the probability of my ever rejecting BT appears very small. Indeed, my perception is that it is God who is enabling me to know that it is God who enables me to know BT. Having accepted JG, its fuller expression in BG, and its yet fuller expression in my personal experience, I am clearly a member of CF who is deep in conviction, yet limited in knowledge, admittedly imperfect in practice, and welcome to receive critical suggestions for improvement as I persevere in the ongoing life-long adventure in which I follow Jesus in the pursuit of growth in my ever-developing relationship with Him in loving and faith-filled obedience to the Torah of God.

This pursuit of truth I find immensely satisfying in my quest to further expand and develop my love of God and others, while urging all to embrace His love as evidenced by following Jesus and His commands. The joy I know in the Holy

Spirit is fulfilling beyond measure! I am compelled to share this Good News with others in obedience to the Great Commission, ever aware of the eternally significant consequences of human choice, and of the need to receive God's gracious free gift of salvation through faith in the sufficiency of the Messiah's atoning blood shed on the cross at Calvary.

What can wash away my sins? Nothing but the blood of Jesus!

Have *you* decided to follow Jesus?

NOTES

1. On JG, see the following: Pentecost, J. Dwight (1981). *The Words and Works of Jesus Christ*. Grand Rapids, MI: Zondervan; Bock, Darrell L. (2002). Jesus *According to Scripture: Restoring the Portrait from the Gospels*. Grand Rapids, MI: Baker; Blomberg, Craig L. (1997). *Jesus and the Gospels: An Introduction and Survey*. Nashville, TN: Broadman and Holman; Stein, Robert H. (1994). *The Method and Message of Jesus' Teachings*. Louisville, KY: Westminster John Knox Press; Lockyer, Herbert (1991). *All the Teachings of Jesus*. Peabody, MA: Hendrickson.

2. Loftus, John W. (2008). *Why I Became an Atheist: A Former Preacher Rejects Christianity*. Amherst, NY: Prometheus Books.

3. Psalm 119:68.

4. Psalm 14:1; Romans 1:28; 1 Corinthians 2:14; 2 Corinthians 4:4; 1 Timothy 6:20-21.

5. On historical evidence for Jesus, see the following: Wilkins, Michael J. and Moreland, J. P., eds. (1994). *Jesus Under Fire: Modern Scholarship Reinvents the Historical Jesus*. Grand Rapids, MI: Zondervan; Komoszewski, J. Ed, and Sawyer, M. James, and Wallace, Daniel B. (2006). *Reinventing Jesus: How Contemporary Skeptics Miss the Real Jesus and Mislead Popular Culture*. Grand Rapids, MI: Kregel Publications; Bock, Darrell L. (2002). *Studying the Historical Jesus: A Guide to Sources and Methods*. Grand Rapids, MI: Baker; Habermas, Gary R. (1996). *The Historical Jesus: Ancient Evidence for the Life of Christ*. Joplin, MO: College Press; France, R.T. (1986). *The Evidence for Jesus*. Downers Grove, IL: InterVarsity Press; Blomberg, Craig L. (2007). *The Historical Reliability of the Gospels*. Downers Grove, IL: InterVarsity Press; Eddy, Paul Rhodes and Boyd, Gregory A. (2007). *The Jesus Legend: A Case for the Historical Reliability of the Synoptic Jesus Tradition*. Grand Rapids, MI: Baker. Montgomery, John Warwick (1986). *History and Christianity*. Minneapolis, MN: Bethany House.

6. Habermas, Gary R. and Licona, Michael R. (2004). *The Case for the Resurrection of Jesus*. Grand Rapids, MI: Kregel. Also, see Craig, William Lane (2008). *Reasonable Faith: Christian Truth and Apologetics*, 3rd ed. Wheaton, IL: Crossway Books, Chapter 8.

7. Geivett, R. Douglas and Habermas, Gary R. (1997). *In Defense of Miracles: A Comprehensive Case for God's Action in History*. Downers Grove, IL: InterVarsity Press.

8. I have personally seen instances of truth-rejection in the lives of very religious persons. Let this be a warning to the religious among us, lest they commit in vain to false religion that is rejected by God. Do not let your pride prevent you from changing your ways! Moreover, Jesus warned that corrupted religious believers will be punished most severely (Mark 12:40; Luke 20:47).

9. John 3:19-21.

10. Matthew 10:37-39; Luke 9:23-25; Luke 14:33-35; John 12:23-26.

11. Joshua 24:15.

12. Amos 4:4; Matthew 23:32; John 13:27; Romans 9:18.

13. Amos 4:2-3; Matthew 12:24; Matthew 13:15; Matthew 23:33; Hebrews 3:7-19.

14. Philippians 2:13; Romans 12:1-2.

15. John 7:17.

16. John 14:15.

17. Matthew 23:34, John 7:17; John 14:26.

18. Numbers 23:19; Psalm 31:5; Proverb 6:17; Isaiah 45:19; John 17:17.

19. Matthew 5:18; Luke 16:17.

20. Geisler, Norman L., ed. (1980). *Inerrancy*. Grand Rapids, MI: Zondervan, pp. 493-502.

21. Many systematic theologies have been written. For example, see Grudem, Wayne (1994). *Systematic Theology: An Introduction to Biblical Doctrine*. Grand Rapids, MI: Zondervan, pp. 1224-1230.

22. Luke 16:16.

23. For further analysis of the nature of this religious experience, including a response to critical comments made by Loftus, see my "Control Beliefs and Religious Experience" section of Chapter 4 on p. 100 of the present volume.

24. See the Atheism Books section of the Bibliography.

25. For example, see Wells, G.A. (1982). *The Historical Evidence for Jesus*. Buffalo, NY: Prometheus Books.

26. See footnote 5 above.

27. Claims of errors and contradictions in the Bible are standard fare in the anti-BT atheist literature. For a sampling, see the following: McKinsey, C. Dennis (1995). *The Encyclopedia of Biblical Errancy*. Amherst, NY: Prometheus Books. Holman, Joe E. (2008). *Project Bible Truth: A Minister Turns Atheist and Tells All*. Morrisville, NC: Lulu Press. Davis, Mike (2008). *The Atheist's Introduction to the New Testament: How the Bible Undermines the Basic Teachings of Christianity*. Denver, CO: Outskirts Press. Long, Jason (2005). *Biblical Nonsense: A Review of the Bible for Doubting Christians*. New York: iUniverse. Barker, Dan (2008). *Godless: How an Evangelical Preacher Became One of America's Leading Atheists*. Berkeley, CA: Ulysses Press.

28. Abdul-Haqq, Abdiyah Akbar (1980). *Sharing Your Faith with a Muslim*. Minneapolis, MN: Bethany House. Shorrosh, Anis A. (1988). *Islam Revealed: A Christian Arab's View of Islam*. Nashville, TN: Thomas Nelson. Geisler, Norman L. and Saleeb, Abdul (2002). *Answering Islam: The Crescent in Light of the Cross*. Grand Rapids, MI: Baker. Parshall, Phil (1983). *Bridges to Islam*. Grand Rapids, MI: Baker. Parshall, Phil (1985). *Beyond the Mosque*. Grand Rapids, MI: Baker. McDowell, Josh and Gilchrist, John (1983). *The Islam Debate*. San Bernardino, CA: Here's Life. Rhodes, Ron (2002). *Reasoning from the Scriptures with Muslims*. Eugene, OR: Harvest House. Campbell, William F. (1992). *The

Quran and the Bible in the Light of History and Science. Published by Middle East Resources. Spencer, Robert (2006). *The Truth About Muhammad: Founder of the World's Most Intolerant Religion.* Washington: Regnery.

29. Brown, Michael L. (2000). *Answering Jewish Objections to Jesus: General and Historical Objections.* Grand Rapids, MI: Baker. Brown, Michael L. (2000). *Answering Jewish Objections to Jesus: Theological Objections.* Grand Rapids, MI: Baker. Brown, Michael L. (2003). *Answering Jewish Objections to Jesus: Messianic Prophecy Objections.* Grand Rapids, MI: Baker. Brown, Michael L. (2007). *Answering Jewish Objections to Jesus: New Testament Objections.* Grand Rapids, MI: Baker. Kac, Arthur (1986). *The Messiahship of Jesus: Are Jews Changing Their Attitude Toward Jesus?* Grand Rapids, MI: Baker. Smith, James E. (1993). *What the Bible Teaches about the Promised Messiah.* Nashville, TN: Thomas Nelson. Ankerberg, John (1989). *The Case for Jesus the Messiah.* Eugene, OR: Harvest House. Kaiser, Walter C. (1995). *The Messiah in the Old Testament.* Grand Rapids, MI: Zondervan.

30. Halverson, Dean C. (1996). *The Compact Guide to World Religions.* Minneapolis, MN: Bethany House. McDowell, Josh and Stewart, Don (1983). *Handbook of Today's Religions.* Nashville, TN: Thomas Nelson.

31. Geisler, Norman L., ed. (1998). *The Counterfeit Gospel of Mormonism.* Eugene, OR: Harvest House. Tanner, Jerald and Sandra (2008). *Mormonism—Shadow or Reality.* Salt Lake City, UT: Utah Lighthouse Ministry. Abanes, Richard (2003). *One Nation Under Gods: A History of the Mormon Church.* New York: Basic Books. Abanes, Richard (2004). *Becoming Gods.* Eugene, OR: Harvest House. Zacharias, Ravi, ed. (2003). *The Kingdom of the Cults.* Minneapolis, MN: Bethany House. McKeever, Bill and Johnson, Eric (2000). *Mormonism 101: Examining the Religion of the Latter-day Saints.* Grand Rapids, MI: Baker. McKeever, Bill (1991). *Answering Mormons' Questions.* Minneapolis, MN: Bethany House. McElveen, Floyd (1997). *The Mormon Illusion.* Grand Rapids, MI: Kregel. Reed, David A. and Farkas, John R. (1992). *Mormons Answered Verse by Verse.* Grand Rapids, MI: Baker. Ankerberg, John and Weldon, John (1992). *Everything You Ever Wanted to Know about Mormonism.* Eugene, OR: Harvest House. White, James R. (1993). *Letters to a Mormon Elder.* Minneapolis, MN: Bethany House. Roberts, R. Philip (1998). *Mormonism Unmasked: Confronting the Contradictions Between Mormon Beliefs and True Christianity.* Nashville, TN: Broadman and Holman. Holding, James Patrick (2001). *The Mormon Defenders: How Latter-day Saint Apologists Misinterpret the Bible.* Proaster Books. Morley, Donna (2003). *A Christian Woman's Guide to Understanding Mormonism.* Eugene, OR: Harvest House. Hutchinson, Janis (1995). *The Mormon Missionaries.* Grand Rapids, MI: Kregel. Hansen, Carol (1999). *Reorganized Latter Day Saint Church: Is It Christian?* Independence, MO: Life Line Ministries. Trask, Paul (2005). *Part Way To Utah: The Forgotten Mormons.* Independence, MO: Refiner's Fire Ministries. Trask, Paul (2006).

32. Reed, David A., ed. (1990). *Index of Watchtower Errors.* Grand Rapids, MI: Baker. Reed, David A. (1986). *Jehovah's Witnesses Answered Verse by Verse.* Grand Rapids, MI: Baker. Reed, David A. (1996). *Answering Jehovah's Witnesses Subject by Subject.* Grand Rapids, MI: Baker. Love, Charles (2005). *20 Questions Jehovah's Witnesses Cannot Answer.* Longwood, FL: Xulon Press. Rhodes, Ron (1993). *Reasoning from the Scriptures with the Jehovah's Witnesses.* Eugene, OR: Harvest House. Rhodes, Ron (2001). *The 10 Most Important Things You Can Say to a Jehovah's Witness.* Eugene, OR: Harvest House. Sire, James W. (1980). *Scripture Twisting: 20 Ways the Cults Misread the Bible.* Downers Grove, IL: InterVarsity Press. Berry, Harold J. (1992). *The Truth Twisters: What They Believe.* Lincoln, NE: Back to the Bible. Ankerberg, John and Weldon, John (2003). *Fast Facts on Jehovah's Witnesses.* Eugene, OR: Harvest House. Bowman, Robert M. (1995). *Jehovah's*

Witnesses. Grand Rapids, MI: Zondervan. Gruss, Edmond (1976). *Apostles of Denial*. Grand Rapids, MI: Baker. Wilson, Diane (2002). *Awakening of a Jehovah's Witness: Escape from the Watchtower Society*. Amherst, NY: Prometheus Books. Morey, Robert A. (1980). *How to Answer a Jehovah's Witness*. Minneapolis, MN: Bethany House. Lingle, Wilbur (2004). *Approaching Jehovah's Witnesses in Love: How to Witness Effectively Without Arguing*. Fort Washington, PA: CLC Publications.

33. A person's strong desire may be defined as a person's desire which is not overridden by any opposing desires of that person.

34. It is assumed that J is not in an epistemic state in which J is justified in choosing to persist in a state in which J knows that J's M-rejection is not necessary; although this assumption may not be universally applicable to the epistemic states of all agents at all times, I do not further explore this special case, as I doubt it poses a serious threat to the general applicability of my position here set forth.

35. I view this fundamental irrationality as a widespread, if not universally present, manifestation of human sin. Since human sin fully matures in BT-rejection, it may be argued that many have acted in ways that would logically entail their rejection of BT, even though they may not even be aware of much at all (if anything) regarding either that logical entailment or the contents of detailed pro-BT arguments. Thus, a person uninformed regarding the detailed nature of BT (e.g., a member of some remote BT-unevangelized African tribe) could, in fact, be justly held liable for rejecting fundamental tenets of BT by virtue of the logical entailment relation between BT tenets and that person's manifested epistemic state. Even the unevangelized are responsible to God (Romans 1:14-16).

36. Hanson, Robin and Cowen, Tyler (2004). *Are Disagreements Honest?* Forthcoming article in Journal of Economic Methodology. Article available online at http://www.gmu.edu/centers/publicchoice/faculty%20pages/Tyler/deceive.pdf (last accessed February 9, 2010).

CHAPTER 6

Loftus and the Bible

Abstract: *The Biblical perspectives espoused by John W. Loftus are examined and found to be logically linked to his unjustified primary control beliefs. The perspectives examined include those pertaining to Genesis, prophecy, Biblical authority, virgin birth, incarnation, atonement, resurrection, evil supernaturalism, and hell.*

The primary control beliefs accepted by John W. Loftus ground his examination of biblical evidence. I have shown in Chapter 4 that those control beliefs are unjustified. It follows that a detailed analysis of Loftus' interpretation of Biblical evidence is not required to show that his interpretation is unjustified. It is sufficient to show that his interpretation is dependent upon his primary control beliefs. If his analysis of Biblical evidence is grounded in his primary control beliefs, we may immediately reject that analysis. Interaction with that analysis at a more detailed level is not required to justify this rejection. Indeed, a more detailed critique of Loftus' interpretation of the Biblical evidence would be somewhat akin to pruning away (in vain) at a weed's branches. Prune it, and it will remain. Uproot it altogether, and it will die. Loftus' analysis deserves not pruning, but uprooting. It follows that I do not bother to argue (in vain) that I have discovered additional evidence[1] that conservative Biblical beliefs are justified from the perspective of Loftus' unjustified primary control beliefs. Rather, I properly emphasize that Loftus' Biblical perspectives may be dismissed due to their logical grounding in those unjustified control beliefs.

Genesis

Either the Genesis creation accounts are theologically false myth,[2] or they are not. If they are not, then Loftus must discontinue acceptance of his primary control beliefs. Thus, acceptance of Loftus' primary control beliefs virtually forces the conclusion that the creation accounts are theologically false myth. If our presuppositions entail that the creation accounts are false (or probably false), then of course we are likely to conclude that the accounts are false (or probably false). Such a conclusion is not derived from a maximally neutral examination of available evidence. Rather, it is merely an unjustified exercise in circular reasoning. We may reject such reasoning, and along with it, Loftus' attempted justification of the claim that the Genesis creation accounts are theologically false mythical stories.

Let MN represent methodological naturalism. Either Genesis 1-11 is consistent with modern science, or it is not. If it is consistent, then science-based critiques of Genesis 1-11 may be rejected. If it is inconsistent, then Loftus either (1) accepts MN-based science and rejects the non-MN-based components of Genesis 1-11, or (2) rejects MN-based science. If Loftus takes option (2), then he discontinues acceptance of his primary control beliefs. Loftus' control beliefs thus force him to take option (1), and along with it, the rejection of the non-MN-based components of Genesis 1-11. Once again, such a conclusion is derived merely from an unjustified exercise in circular reasoning, not from a maximally neutral examination of available evidence. We may reject such reasoning, and along with it, Loftus' attempted justification[3] of the claim that Genesis 1-11 is inconsistent with modern science.

Prophecy

Since Biblical prophecy fulfillment is often used to aid in the justification of claims that Biblical information is divinely authoritative, investigators of Biblical truth claims often examine the nature of Biblical prophecy. Unfortunately, Loftus' examination of Biblical prophecy begins with an incorrect philosophical approach. Loftus reasons, in effect, that his knowledge of the means M by which God (if God exists) foreknows free actions is a necessary condition of Loftus not being justified in thinking God (if God exists) does not foreknow free actions.[4] In response, one can know the sun shines, yet not understand the means by which it shines. One can possess knowledge of some features of an actual process, even if one does not understand how that process operates. Thus, there exists the possibility Q that a person could know that God (if God exists) foreknows free actions, even if that person does not know M. Loftus does not justify his presumption that Q is unlikely, nor does he even consider the rational implications of the nature of Q or the means by which Q could potentially be properly identified in a noetic structure as likely. Rather, he merely infers (incorrectly) that his lack of knowledge of a probably existing M justifies the belief that God can not foreknow human history with certainty.[5]

It is wrong of Loftus to assume, in effect, that "If God foreknows future free actions, then Loftus likely knows how God has such foreknowledge." It is wrong because we simply have no good reason to insist that Loftus would have any detailed understanding of how God possesses *any* knowledge, if God exists. This is especially evident in light of the nature of the physical universe itself, since the nature of that universe is such that if God is its creator-sustainer-designer, then God's knowledge is likely far greater than that of any mere man, thereby exposing the rational basis for the assumption that such a God would likely have knowledge not possessed by Loftus, where that knowledge may well include foreknowledge by some means unknown to Loftus. Furthermore, the hypothesis "The Biblical God exists" entails that Loftus (and the rest of us mere humans) are unlikely to possess more than a highly limited understanding of the ways of God,[6] thereby exposing further the rational basis for supposing that Loftus is unlikely to know M, if the Biblical God exists. For these reasons, Loftus' position stands unjustified and in need of serious revision, or better yet, rejection.

The situation for Loftus is even worse, however, since the Biblical God (if the Biblical God exists) may reveal to particular individuals truths by the Spirit, where those truths are incomprehensible foolishness to those who are without the Spirit.[7] Again, this opens the door to the possibility that if Biblical theology is true, then some who accept it may be divinely enabled to be justified in knowing truths unknown by Loftus. Thus, Bible-believers could know God foreknows future free actions, even if Loftus has no clue how God could have such foreknowledge.

Loftus considers the possibility that God's foreknowledge is deduced from God's knowledge of present conditions.[8] Loftus concludes that this option leads to the belief that humans are analogous to "programmed rats" without freedom.[9] In response, I would like to briefly explore two inferential views in which God's foreknowledge may be deduced from God's present knowledge of God's decision to perform actions that will insure that God has sufficient foreknowledge of all events to facilitate the fulfillment of every divinely inspired prophecy via human prophets. In both views, significant human freedom may be preserved.

The first inferential view I set forth here relates to the idea that if God predicts future events based on God's knowledge of both present and future conditions, then we need not infer that humans are wholly determined creatures with no freedom. After all, if the Biblical God exists, then we may infer that God knows that present and future conditions obtain by virtue of God's decision to permit those conditions. Since all future conditions may be contingent upon God's permitting-power (i.e., all future conditions may, at all times, be understood to be subject to God's continuous supply of power necessary for the obtaining of those contingent conditions), God may be able to predict the future state of all conditions simply by virtue of God's knowledge of the future actions God knows God has decided to perform in the future. So long as God possesses such self-knowledge, then, we may presume that God may foreknow future actions.

To see how this version of the "inferential view" works, let's consider an example. Suppose God enabled a prophet to prophesy, today, that I will eat a cheeseburger tomorrow. God could foreknow this future action, and God could enable a prophet to predict this future action. How? By virtue of God's knowledge that either (1) God will cause me to eat a cheeseburger tomorrow, or (2) God will not cause me to eat a cheeseburger tomorrow, if I freely choose to eat a cheeseburger tomorrow. In this case, God foreknows that I will eat a cheeseburger tomorrow, even if God does not presently know whether that cheeseburger will be eaten by virtue of my free choice or by God's overpowering causal action. Incidentally, I rather doubt this is the means by which God may foreknow future actions, but it is, nevertheless, a plausible means by which God could conceivably choose to foreknow future actions, and it is sufficient to justify rejection of any critical claim that God can not possibly foreknow future actions.

It is critical to note, too, that even if God takes option (1) so as to insure that I eat a cheeseburger tomorrow (say, due to the fact that if God didn't choose option (1), then I would not freely choose to eat a cheeseburger tomorrow), it does not follow that I am merely a programmed rat without freedom.[10] I could have significant human freedom, yet be occasionally caused by God to perform actions which might be contrary to what I would otherwise have freely chosen. For example, if I choose to walk from region A to region B, and if I do not particularly care whether I take 273 steps or 274 steps during that walk, then God could cause me (for good reasons I don't know) to take the number of steps God prefers, even if I am completely oblivious to such divine intervention in my walk. In this case, no significant loss of freedom obtains, yet divine action nevertheless manifests in the physical world. If God causes me to take 273 steps during the walk, then it hardly follows that I may be likened to a programmed rat! After all, I am the one who chose to take the walk, and I was not programmed to take a walk; God merely influenced that walk in ways I did not detect. Thus, even if God takes option (1) to insure that I eat a cheeseburger tomorrow, all my other actions tomorrow could still be freely performed by me, in which case I will still have significant freedom tomorrow.

My definition of "free" is such that "Person J freely performs action A" if and only if "J causes A, and J is not caused to cause A". Note carefully that my definition of freedom does not entail "If J freely causes A at time T, then J at T had the power to not cause A at T", as is often erroneously assumed to be essential to human freedom. If J freely ate a cheeseburger yesterday, then it need not be the case that J could have not eaten a cheeseburger yesterday. Why? Because it could be true that if J did not cause J to eat a cheeseburger yesterday, then God would have caused J to eat a cheeseburger yesterday. In this way, J's human action A could be free (since J was not caused to cause A), where that freedom does not entail that A could have not occurred. In like manner, God could foreknow all future human actions, where only some of those foreknown actions are freely performed by humans. There is evidently no reason to suppose such a God would have any problem at all divinely enabling prophetic revelation of future events through God-inspired human prophets.

A second possible divine foreknowledge mechanism that deserves evaluation, here, is the consideration that God may have sufficient power to influence conditions relevant to free human choices such that God could lead a person to make any free choice God desires. God could, for example, know that God only creates humans such that human free will can be determined by physical events freely caused by God. In this case, God's knowledge of the future actions God will perform may be sufficient to determine the future free actions of all humans. God's self-knowledge may, therefore, be sufficient to explain God's foreknowledge of free actions; so long as God knows that God will perform (in the future) the actions God knows God intends to perform in the future, God may infer the results of all future free human actions from that divine self-knowledge. In this scenario, it may be that no human always performs free actions at all times, and it may be that every human performs some free actions at some times. Thus, prior to God's creation of any person, God could have recorded and determined the future actions of all persons, including the names of all persons who would freely enter into proper relationship with God.[11] Again, there is evidently no reason to suppose such a God would have any problem at all divinely enabling prophetic revelation of future events through God-inspired human prophets.

In summary, I have explored two possible means by which God could foreknow future human actions, where that foreknowledge need not be taken to preclude significant human freedom. Pending good reasons to suppose these possibilities are not likely, we may not arbitrarily presume they are unlikely. Since Loftus has not shown that these possibilities are unlikely, therefore, it does not follow that absence of his knowledge of evidence for possibly existing divine foreknowledge of future free actions is evidence of the absence of possibly existing divine foreknowledge of future free actions. In fact, my considerations here establish that we do have evidence for possibly existing divine foreknowledge of future (free and not free) actions. In turn, it is improper of Loftus to infer he is justified in maintaining the belief that no possibly existing mechanism facilitates (for any possibly existing god) divine foreknowledge of future free actions.[12]

My position is not that Loftus may rationally reject divine foreknowledge only if he shows that every possibly existing divine foreknowledge mechanism (let R denote the set of all such mechanisms) is impossible.[13] Rather, my position is that Loftus may rationally reject the members of R only if he shows that he is justified in supposing those members are all improbable. After all, if a member of R is a highly probable mechanism by which God (if God exists) could foreknow future free actions, then Loftus' inference is, of course, incorrect that God (if God exists) has no available mechanism by which God could foreknow future free actions. We can perceive sun-derived light, yet a necessary condition of that perception is surely not our knowledge of physical nuclear fusion and stellar dynamics processes that ultimately lead to light transmission. We may not, therefore, presume that our failure to discover a physical process that explains solar light transmission justifies our rejection of the existence of solar light transmission. After all, even a child perceives solar light transmission, yet a child generally does not understand physical laws that describe that transmission process. Somewhat analogously, we may not rationally reject the members of R, especially since (1) we have identified two mechanisms by which possibly existing divine foreknowledge may obtain for a possibly existing God, (2) it is not established that those possibly existing mechanisms are (for a possibly existing God) improbable, and (3) the nature of one's noetic structure could justify particular beliefs (including the belief that a member of R is probable), regardless of whether the details of the mechanisms entailed by those particular beliefs are well understood.

I have not resorted to a "merely possible" defense.[14] Consider claim D: "Divine foreknowledge is sufficient (for a possibly existing God) to facilitate divinely inspired Biblical prophetic revelation via human prophets". Now, my position is not "D is improbable (yet possible), therefore we may not consequently accept that D is unknown". Rather, my position is "Since it is not known that all members of R are improbable, it is not known that D is unknown". That is, I have properly employed the *unknown probability of a possibility* (UPOAP) defense. The purpose of the UPOAP, here, is not to show that D is likely, but to show that D is not known to be unlikely as a consequence of objections raised by Loftus. Specifically, it is not the case that D is known to be unlikely by virtue of Loftus' lack of knowledge of a member of R that would function as the means by which D obtains for a possibly existing God; this follows because Loftus has not examined all members of R, and because Loftus has not justified the claim that his examination of a subset of the members of R renders D unlikely. This result is especially evident, given that Loftus has only considered several members of R.[15] There is more for Loftus to do. He could attempt to justify the claim that all members of R are known to be improbable. My point is that since all members of R are not known to be improbable, D is not known to be improbable. Of course, this does not entail that D is known to be probable, but this is beside the point. The purpose of an inductive defense is not to show "Reasons examined in a defense entail that a disputed claim is known to be likely", but to show "Reasons examined in a defense entail that a disputed claim is not known to be unlikely".

Even if my brief exploration, above, of the means by which God could foreknow free human actions is flawed for some unknown reason, there is a much more fundamental reason which precludes Loftus' acceptance of divinely enabled predictive Bible prophecy fulfillment. Specifically, Loftus' acceptance of his control beliefs requires that he immediately reject any claims of divinely-enabled Bible prophecy fulfillment, even prior to any more detailed analysis.[16] After all, the truth of a religious belief system can not be likely to be confirmed by analysis of possible instances of Bible prophecy fulfillment, if we must begin that analysis with a control belief (i.e., Loftus' control belief CB1) that entails all religious beliefs systems under investigation are likely false. Also, God likely can not facilitate Bible prophecy fulfillment, if all events likely have a natural cause (Loftus' control belief CB2). In addition, scientific analysis of possible instances of divinely-enabled prophecy fulfillment will likely conclude that no such instances likely exist, if scientific analysis must begin with the assumption of methodological naturalism (Loftus' control belief CB3). In other words, the nature of the detailed evidence relevant to Bible prophecy is not critical to Loftus' analysis, since he could always resort to the fall-back position that his control beliefs entail that divinely-enabled Bible prophecy fulfillment is unlikely. Once again, we have exposed the question-begging nature of Loftus' control beliefs. Therefore, we may proceed to reject Loftus' analysis of Biblical prophecy, since it is fundamentally couched in the context of presumed control beliefs which I have shown, in Chapter 4, to be unjustified.

Biblical Authority

Biblical information is taken by many believers to be divinely inspired, facilitating a Bible-based worldview. Fundamentally, Loftus is virtually guaranteed to reject such a worldview, since his control beliefs blind him from seeing evidence for divine inspiration of the Bible. Specifically, Loftus' control belief CB1 insists that examination of a religious belief system begin with the assumption that that system is probably false. Well, of course, such an assumption leads to rejection of religious belief systems (including any traditional conservative Bible-based systems), but this merely exemplifies the consequences of circular (and unjustified) reasoning. Also, Loftus' control belief CB2 requires that all events probably have a natural cause, entailing the probable nonexistence of any divine cause (including any possible divine cause of any Scripture's inspiration and authority). Thus, we see that even without a critique of Loftus' detailed analysis of the case for divine Biblical authority and inspiration, we may make the critical observation that his control beliefs preclude acceptance of any such possibly existing authority and inspiration. We may rightly reject such analysis, especially given the unjustified nature of the control beliefs grounding that analysis, as shown in Chapter 4.

Virgin Birth

If Loftus accepts his primary control beliefs, then it is reasonable to infer that Loftus would likely reject that Jesus was born of a virgin in Bethlehem. So, Loftus' acceptance of such a birth would require that Loftus infer that his primary control beliefs are unlikely. It follows that Loftus' acceptance of his primary control beliefs virtually forces the inference that it is unlikely that Jesus was born of a virgin in Bethlehem, regardless of the nature of the available evidence. Again, we see circular (and unjustified) reasoning in action. We may not reject the virgin birth by using reasoning grounded in the presupposition that virgin births are highly improbable (if not impossible). Since Loftus presupposes his primary control beliefs, he must conclude that the virgin birth is improbable, regardless of the nature of the available evidence. The problem with Loftus' analysis is that it is ultimately grounded in unjustified control beliefs. Those historians seriously concerned with reconstructing plausible models of past events, therefore, may reject Loftus' fundamentally question-begging approach.

Incarnation

If Jesus was God Incarnate, then supernatural causes of events surely exist. Since Loftus accepts a control belief (CB2) that entails all events likely have natural causes, it follows that Loftus' acceptance of CB2 virtually forces the conclusion that the probability is small that any person is ever God Incarnate at any time. So, regardless of the nature of the historical evidence for the Biblical claim that Jesus was God Incarnate, Loftus is virtually bound to conclude that

Jesus was not God Incarnate. Once again, we see that Loftus' failure to maximize the degree to which neutral presuppositions are brought to historical analysis skews him towards rejection of a fundamental Biblical belief. Loftus' rejection is, itself, to be properly rejected, however, since his analysis is fundamentally an unfortunate case of circular (and unjustified) reasoning. He uses unnecessary and unjustified anti-Biblical presuppositions to draw anti-Biblical conclusions.

It is no surprise that Loftus is unable to make sense of the Biblical doctrine of Jesus' Incarnation.[17] His unjustified presuppositions virtually guarantee this result. Those interested in seeing where the evidence may lead a person who begins from a more nearly neutral starting point, however, may well draw considerably different conclusions. We may urge Loftus to exchange his unjustified skeptical agnosticism for neutral agnosticism so that he may reevaluate the nature of the evidential considerations relevant to Biblical history, theology, and philosophy by beginning from a much better justified starting point.

Atonement

If the Biblical God exists, then there exists a good atonement theory (GAT) grounded in God's good actions, regardless of whether we fully understand either GAT or the divine decision procedures involved in God's performance of actions which pertain to GAT. If we accept Loftus' control beliefs, then GAT must be immediately rejected, since GAT entails the existence of God-caused events and the truth of a religious belief system, both of which are improbable on the assumption that Loftus' control beliefs are true. Thus, it is evident that Loftus' control beliefs refuted in Chapter 4 lead him to reject the existence of GAT. It is no surprise, and to be expected, that it makes no sense to Loftus[18] to suppose GAT exists.

Conservative Bible-believers need not suppose that Loftus' rejection of GAT implies GAT does not exist, and in fact, Loftus' confusion regarding how GAT could be true is even consistent with the hypothesis that Biblical beliefs are true.[19] Thus, Loftus' confusion is hardly evidence against the existence of GAT, especially in light of the fact that Loftus has failed to justify the claim "If GAT exists, then Loftus would know GAT exists." Since Loftus is a champion of skeptical thinking, let us invoke that very skepticism to the effect that we may doubt that Loftus would know either that GAT exists or the nature of the divine decision procedures involved in God's performance of actions which pertain to GAT, even if GAT exists. This skepticism is especially warranted, given that a Biblical belief system entails we are unlikely to fully understand divine decision procedures.[20] So, once again, it follows that Loftus' ignorance of GAT is not evidence for the nonexistence of GAT, especially since his analysis is fundamentally grounded in anti-Biblical presupposed control beliefs which lead to unjustified anti-Biblical conclusions via circular reasoning.

Resurrection

Consider the historical-theological belief R: "God bodily raised Jesus from the dead out of the tomb in which he was buried." Loftus evidently accepts that R is a supernatural explanation.[21] If R is true, then Loftus' primary control beliefs are false. If Loftus accepts his primary control beliefs CB, then it follows that R may be rejected,[22] regardless of the nature of any available evidence relevant to R that might further "disconfirm" R. Thus, the control beliefs CB almost inevitably force Loftus to the conclusion that R is false, for even if R were highly likely on some body of evidence E, Loftus could always invoke his control beliefs in support of his claim to "know" that R is unlikely on evidence E + CB.

In response, the control beliefs CB are shown, in detail, to be unjustified in Chapter 4. It follows that Loftus may not punt to evidence E + CB as a virtually guaranteed fall-back position to justify his rejection of R. Rather, Loftus needs to pursue the maximization of the degree to which he may objectively begin evidential analyses with neutral control beliefs so that he may subsequently reevaluate evidence from history, science, philosophy, etc., in the light of those better justified control beliefs. Failure to do so simply renders Loftus' analysis an interesting, but unjustified, exercise in circular reasoning which we may consequently reject.

Evil Supernaturalism

If satanic-demonic beings actually exist and cause events as described in the Bible, then Loftus' control beliefs are false. Those control beliefs, therefore, virtually inevitably lead to rejection of the existence of such evil supernatural beings, regardless of the degree to which available evidence (apart from those control beliefs) may confirm or disconfirm belief in the existence of such evil supernaturalism. It is no surprise, therefore, that Loftus concludes that the

Biblical description of a satanic kingdom is a human invention.[23] Indeed, Loftus' control beliefs virtually guarantee that he will not accept the existence of evil supernatural beings, regardless of the strength of any Biblical or empirical evidence.[24] In other words, Loftus presupposes anti-Biblical control beliefs and proceeds to draw anti-Biblical conclusions. We may reject, once again, Loftus' circular reasoning as unjustified.

Hell

If the traditional view of hell is correct,[25] then God acts so as to permit the unending conscious torment of some people. If Loftus accepts his primary control beliefs, then he, of course, is led to conclude that there is no God who acts. It follows that acceptance of Loftus' control beliefs leads to the rejection of the traditional view of hell, regardless of the nature of any possible Biblical[26] or extra-Biblical[27] evidence for it. Yet again, Loftus fundamentally relies upon anti-Biblical control beliefs to justify anti-Biblical conclusions. Once more, we may reject such reasoning as circular and unjustified.

Summary

It is clear that Loftus' control beliefs logically undergird his rejection of conservative Biblical theology. By revealing this logical connection, and by emphasizing that his control beliefs are unjustified, it is shown that his rejection of conservative Biblical theology is, itself, unjustified.

NOTES

1. Loftus, John W. (2008). *Why I Became an Atheist: A Former Preacher Rejects Christianity*. Amherst, NY: Prometheus Books, p. 58:18-20.
2. Ibid., p. 279:6-7.
3. Ibid., p. 281:1-288:30.
4. Ibid., p. 292:9-12.
5. Ibid., p. 292:13-16.

6. Psalm 145:3; Psalm 147:5; Isaiah 40:28; Isaiah 55:8-9; Romans 11:33; 1 Corinthians 13:9-12.

7. 1 Corinthians 2:12-14.

8. Loftus (2008), p. 291:13-14.

9. Ibid., p. 291:17-19.

10. Ibid.

11. Psalm 139:16; Revelation 20:12.

12. Loftus (2008), p. 292:11-12.

13. Ibid., p. 292:4-6.

14. Ibid., p. 61:40-41.

15. Ibid., p. 292:6-7.

16. Ibid., p. 292:20-302:43.

17. Ibid., p. 341:21-22.

18. Ibid., p. 349:21-23.

19. 1 Corinthians 1:18; 1 Corinthians 2:14.

20. Psalm 145:3; Psalm 147:5; Isaiah 40:28; Isaiah 55:8-9; Romans 11:33.

21. Loftus (2008), p. 371:33-35.

22. Ibid., p. 377:41-378:2.

23. Ibid., p. 386:7-9.

24. Murphy, Edward F. (2003). *The Handbook for Spiritual Warfare*. Nashville, TN: Thomas Nelson. Rische, Jill Martin (2008). *The Kingdom of the Occult*. Nashville, TN: Thomas Nelson. Unger, Merrill F. (1994). *Biblical Demonology: A Study of Spiritual Forces at Work Today*. Grand Rapids, MI: Kregel Publications. Unger, Merrill F. (1971). *Demons in the World Today*. Wheaton, IL: Tyndale House. Koch, Kurt (1969). *Occult Practices and Beliefs*. Grand Rapids, MI: Kregel Publications. Koch, Kurt (1972). *Occult Bondage and Deliverance*. Grand Rapids, MI: Kregel Publications.

25. Loftus (2008), p. 392:1-394:4.

26. Blanchard, John (1995). *Whatever Happened to Hell?* Wheaton, IL: Crossway Books.

27. Rawlings, Maurice S. (1993). *To Hell and Back*. Nashville, TN: Thomas Nelson. Wiese, Bill (2006). *23 Minutes in Hell*. Lake Mary, FL: Charisma House. Also, I personally know an individual who has described an experience of going to hell and subsequently returning.

CHAPTER 7

Theism, Atheism, and STONE

Abstract: *The nature of neutral agnostic reasoning is explored with the ultimate objective of outlining a newly developed procedure, STONE (Stone's Test Of Neutral Evidence), which is designed to provide practical assistance to those interested in resolving debates regarding the merits of Stone's Minimalist Theism relative to a denial of that position. STONE is then applied to the atheism advocated by John W. Loftus, and his atheism is shown to fail the test.*

Neutral Agnostic Reasoning

Loftus recalls a position taken by a former instructor of his (James D. Strauss) and describes that position, in effect, as consisting of the fundamental claim that a theistic assumption better explains the evidence available from the Bible and the world than any alternative assumption.[1] Loftus considers this to be an approach "from above", but it need not be construed as such. Let A1 be an advocate of theory T1, and let A2 be an advocate of theory T2, where A1 ≠ A2, where T1 ≠ T2, and where A1 and A2 disagree regarding which of T1 and T2 is best, given all available evidence. A1 and A2 are defined as persons whose positions are in disagreement regarding which of T1 and T2 is best, and each of T1 and T2 is defined as a theory not known by A1 or A2 to be internally logically inconsistent. NE (neutral evidence) is defined as the set of evidential considerations mutually agreeable to both A1 and A2 to be neutral with respect to both T1 and T2. So defined, NE presumes we set aside any alleged theory-favoring background knowledge regarding the probability of T1 (or of T2) so that we may see where the evidence leads us from this neutral starting point.

Now, if A1 and A2 begin "from the middle" via neutral agnosticism, then they could agree to assess the relative rational superiority of T1 and T2 by testing the degree to which each presupposed theory coheres with NE. Then, the more probable theory, given NE, would be favored, resolving the dispute between A1 and A2. This approach, as I have described it, is not rightly characterized as "from above", since the "from above" and "from below" perspectives are both neutrally analyzed from the starting point of neutral agnosticism.

Granted, some presuppositions are necessary in all debates, but this fact does not entail the nonexistence of a methodology in which proponents of opposing viewpoints may agree upon a mutually acceptable neutral starting point in a dialogue aimed at debate resolution. Such a methodology may not exist in a form that is universally accepted, but this does not entail that individual advocates of opposing perspectives can never justify a mutually accepted methodology that may lead to the attainment of debate resolution between those particular individuals.[2] In addition, the fact that some such methodology may not be universally accepted could derive merely from the fact that not all inquirers are cognizant of the reasonable basis for supposing that it should be universally accepted. The mere fact of the nonexistence of a universally accepted methodology, therefore, does not justify rejection of the claim that no methodology should be universally accepted by adequately informed inquirers. The pursuit of a methodology that should be universally accepted by such inquirers is a worthwhile objective.

In the context of the theism-atheism debate, if an atheist B and a theist C together identified NE, then B and C could work towards agreeing upon the more probable theory as determined from a neutral agnostic starting point, and the dispute between them could be resolved, provided the two theories do not ultimately end up as approximately equiprobable in the perception of both B and C (in which case, the analysis would conclude with an agnostic ending point, leaving the dispute unresolved by that analysis). It is also assumed, of course, that B and C achieve mutual agreement regarding the contents of NE, and attainment of this agreement may itself require a considerable measure of mutual response and counter-response. It is additionally assumed that mutual agreement can be achieved regarding the proper procedure for using a neutral agnostic starting point to assess the relative probabilities of theism and atheism once the contents of NE have been identified by B and C. For several reasons, therefore, it is evident that dialogue beginning from a neutral agnostic starting point is not obviously guaranteed to quickly resolve all disputes between advocates of theism and atheism. Further explication of practical procedures for achieving such ends could, thus, reduce the probability of failed debate resolution between persons employing this approach.

This neutral agnostic ("from the middle") approach I am exploring here may be expressed through conditional probabilities as:

(1) $[\, P(NE \mid T1) > P(NE \mid T2) \,] \rightarrow T1$ is rationally superior.[3]

Using Bayes' Theorem, (1) may be rewritten as:

(2) $[P(T1 | NE) / P(T1) > P(T2 | NE) / P(T2)]$ → T1 is rationally superior.

The initial assumption $P(T1) \approx P(T2)$ may then be used to achieve further simplification:

(3) $[P(T1 | NE) > P(T2 | NE)]$ → T1 is rationally superior.

The simplifying assumption used to obtain (3) is derived from the neutral agnostic approach which presumes we set aside, for the sake of argument, any alleged theory-favoring background knowledge regarding the probability of T1 (or of T2), thus enabling the consideration of the epistemological consequences of a fresh reexamination of NE in a mutually agreed upon context in which the following neutral presumptions are made: (1) For both A1 and A2, T1 is not more or less probable than T2 prior to examination of NE; and (2) For both A1 and A2, T1 and T2 will be approximately equiprobable after examination of NE unless that examination yields a different result. The problem of justifying prior probabilities is, therefore, avoided, and an objective approach to attaining mutual agreement upon posterior probabilities emerges.

If a theory is not logically inconsistent (either internally within itself or externally with respect to available evidence), then that theory is technically compatible with all available evidence. This fact need not lead to the supposition that all logically possible theories are equally well justified. Nor does this fact require that debates between opposing viewpoints are hopelessly mired in their respective presuppositional contexts, being unable to identify an objective basis for preference of one context over the other. Rather, (1) expresses the reasonable intent to properly proportion one's presupposed beliefs in accordance with available evidence, and Bayes' Theorem in conjunction with a simplifying assumption grounded in acceptance of neutral agnosticism leads to (3), which identifies a means by which the best presuppositional belief-context may be identified, and mutually agreed upon, in an approach to the resolution of debates between advocates of opposing theories.

Neutral Evidence

Given a debate between A1 and A2 regarding whether T1 or T2 best explains neutral evidence NE, it would be helpful to identify the set NC of conditions jointly sufficient to justify mutual acceptance that $e_i \in$ NE, where e_i is some individual evidential element under consideration for NE membership. It would not appear to be controversial to propose the following member of NC:

> NC1 $\equiv$ Neither e_i nor a constituent component of e_i is identical in meaning to T1 or T2 or ~T1 or ~T2.

The purpose of NC1 is to impose a restriction upon NE membership which prevents the use of circular reasoning to "evidentially support" a theory. The use of the term "or" in NC1 is in the inclusive sense of that term. One might suppose that the restriction as stated in NC1 overdetermines the desired condition, but this supposition is not well founded, since theories T1 and T2 have not been defined such that each must be precisely a contradiction of the other. Sometimes individuals debate theories, where the opposing theories provide alternative explanations of evidence, but where one of the theories in question is not, itself, precisely the negation of the alternative theory in question.

The following condition is also proposed as a member of NC:

> NC2 $\equiv$ Neither e_i nor a constituent component of e_i is a premise or inductive argument which probabilistically presupposes meaning identical to T1 or T2 or ~T1 or ~T2.

The purpose of NC2 is to block any question-begging premise which is accompanied by the presupposition that one of the theories debated by A1 and A2 is probably true or probably false. Also, NC2 is designed to block any inductive argument which is not technically deductively circular, but which is *inductively circular* in the sense that the force and success of the argument is grounded in theory-favoring (or theory-disfavoring) probabilistic presuppositions.

So, NC1 and NC2 together insure that no member of NE either deductively begs the question or inductively begs the question. These conditions require that neutral evidence be sufficiently logically removed from the debated theories that question-begging presuppositions do not arbitrarily favor (or disfavor) either T1 or T2.

A third proposed member of NC is derived from the definition of NE:

NC3 $\equiv$ e$_i$ ϵ NE only if A1 and A2 both agree that e$_i$ ϵ NE.

This condition emphasizes the need for opposing parties to agree upon the contents of NE, lest the neutral agnostic reasoning approach fail to assist A1 and A2 in their practical efforts to achieve debate resolution.

Theory Confirmation

Given that A1 and A2 achieve mutual recognition of a nonzero number of NE elements, there remains the task of attaining mutual agreement regarding the degree to which each of T1 and T2 is probable. One way that a theory could be justifiably identified as rationally superior to a competing theory is by examining likelihoods (explanatory power) to see which theory, if true, is more likely to render NE probable. If $P(NE \mid T1) > P(NE \mid T2)$, then it is confirmed to some degree that T1 is rationally superior to T2. This "explanatory power" degree of confirmation C1 is proportional to the difference $P(NE \mid T1) - P(NE \mid T2)$, and it is derived from (1).

The value of C1 might be approximately zero or it might be undetermined. Even if, initially, $P(NE \mid T1) \approx P(NE \mid T2)$, or even if $P(NE \mid T1)$ or $P(NE \mid T2)$ is initially undetermined, then neutral agnostic reasoning might nevertheless be used to establish that it is subsequently confirmed, to some degree, that T1 is rationally superior, if we have good arguments showing that $P(T1 \mid NE) > P(T2 \mid NE)$. The degree of confirmation would be proportional to the difference $P(T1 \mid NE) - P(T2 \mid NE)$, and this "evidential support" confirmation measure C2 is derived from (3).

If C1 and C2 are both approximately zero, and if A1 and A2 agree that T1 is simpler than T2, then it is confirmed, to some degree, that T1 is rationally superior. The notion of "simplicity", here, is a function of both the number q of distinct theoretical components of a theory, and also the maximum number r of those components which can be successively removed from that theory while preserving (within a suitably narrow range of marginal deviation from) the established value of the probability of NE conditional upon the theory. The measure S1 of simplicity for theory T1 would be proportional to the ratio $(q1-r1)/q1$, and S2 for T2 would be proportional to $(q2-r2)/q2$. This "simplicity" confirmation measure C3 would be proportional to $S1 - S2$, and it captures a feature of the often discussed Occam's Razor principle of parsimony.

If C1 and C2 are both approximately zero, and if A1 and A2 agree that T1 has greater explanatory scope, then it is confirmed, to some degree, that T1 is rationally superior. The notion of "scope" here is a function of both the number w of elements of NE, and also the maximum number v of successive elements of NE that can be removed from NE while preserving (within a suitably narrow range of marginal deviation from) the established value of the probability of NE conditional upon the theory. The measure U1 of scope for theory T1 would be proportional to (w1-v1)/w1, and U2 for T2 would be proportional to (w2-v2)/w2. This "scope" confirmation measure C4 would be proportional to the difference U1 − U2, and it provides a relative measure of the degree to which the elements of NE are explained by the competing theories.

An additional confirmation measure could be derived from reasoning which confirms a theory by disconfirming a competing theory. If, for example, one of the debated theories (say, T2) entails NE would likely differ from its actual form, then the likely actual form of NE entails (with probability x, as quantified by my QLMT argument structure[4]) T2 is unlikely. Then, if "T2 is unlikely" implies (with probability y) that T1 is likely, T1 is thus confirmed, to some degree, to be rationally superior. This degree of confirmation C5 would be proportional to the product xy. Note that even if y is not much greater than 0.5, a sufficiently large x could significantly disconfirm T2, even though T1 would not be significantly confirmed in this case. An individual theory may be directly confirmed (or disconfirmed) by evidential considerations, and the degree to which a competing theory may be consequently confirmed (or disconfirmed) will be a function of the degree to which both theories span the entire partition (probability space) of possibilities, and will also be a function of the degree to which the respective partition-spans overlap.

In the development of my QLMT argument in Chapter 1, I argued that theory confirmation need not be presumed to be grounded merely in relative comparative measures, but must also leave room for the possibility that evidence could directly confirm or disconfirm a particular theory. The measures of theory confirmation proposed above are grounded not merely in a theory-comparative conception of evidence, but also include a means (C5) by which an argument (e.g., a QLMT argument) could individually "pick off" a single theory (e.g., T2), whose being picked off may even happen to largely confirm the alternative debated theory (T1).

I do not presume that I have identified all reasonable means by which A1 or A2 might agree that T1 or T2 is confirmed or disconfirmed; indeed, QLMT represents a probabilized *modus tollens* that could be structured to individually confirm or disconfirm a single theory, and I see no reason to suppose that other deductive inference forms could not also be probabilized to achieve the same objective. In addition, I have specified neither the relative weights which ought to be assigned to the distinct confirmation measures, nor the range of possible conditions of which those weights may be a function. Nevertheless, given the above measures of theory confirmation, and given any additional measures that A1 and A2 may come to accept in some debate, a cumulative case could be made for the overall best-confirmed theory. The best-confirmed theory would, in turn, become established as the rationally superior theory mutually accepted as such by both A1 and A2.

Theory-Evidence Resolution

In the preceding section it was assumed that T1, T2, and NE can be resolved into distinct elemental components in a manner not rightly susceptible to charges of question begging or circularity. This assumption is reasonable, if we have an acceptable approach to such resolution, and I now briefly consider how such a project might be undertaken.

The idea of resolving a theory, or of resolving NE, into elemental components has not been well defined in my analysis thus far, and the prospects for identifying an appropriately concrete procedure are evidently contingent upon the overall motivation for resolution in the first place. Neutral agnostic reasoning is motivated by the pursuit of the best justified evidentially informed theoretical explanation. It is true that "A explains B" does not entail "A causes B", since the nature of the term "explanation" in the English language does not always refer to causal explanations, but sometimes refers to noncausal descriptive features. In the theism-atheism debate, however, a routine focal point of dispute is the question of whether there exists a divine being who is the cause of some specified physical phenomena. So, it is appropriate to presume that a causal nature of explanation is operative in this debate.

T1, T2, and NE may be resolved into their constituent elemental components, then, keeping in mind that the relevant mode of explanation is *causal* explanation, and specifically, causal explanation as it pertains to the causation of physical events. The nature of physical event causation, therefore, is of critical importance as it relates to theory-evidence resolution in the context of theism-atheism debates.

My AFTLOP establishes that physical event causation is known to occur only in the context of causal agency theory, where physical events are known to be caused by a person's exercise of power. Given the absence of an alternative successful theory of physical event causation, we may presume that my causal agency theory is the best available and is well justified from all we know.[5] It is natural, then, to seek to resolve T1, T2, and NE into the following components: *physical events* and *physical-event-causing agents*. If it turns out that such resolution favors (or disfavors) either of T1 or T2, then this is not to be rejected as a non-neutral procedure, but is to be viewed as a consequence of a neutral examination of the nature of theory-evidence resolution, where my philosophy of physical event causation is neutrally established independent of this resolution. Once so resolved, the way will have been paved to facilitate a more precise evaluation of the relative merits of T1 and T2 on such counts as explanatory power, best NE support, simplicity, and scope.

STONE

STONE (Stone's Test Of Neutral Evidence) is designed to resolve debates between individuals who mutually agree to begin from a neutral agnostic starting point and examine neutral evidence, without question-begging assumptions, to see where the evidence leads. The result is the proportioning of one's beliefs in accordance with available evidence by justifying acceptance of the best presupposed theory explaining NE. Although STONE may be adapted to debates in virtually any context, it is here developed and applied to the context of the theism-atheism debate.

Let T1 represent Minimalist Theism (MT), defined as follows: (1) A person created the physical world and designed some of its features; and (2) A person sustains the existence of the physical world by causing physical events (except any physical events caused by humans) to continue to generally occur in accordance with physical laws, including all such laws identified via the scientific method. Note that the moral nature (or lack thereof) of the person ("God") of T1 is undetermined by T1. It follows that the God of T1 is not presumed to possess (and is not presumed not to possess) the property *omnibenevolence* often associated with theistic belief, but is simply taken to possess the properties identified in the definition of T1. The other typically theistic "omni" properties (e.g., omniscience and omnipotence) are also not assumed. Subsequent analysis might reveal (and I believe it successfully can) that the God of T1 may be shown to be a personal being more along the lines of a traditional "omni" theistic God, but such analysis deserves consideration elsewhere, and is not essential to my position developed here.

We may define T2 as follows: It is not the case that T1 is true. From this definition it should not be controversial to assume that most (if not all) informed atheists would be likely to believe T2. Then, with T1 and T2 now defined in STONE, we may identify each of A1 and A2 as an advocate of T1 and T2, respectively.

The identification of the members of NE is debate-dependent (NC3), and can not always be presumed prior to an actual debate. Nevertheless, I submit that my theistic arguments (Chapters 1 and 2) assume more than the requisite burden of proof sufficient to argue that the following proposed NE members in STONE deserve identification as NE members in a theist-atheist debate:

NE1 $\equiv$ For each physical event known to be caused, it is known to be caused by a person.

NE2 $\equiv$ No known physical law describes the physical conditions that are identified as "fine-tuned" in Stone's teleological arguments.

NE3 $\equiv$ It is likely that there is not a good anti-MT argument.

Each of NE1, NE2, and NE3 clearly satisfies both NC1 and NC2. Also, pending support from any prospective A2 member to the contrary, each of NE1, NE2, and NE3 will be presumed to satisfy NC3 in a theist-atheist debate. The burden rests upon A2 to either dispute my proposed NE members or propose other members.

Given my theistic arguments (Chapters 1 and 2), it is evident that T1 has greater explanatory power (greater likelihood) than T2, and it is evident that, given NE, T1 is more probable than T2 (T1 has greater evidential support). I also cite Chapter 3 for the purpose of blocking any QLMT-structured argument from evil intended to either directly disconfirm T1 or indirectly confirm T2.

I have suggested that scope and simplicity considerations may tip the balance in favor of T1 (or T2) in cases in which explanatory power and evidential support from NE yield roughly equiprobable results for each of the debated theories. However, in cases in which T1 is confirmed (and T2 is disconfirmed) by virtue of considerations pertaining both to evidential support from NE and explanatory power (as in the case I have set forth above), the confirmation considerations relevant to scope and simplicity are of arguably relatively small additional value. However, it is worth noting that T2's denial of a single personal cause of the caused physical events in NE1 and NE2 implies that a person who accepts T2 probably also theorizes a larger number of causes of the caused physical events described in T1, and this implies T1 acceptance is characterized by greater simplicity than T2 acceptance.

In the present context, T2 is simply the denial of T1, and both theories would appear to have approximately equal measures of scope, since both consist of either an affirmation or denial of the existence and operation of the same quantity of causal agents and associated caused entities. If, instead, we were in the context of a debate between a theory such as T1 and some rival theory (in which an alternative, presumably non-agent-centered, causal explanatory theory is proposed), these quantities might significantly differ, yielding a greater difference between relative scope measures.

I conclude that T1 is strongly confirmed and T2 is strongly disconfirmed. In turn, this implies that T1 is rationally superior.

STONE is, therefore, a challenge to all who reject MT to achieve at least one of the following four objectives:

> (ST1) Show that one or more of NE1, NE2, and NE3 should not be accepted as NE members in a debate between adequately informed A1 and A2.

> (ST2) Show that proper analysis of NE1, NE2, and NE3 does not actually favor T1 (and disfavor T2) even if accepted.

> (ST3) Show that NE members (other than NE1, NE2, and NE3) deserve acceptance in a debate between adequately informed A1 and A2, where those proposed members may be used to favor T2 or disfavor T1.

> (ST4) Show that STONE methodology is better replaced by some alternative.

Unless, or until, an MT-critic passes STONE by achieving one or more of the above objectives, I submit that I have justified my claim that T1 is rationally superior to T2.

STONE and Loftus

It is clear that Loftus does not use neutral agnostic reasoning as a starting point, but rather starts with skeptical agnostic reasoning grounded in acceptance of his control beliefs. Loftus' book may be interpreted as a failed attempt to pass STONE, given my critique (Chapter 4) which establishes that he has (1) not established that his control beliefs deserve NE acceptance, and (2) not shown that any prospective NE-worthy evidential elements may be used to establish that his control beliefs deserve NE acceptance.

If Loftus' atheism is probably true, then it is unlikely that T1 is rationally superior to T2. It is likely that T1 is rationally superior to T2. Therefore, it is likely false that Loftus' atheism is probably true.

If Loftus' atheism is neutrally established, then it should pass STONE. It doesn't pass STONE. Therefore, Loftus' atheism is not neutrally established. We may reject Loftus' atheism as fundamentally arbitrary and unjustified question-begging. Given my acceptance of conservative Biblical theology, it is proper for me to cite John 3:19 as the description of the plausible underlying motive of anyone who, though understanding my position is justified, persists in rejection of my conclusions.

Loftus asks us to take the (unjustified) Outsider Test. We may now ask Loftus to take STONE. Please join me in my effort to elicit Loftus' response to the position I have defended by visiting Loftus' blog[6] and urging Loftus to provide a detailed response that is "set in stone", so to speak, by virtue of being a physically printed (e.g., book) response. I desire to respond to a fixed response from Loftus, but not if his response is merely an easily changeable Internet-based moving target. I await a book response from him. Until (or unless) he responds, I submit that my analysis shows that Loftus' atheism is false.[7]

Summary

In an effort to help insure that Loftus does not fail to perceive the full import of my critique, I have listed seven questions I would expect a thorough response from him to address. I submit that until (or unless) Loftus responds to the following issues, his atheistic anti-Biblical position stands refuted and in need of substantial revision (or better still, rejection):

1. How do you justify rejection of David Reuben Stone's ACPO metaphysics?

2. How do you answer Stone's HIP defense?

3. How do you defend the Outsider Test against STONE?

4. How do you defend your control beliefs against Stone's critique?

5. How do you justify your Standard Objection to Messianic Israelism?

6. If the Biblical God exists, would you strongly desire to know, serve, and love Him? Why or why not?

7. Won't you convert and follow Yeshua? Please join us! You have much to contribute. We need your help to advance the cause of the Gospel. The Lord loves you and desires to richly bless you. He died to save you from your sins. Won't you live for Him?

I wish to formally announce my invitation to John W. Loftus to publish in book format (not in some changeable moving-target online format) a response to my critique. I trust that I could learn much from him, and I'm confident that a charitable dialogue could benefit us both in our search for truth.

NOTES

1. Loftus, John W. (2008). *Why I Became an Atheist: A Former Preacher Rejects Christianity.* Amherst, NY: Prometheus Books, p. 58:7-10.
2. For an example of how communicating agents might conceivably achieve a common posterior probability, given a common prior probability assumption, see Geanakoplos and Polemarchakis, "*We Can't Disagree Forever*", Journal of Economic Theory, v. 28, no. 1, 1982, pp. 192-200.
3. The symbol "→" denotes a conditional expression; thus "X → Y" represents "if X, then Y".
4. See Chapter 1 for QLMT details.
5. Of course, those who disagree are challenged to justify an alternative theory of physical event causation so that I may respond to that position.
6. Loftus' blog may be found at http://debunkingchristianity.blogspot.com
7. Or, as a quipster might remark: Stone uses STONE to stone the Outsider Test.

CONCLUSION

The purpose of this study has been to participate in the project of answering critical questions about God by presenting and expanding new arguments for the existence of God and for the truth of conservative Biblical theology, and by refuting contemporary arguments for atheism, in the context of a detailed refutation of the distinctively anti-Biblical atheism recently set forth by John W. Loftus. I submit that my analysis has shown that good reasons exist for believing in the existence of God, where "God" is here defined as the person who is the creator-sustainer-designer of the physical world, and who possesses immensely greater power and knowledge than that of man. I submit, also, that despite widespread ill-founded objections to conservative Biblical belief systems, my arguments provide a broadly outlined means by which such systems may be justified.

Biblical theology is true, atheism is false, and the reader is encouraged to examine the arguments in the atheism books listed in the Bibliography to verify that my position, somewhat novel as it may be in its detailed formulation, stands firm and unchallenged by any atheistic argument found in those referenced sources. Please also visit http://www.loftus-delusion.com for author contact details, as I appreciate any feedback you may wish to provide.

Given the existence of God and the truth of Biblical theology, we may naturally desire to acquire, in greater measure, a deeper understanding of God's ways and their implications for our lives. My AFTLOP and fine-tuning arguments (see Chapters 1 and 2) may be understood as a perception of a form of divine revelation in which the nature of God's causal activity in the physical world is revealed. Since, in addition to this natural theology, God has provided special revelation through the Bible, this revelation may help us determine the answers to such fundamental questions as: What does God's Torah require of me? Will I give account of my life to God on a future day of judgment? Does eternal heaven (or hell) exist? Can I form a proper relationship with a God of immeasurably great love and justice? What are the benefits and requirements of my being properly related to God?

A theologically conservative Biblical worldview contains answers to these and many other questions. Although a full-blown explication and defense of this position, in all details, lies beyond the scope of the present analysis, I have sketched an outline, in Chapter 5, of a rational basis for the belief that this view of the world is true and deserving of your serious consideration and acceptance.

The implications of accepting this worldview are immense, and bring into focus our great need to grow in knowledge of divine revelation so that we may acquire enhanced insight into the nature and purposes of the supremely loving God who commands us to repent and receive, by grace through faith, the free gift of eternally joyous and abundant life that is available to us through our personal identification with the life, death, and resurrection of Messiah Yeshua, whose atoning sacrifice for our sins is alone sufficient to secure for us forgiveness and reconciliation unto God, and sufficient to bring us into the company of the redeemed who attain the fullest possible measure of human fulfillment in their love of God and others expressed through service and obedience to the gospel by which we are saved from the wrath to come. Since the Biblical Gospel is true, loving God must be our central focus as we fully integrate a conservative Biblical worldview into our personal lives. Loving others must also be a central focus as we defend and promote this worldview in the marketplace of ideas, with special emphasis on global evangelization and discipleship.

Do you desire that the Lord of the physical world be the Lord of your personal life?

Repent and follow Yeshua in loving and joyous obedience to His commands!

APPENDIX – Messianic Israelism

www.messianic-israelism.com

Abstract: *The five core truths of Messianic Israelism are stated, and reasons for their acceptance are provided. Seven prominent systems challenged by Messianic Israelism are identified. Recent objections raised by Michael L. Brown are critiqued. The relationship between the Torah and the Biblical Gospel is examined.*

There has emerged during the past century a significant "Messianic Movement", which now comprises individuals, small groups, congregations, synagogues, and also larger organizations often associated with such labels as *Messianic, Messianic Judaism, Jewish Christian, Hebrew Christian, Hebrew Roots,* and *Torah Communities.* These groups are typically characterized by an emphasis upon the rediscovery of genuine Biblical faith as originally expressed in its ancient context. Although this movement is relatively new in its modern manifestation, it may actually be viewed as an effort to *restore* fundamental theological understanding to conservative Biblically-grounded communities. The result has been the reinstituting of theology and practices which have been largely neglected and forgotten throughout much of the past 2000 years. There exists considerable diversity within this maturing movement along many theological dimensions, and the constituent organizations within the movement (and even specific individuals within a given organization) must be evaluated on a case-by-case basis so as to accurately identify positions. Although there has been no clear and unifying doctrinal statement which all members of the movement have formally embraced, I have identified what I perceive to be the five components of a conservative theological system that has been informed by the Biblically essential features of these ongoing developments. I offer the term "Messianic Israelism" as a label for the position here briefly set forth.

Five Core Truths

Messianic Israelism (MI) is characterized by five core truths which motivate its adherents to embrace authentic Biblical faith. The five truths include the following:

(1) There exists a personal creator-sustainer-designer of the physical world.
(2) YHVH is the personal creator-sustainer-designer of the physical world, and He exists as described in the Tanach and Messianic Scriptures.
(3) Israel is YHVH's family.
(4) Yeshua is Israel's Savior and Messiah.
(5) Torah obedience is the proper manifestation of New Covenant faith.

Thus, MI is theistic, creationist, and Biblical. "YHVH" denotes the self-revealed name of God in the Tanach ("Old Testament"). The Messianic Scriptures ("New Testament") and Tanach are jointly taken to constitute the divinely inspired and authoritative Biblical Scriptures. The covenants of promise between YHVH and the family of living Israel reveal the divine ideal purpose to bless all nations through that family, and to bring individual and corporate salvation through Yeshua ("Jesus"), Israel's Savior and Messiah, whose gracious initiation of the New Covenant brings the promise of forgiveness of sins to the faithful, and facilitates the blessings of Torah obedience in sanctification directed by the Holy Spirit.

Reasons for MI-Acceptance

The first core truth in MI is that there exists a personal creator-sustainer-designer of the physical world. This present volume, and in particular, my ACPO theistic metaphysics detailed in Chapters 1 and 2, provides a rational basis for embracing this component of MI.

The second core truth in MI is that YHVH is the personal creator-sustainer-designer of the physical world, and He exists as described in the Tanach and Messianic Scriptures. In short, the personal Creator of the world is the God of the Bible. I have outlined, in Chapter 5, a means by which the truth of conservative Biblical theology may be justified. It follows, from such reasoning, that assertions contained in the Bible are true. Since it is asserted in the Bible that the Biblical God (YHVH) is the creator-sustainer-designer of the physical world,[1] it then follows that it is true that YHVH is the creator-sustainer-designer of the physical world.

The third core truth in MI is that Israel is YHVH's family. Given the truth of conservative Biblical theology,[2] it follows that the people (children) of Israel comprise the only family YHVH has chosen or known.[3] This Israel is not identical to the physical descendants of Abraham,[4] since the unbelieving and disobedient physical descendants are cut off,[5] and since those not physically descended from Abraham through Israel are grafted by faith[6] into this *living* Israel, the family (house) of God[7] which constitutes Abraham's seed of promise in Yeshua.[8] Living Israel is the corporate church, the set of all who believe and obey YHVH and Messiah Yeshua, who has been building the church[9] since its assembly with Moses.[10] YHVH's covenants are not made with any non-Israelite church, but are made *with living Israel*.[11] Yeshua did not come to begin a new church or start a new religion; rather, He has initiated with the House of Israel the New Covenant in His blood[12] and He will restore the kingdom to Israel at some future point in time.[13] Those excluded from living Israel, therefore, are excluded from the covenants of promise, excluded from hope, and excluded from God.[14]

The fourth core truth in MI is that Yeshua is Israel's Savior and Messiah. Given the truth of conservative Biblical theology,[15] it quickly follows that Yeshua is the Savior[16] and Messiah[17] of His people, the citizens of living Israel.[18]

The fifth core truth in MI is that obedience to the Torah (i.e., instruction, direction, doctrine, law) of God is the proper manifestation of New Covenant faith. Given the truth of conservative Biblical theology,[19] it follows that the set of all Biblical commandments which may be used to determine one's personal moral obligations as maturing participants in the New Covenant with Israel includes not only those commandments found in the Messianic Scriptures,[20] but also the commandments found throughout the Tanach, including those in the Psalms, Prophets, and the Torah. My use of "Torah" may be taken to refer to the Pentateuch, and especially the 613 commands typically identified therein.

Conservative Biblical theology accounts for the many reasons which jointly comprise a compelling basis for Torah observance as morally obligatory for the New Covenant participant. What follows is a brief outline of 131 distinct arguments which constitute much of the Biblical evidence in favor of this position:

1.   If New Covenant believers should not observe the Torah, then Yeshua abolished the Torah. Yeshua did not abolish the Torah.[21] Therefore, it is false that New Covenant believers should not observe the Torah.

2.   Since Yeshua fulfills the Torah,[22] Yeshua does not teach us to subtract from the Torah.[23]

3.   Yeshua taught that nothing from the Torah will pass away until the Earth passes away.[24] The earth has not yet passed away. Therefore, nothing from the Torah has passed away.

4.   Yeshua taught that the Torah is more permanent than heaven and earth,[25] implying that He does not abolish the Torah for those who follow Him.

5.   If anyone breaks Torah commands and teaches others to do the same, then he will be called least in the kingdom of heaven.[26] I do not want to be called least! Therefore, I desire a Torah-observant life, and I urge others to desire the same.

6.   Yeshua urged Torah observance.[27]

7.   Yeshua commanded that His disciples pray for God's will to be done.[28] Doing God's will is properly accompanied by having the Torah within one's heart.[29] Therefore, Yeshua's disciples should observe the Torah in pursuit of the accomplishment of God's will.

8.   Yeshua associated Torah observance with obtaining eternal life.[30] We need not deny that salvation is by grace through faith, but Yeshua's high regard for Torah-observance constitutes implicit acknowledgement that genuine saving faith manifests itself through growth in obedience to the commands of the Torah as one perseveres in one's doctrine.

9.   If New Covenant believers must not observe the Torah, then they must not live by every word that proceeds from the mouth of God. Since Yeshua taught that man must live by every word that proceeds from the mouth of God,[31] it is false that New Covenant participants must not observe the Torah.

10.   Yeshua taught that the Torah and the Prophets are summed up to equal the Golden Rule.[32] Since the Golden Rule is not abolished, neither are the Torah and Prophets.

11.   Yeshua taught that workers of lawlessness (Torah-lessness) will not enter the kingdom of heaven, even if they are prophetic miracle-working exorcists in Yeshua's name.[33] This implies Torah observance is associated with entrance into the kingdom of heaven. Again, we need not deny that salvation is by grace through faith, but Yeshua's high regard for Torah-observance

constitutes implicit acknowledgement that genuine saving faith manifests itself through growth in obedience to the commands of the Torah as one perseveres in one's doctrine.

12.　　Yeshua taught that increasing lawlessness (Torah-lessness) in the last days will lead to a widespread decreasing measure of love.[34] Since Torah-lessness leads to a love-less condition, our obligation to be loving requires rejection of Torah-lessness.

13.　　Yeshua embraced the authority of Scripture.[35] The Torah is Scripture. Therefore, Yeshua embraced the authority of the Torah.

14.　　Yeshua taught that the Sabbath will be observed even during the Last Days.[36]　This disconfirms those positions opposed to ongoing Torah observance.

15.　　Yeshua did not reject proper observance of the Sabbath. Rather, He emphasized that He is the Lord of the Sabbath,[37] and He was careful to shed light on how to be Torah-observant on the Sabbath.[38]

16.　　Yeshua commanded obedience to the Torah as it pertained to cleansed lepers.[39]

17.　　The preaching of repentance in first century Judaism would be tantamount to a command to turn from wickedness and turn toward obedience to God[40] whose commands are set forth in the Torah. Yeshua commanded repentance.[41] Therefore, Yeshua commanded Torah observance.

18.　　Yeshua authenticated the ministry of John the Baptist.[42] John preached repentance.[43] The preaching of repentance in first century Judaism would be tantamount to a command to turn from wickedness and turn toward obedience to God[44] whose commands are set forth in the Torah. Therefore, Yeshua commanded Torah observance by authenticating John's ministry.

19.　　Yeshua said that the greatest commandments in the Torah[45] are love for God[46] and love for others.[47]　Yeshua did not say that these two commandments are the *only* commandements. Thus, Yeshua implied that the other Torah commandments are not as great, but still in force.

20.　　Yeshua prayed that all believers[48] would be sanctified by the truth (i.e., the Torah).[49] Therefore, all believers should seek sanctification by the Torah.

21.   Yeshua commands Torah observance (as seen in the above points). If we love Yeshua, then we obey Yeshua's commands.[50] Therefore, if we love Yeshua, we observe the Torah.

22.   Yeshua commands global evangelization with discipleship in the fullness of His teachings.[51] Yeshua's teachings include the command that his disciples observe Torah (as seen in the above points). Therefore, Yeshua commands global evangelization with discipleship in Torah observance.

23.   Yeshua commanded perfection.[52] The Torah is perfect.[53] Therefore, Yeshua commanded Torah observance.

24.   Yeshua commands Torah observance (as seen in the above points). Yeshua is the Torah-observant teacher of those who follow Him.[54] Yeshua's students will be like Him when fully trained.[55] Therefore, followers of Yeshua seek Torah observance in pursuit of attainment of full training.

25.   Yeshua's teachings in the synagogues received widespread praise.[56] Since anti-Torah teachings in the synagogues would not receive widespread praise, Yeshua's teachings must have been Torah-observant.

26.   Yeshua commands Torah observance (as seen in the above points). The islands (which would include both Gentiles and any non-Gentiles living in the islands) will put their hope in Yeshua's law.[57] Yeshua's law included Torah observance. Therefore, Torah observance is for Gentiles *and* non-Gentiles.

27.   Yeshua did not violate kosher dietary laws[58] when He declared all foods clean.[59] After all, "all foods are clean things" does not entail "all things are clean foods". Since the Torah defines food restrictions for us,[60] we may be free to live, knowing that all Torah-compliant foods are clean, regardless of whether we have first followed the man-made rule of ceremonially washing our hands in accordance with the tradition of the elders.[61] Therefore, let no one declare as unclean what the Torah declares is clean! On the other hand, we should not use our freedom inappropriately. There may be practical loving considerations which require that we restrain from exercising our freedom openly. In general, such restraint may be imposed for such purposes as evangelistic expediency,[62] protection of a brother whose faith is weak,[63] or adaptive accommodation to local customs.[64]

28.   Yeshua is the purpose (goal) of the Torah.[65]

29.   It is good to be blessed. Those who are properly Torah-observant will be blessed.[66] It is good to satisfy a sufficient condition of being blessed. Therefore, it is good to be Torah-observant so as to insure blessing upon one's life.

30.   Yeshua did not violate the tzitzit Torah command.[67] Yeshua's disciples should imitate Yeshua[68] and not violate this command.

31.   Yeshua is the living word of God.[69] The Torah is the word of God. Therefore, Yeshua is the living Torah, and His sheep hear His Torah voice.[70] Just as Abraham heard God's voice[71] and kept God's Torah,[72] the disciples of Yeshua hear His voice as Abraham's children[73] and keep His Torah.

32.   Yeshua commanded that we store up for ourselves a reward of treasures in heaven.[74] Torah observance brings great reward.[75] Therefore, Torah observance is a good practical means by which we may meet our reward-storing obligations.

33.   Yeshua manifested his Torah observance by citing the Torah in defense of his position.[76] Yeshua's disciples should imitate Yeshua.[77]

34.   Yeshua referenced even the Psalms of Scripture as authoritative Torah.[78] The Psalms advocate Torah observance.[79] Therefore, Yeshua viewed Torah observance as a Scripturally-derived obligation.

35.   If Yeshua were not Torah-observant, then a Torah teacher would not express willingness to follow Yeshua. A Torah teacher expressed willingness to follow Yeshua.[80] Therefore, Yeshua was Torah-observant.

36.   If Yeshua's teachings were anti-Torah, then acceptance of Mosaic Torah would not be a sufficient condition of acceptance of Yeshua's teachings. Acceptance of Mosaic Torah is a sufficient condition of acceptance of Yeshua's teachings.[81] Therefore, Yeshua's teachings were not anti-Torah.

37.   If Yeshua were not Torah-observant, then Nicodemus would not refer to Yeshua as "Rabbi". Nicodemus referred to Yeshua as "Rabbi".[82] Therefore, Yeshua was Torah-observant.

38.   Yeshua celebrated the Passover in obedience to the Torah.[83]

39.   Torah-rejection precludes belief in Yeshua.[84] We should believe in Yeshua.[85] Therefore, we should not reject the Torah (written by Moses[86]), but observe it.

40.   If Yeshua were not Torah-observant, then a large number of Torah-observant priests would not become faithful disciples of Yeshua. A large number of Torah-observant priests became faithful disciples of Yeshua.[87] Therefore, Yeshua was Torah-observant.

41.   Yeshua was Torah-observant (as seen in the above points). His followers should imitate Him.[88] Therefore, disciples of Yeshua should also be Torah-observant.

42.   The Old Covenant is an ongoing treasure,[89] not an abolished thing of the past.

43.   The New Covenant has been given as Torah,[90] implying Torah is not abolished.

44.   If the Torah were abolished in the New Covenant, then the Torah would not be the legal foundation of Yeshua's forthcoming Millennial Reign. The Torah will be the legal foundation of Yeshua's forthcoming Millennial Reign.[91] Therefore, the Torah is not abolished in the New Covenant.

45.   The Old Covenant will soon disappear,[92] implying it has not yet disappeared. It follows that Torah observance associated with the Old Covenant has not disappeared.

46.   The Torah is summed up (not substituted!) by the command to love your neighbor as yourself.[93] Torah observance and neighborly love are synonymous; they stand together. Neighborly love is not abolished in the New Covenant, so neither is Torah observance.

47.   In the New Covenant in Yeshua's blood,[94] God writes the Torah on the minds and hearts of men.[95] The Torah is not abolished in the New Covenant.

48.   The blood of Yeshua does not abolish the covenants, but facilitates the joint access by both Gentiles and non-Gentiles to the covenants of promise.[96] Thus, the blood of Yeshua does not abolish the Torah in the New Covenant.

49.   Repentance is commanded of all peoples regardless of ethnicity.[97] Repentance and turning to God is characterized by obedience to the God whose commands are found in the Torah. Therefore, all peoples (Gentiles and non-Gentiles) are commanded to repent and obey God in observance of the Torah.

50.   Gentile believers are included as saints.[98] Saints are commanded to sing to the Lord and praise His holy name.[99] The Torah is a proper basis for singing to the Lord.[100]   The Torah is a proper reason for praise to the Lord.[101] Therefore, Gentiles may join together with non-Gentiles in Torah observance with singing and praise.

51.   Gentile believers are included as saints.[102] Saints are commanded to love the Lord.[103]   Loving the Lord is properly accompanied by Torah observance.[104]   Therefore, Gentiles may join together with non-Gentiles in Torah-observant love of the Lord.

52.   Gentile believers are included as saints.[105] Saints are commanded to fear the Lord.[106] To fear the Lord is to hate evil.[107] Turning from evil entails observing the Torah and Prophets.[108]   Therefore, Gentiles and non-Gentiles must join together in observance of the Torah and the Prophets.

53.   Gentile believers are included as saints.[109] Saints are commanded to fear the Lord.[110] Fear of the Lord is properly accompanied by standing in awe of the Torah.[111]   Therefore, Gentiles and non-Gentiles may together fear the Lord in Torah-observant awe.

54.   Gentile believers are included as saints.[112]   Saints are properly characterized by faithfulness to Yeshua and obedience to God's commandments.[113] God's commandments include the Torah. Therefore, it is proper for Gentiles and non-Gentiles to join together in faithfulness to Yeshua and in Torah observance.

55.   Torah observance is commanded for both Gentiles and non-Gentiles.[114]

56.   Gentiles should praise God for His mercy.[115] God has mercy on those who love His name.[116]   Loving God's name is properly characterized by embracing God's Torah covenant.[117]   Therefore, Gentiles and non-Gentiles should jointly observe the Torah and praise God for His mercy.

57.   Torah blessings are conditional upon Torah observance.[118]   Gentiles should not be denied Torah blessings.   Therefore, Gentiles should not be prohibited from observing the Torah.   Rather, Gentiles and non-Gentiles should together observe the Torah and jointly share in the blessings that come from its observance.

58.   Paul taught that the Torah plays an important role in bringing wisdom for salvation.[119] Therefore, we should not disregard the Torah.

59.   Paul taught that all Scripture (including the Torah) is useful for instruction in righteous living.[120] We should imitate Paul.[121]

60.   Paul obeyed the Torah[122] and we should imitate Paul.[123]

61.   Paul taught that love fulfills (not replaces or abolishes) the Torah.[124] If we need not be Torah-observant, then we need not fulfill the law. We need to fulfill the law (via love). Therefore, we need to be Torah-observant.

62.   Paul urges that the Torah be upheld, not nullified.[125] We should imitate Paul.[126]

63.   Paul delights in (fully agrees with) the Torah.[127] We should imitate Paul.[128]

64.   Paul persisted as a Pharisee.[129] Pharisees are taken to advocate Torah observance.[130] We should imitate Paul by being Torah-observant.[131]

65.   Paul was careful to meet ceremonial Torah requirements.[132] We should imitate Paul.[133] Therefore, we should also meet ceremonial Torah requirements insofar as such obedience is possible.

66.   Paul agrees with everything written in the Torah and the Prophets.[134] We should imitate Paul.[135]

67.   Paul said that he did nothing wrong against the Torah.[136] We should imitate Paul.[137]

68.   Paul urged keeping the Passover Festival.[138] This confirms Torah-observant Biblical ethics, and disconfirms alternative systems.

69.   Paul was careful to speak in obedience to Torah speech commands.[139] We should imitate Paul.[140]

70.   Paul used the Torah to identify applicable ethical principles[141] regarding material support and compensation. We should imitate Paul.[142]

71.   Paul used the Torah to identify applicable ethical principles regarding the role of women.[143] We should imitate Paul.[144]

72.   Paul prayed that all (Gentiles and non-Gentiles) in his audience would attain the Torah-observant understanding and position which he clearly manifested.[145] We should imitate Paul[146] and pray the same for all peoples.

73.   Paul stated that Torah observance is a sufficient condition of one's attainment of righteousness in God's sight.[147] For those who strongly desire assurance regarding one's election and calling, it is prudent to seek to satisfy a sufficient condition of attainment of righteousness in God's sight.[148] Therefore, it is prudent to seek a life of Torah observance.

74.   Paul would have been rejected by the Bereans, if he were anti-Torah.[149] Paul was not rejected, but was accepted by both Jewish and Greek Bereans.[150] Therefore, Jews and Greeks accepted Paul's Torah-observant message.

75.   Paul said he had done nothing against the Jews or the Jewish customs of his ancestors,[151] implying he was Torah-observant. We should imitate Paul by being Torah-observant.[152]

76.   Paul's ministry is instrumental in leading Gentiles to obey God.[153] God's commands are in the Torah. Therefore, Paul's ministry is instrumental in leading Gentiles to obey the Torah.

77.   Paul taught obedience to God's commands.[154] God's commands are in the Torah. Therefore, Paul taught obedience to the Torah. We should imitate Paul by being Torah-observant.[155]

78.   Paul, Silas, and Timothy submitted to the verdict of the Jerusalem Council and helped spread the message regarding the conclusions reached by Peter, James, and the apostles and elders of the Jerusalem church.[156] Since Paul taught Gentiles and non-Gentiles to observe the Torah (as seen from many of the above points), it follows that Peter, James, and the apostles and elders of the Jerusalem church must also have embraced a doctrine of Torah-observance for both Gentiles and non-Gentiles.

79.   Paul's Torah-observant way of life corresponds to his Torah-observant teachings in all the churches.[157] We should imitate Paul.[158]

80.   Righteousness is by faith[159] and is properly proclaimed from a Torah-observant heart.[160]

81.   Salvation by grace through faith[161] is not opposed to an obedient heart which pursues maximal faith-derived Torah-observance.[162]

82.   Sin is characterized by rejection of God's law.[163] We should not sin. Therefore, we should embrace God's law and obey it. The Torah is God's law. Thus, we should embrace the Torah and obey it.

83.   The Torah is holy.[164] We should be holy.[165] Therefore, we should obey the Torah.

84.   Unrighteous acts are anti-Torah.[166] We should not act unrighteously. Therefore, we should act in obedience to the Torah.

85.   The Torah is good.[167] We should be persistent in doing good.[168] Therefore, we should do good in obedience to the Torah.

86.   Since we should not go beyond what is written,[169] the written Scriptures (including the Torah) should be used to determine our faith and actions.

87.   Witnesses falsely testified that Stephen was anti-Torah.[170] Therefore, Stephen's teachings were actually Torah-observant teachings. Since Stephen was full of faith and of the Holy Spirit[171] and full of God's power and grace,[172] it is wise to heed Stephen's Torah-observant New Covenant era teachings.

88.   Witnesses falsely testified that Stephen had embraced such anti-Torah teachings as that Yeshua would alter Mosaic customs.[173] Therefore, Stephen must have actually taught that Yeshua did not come to alter the Torah. Since Stephen was full of faith and of the Holy Spirit[174] and full of God's power and grace,[175] it is wise to heed Stephen's Torah-observant New Covenant era teachings regarding Yeshua's ongoing acceptance of Mosaic customs.

89.   Disobeying the Torah[176] is characterized by resistance to the Holy Spirit.[177] We should not resist the Holy Spirit. Therefore, we should obey the Torah.

90.   We are going to be judged by the Torah.[178]

91.   It is not good to speak against the Torah or fail to keep it.[179] Therefore, it is good to not speak against the Torah, and it is good to keep the Torah.

92.   We are commanded to do what is commanded in the word of God.[180] The Torah is the word of God. Therefore, we are commanded to obey the Torah.

93.   Ongoing Torah observance leads to freedom, liberty, and blessing.[181]

94.   The Torah is for all Israel.[182] Gentile and non-Gentile participants in the New Covenant together comprise Israel[183] and jointly share in the blessings.[184]   Therefore, the Torah is for all Gentile and non-Gentile participants in the New Covenant.

95.   It is good to revive the soul. Torah observance revives the soul.[185] Therefore, Torah observance is good.

96.   We should be wise. Torah observance brings wisdom.[186]   Therefore, we should observe the Torah.

97.   We should do what is right. The precepts of the Torah are right.[187] Therefore, we should obey the precepts of the Torah.

98.   We should rejoice and be glad. Torah observance gives joy to the heart.[188] Therefore, we should observe the Torah with rejoicing and gladness.

99.   We should seek to bring light to the eyes. Torah observance gives light to the eyes.[189]   Therefore, we should seek to bring light to the eyes in observance of the Torah.

100.   Our actions should be grounded in sure and righteous ordinances. The Torah ordinances are sure and righteous.[190]   Therefore, our actions should be grounded in the Lord's Torah ordinances.

101.   Torah commands are true.[191] We should live in accordance with the truth. Therefore, we should live in obedience to Torah commands.

102.   All nations are commanded to praise the Lord.[192] Such praise includes praising God for the Torah which sustains us.[193]   Therefore, all nations (Gentiles included) should engage in Torah-observant praise to God.

103.   The kingdoms of the earth are commanded to sing to God.[194] Such song includes singing of God's righteous words and commands.[195] The commands include the Torah.

104.   Gentiles should praise the Lord[196] together with non-Gentiles. Praise to the Lord is properly associated with (and accompanied by) Torah observance.[197] Therefore, Gentiles and non-Gentiles should jointly praise the Lord in observance of the Torah.

105.   All the people of the earth should fear and revere the Lord,[198] and stand in awe of the Torah.[199]

106.   All the people of the earth should fear the Lord.[200] To fear the Lord is to hate evil.[201] Turning from evil entails observing the Torah and Prophets.[202] Therefore, all the people of the earth should observe the Torah and Prophets in ever-maturing faith.

107.   God desires prayer that is deserving of reward and not detestable.[203] The prayers of those who reject the Torah are detestable.[204] Therefore, we who strongly desire prayer that is deserving of reward should not reject the Torah.

108.   We are commanded to fear God and obey his commands.[205] The Torah contains God's commands.[206] Therefore, we are commanded to obey the Torah.

109.   The wrath of God's judgment comes against those who disobey the commands in the Torah[207] and refuse to repent.[208] God desires that we repent.[209] Therefore, God desires that we observe the Torah.

110.   Blessings are promised to those who are Torah-observant.[210] The promises of God are "Yes" in Yeshua.[211] Therefore, Torah blessings are available to those who are Torah-observant in Yeshua.

111.   Torah observance brings spiritual blessing.[212] All in Yeshua have access to all spiritual blessings in Messiah.[213] Therefore, all who are in Yeshua (both Gentiles and non-Gentiles) are free to enjoy the blessings of Torah observance.

112.   Sin is Torah-lessness.[214] We should not continue to sin.[215] Therefore, we should reject Torah-lessness.

113.   Torah-lessness is associated with the spirit and power of the anti-Messiah to come.[216] Since the Torah-lessness of the anti-Messiah is identified

with the evil work of Satan, it is reasonable to infer that Torah observance must be good.

114.   We want God's love,[217] so we keep the Torah in a covenant[218] which has not yet disappeared.[219]

115.   Torah observance is for Gentiles *and non-Gentiles*.[220]

116.   Torah statutes should be obeyed because they are wonderful.[221]

117.   Torah observance assures deliverance from suffering.[222]   We desire deliverance from suffering. Therefore, we desire Torah observance as a means by which we may be assured of deliverance from suffering.

118.   The wickedness of failure to seek Torah decrees is characterized by being far from salvation.[223] Therefore, we seek Torah observance so as to avoid such wickedness.

119.   We desire preservation of life. Torah observance makes provision for preservation of life.[224] Therefore, we desire Torah observance.

120.   If Torah observance were not applicable to New Covenant believers, then the righteous laws of the Torah would not be eternal. The righteous laws of the Torah are eternal.[225] Therefore, Torah observance is applicable to New Covenant believers.

121.   If Torah observance were not applicable to New Covenant believers, then the statutes of the Torah are not forever right. The statutes of the Torah are forever right.[226]   Therefore, Torah observance is applicable to New Covenant believers.

122.   The New Covenant does not abolish knowledge and truth. Knowledge and truth are found within the Torah.[227] Therefore, the New Covenant does not abolish the Torah.

123.   The Davidic Covenant upholds Torah observance.[228]   The Davidic Covenant lasts as long as day and night persist.[229] Therefore, the Torah has not been abolished, but remains in force.

124.   The Torah was changed regarding the priesthood,[230] not abolished.[231] We must still fulfill the Torah, understanding that Yeshua is our High Priest and the perfect sacrificial Lamb of God as foreshadowed[232] in the Torah. There is a

temple to come[233] in which only Levites[234] shall preside over the reinstituted sacrificial system[235] throughout the Millennium,[236] proving sacrificial Torah laws have not been abolished. New Covenant believers understand that this depicts an ongoing memorial of the unblemished Lamb who was sacrificed once for all[237] for the forgiveness of sins and eternal life to those who believe[238] and who remain in (and manifest) this love of God which is in Yeshua.[239] After the Millennium, our physical universe will pass away[240] and it will be replaced with a new spatial expanse and a new ocean-less earth[241] with the New Jerusalem[242] moving from God (where Yeshua has prepared a place for His disciples[243]) to the new earth, where a temple is no longer needed[244] as a copy[245] of the new reality of God dwelling together with men,[246] and where portions of the Torah will evidently pass away (but not until then), as prophesied by Yeshua.[247]

125.   There is apparently no Torah command requiring non-infant Gentile male converts to be circumcised either as a condition of conversion or as an eventual outward manifestation of a mature and sanctified faith. Paul's claim that physically uncircumcised persons can be Torah-observant[248] confirms this position. Also, this position is not in violation of the Torah command regarding circumcision of newly born males on the eighth day,[249] since uncircumcised persons coming to faith in Yeshua are older than eight days. Neither is this position in violation of the Abrahamic covenant of circumcision in which adult males were circumcised,[250] since the ongoing mark of the Abrahamic covenant was to be instituted via circumcision of newly born (not adult!) males on the eighth day,[251] and since the righteousness imputed to Abraham prior to his circumcision[252] symbolizes the righteousness granted to uncircumcised Gentiles who come to faith in Yeshua and attain righteousness even though they are without circumcision[253] and may remain without circumcision in their Torah observance;[254] it is Yeshua's circumcision of one's heart that is sufficient to achieve praise from God for all persons.[255] The stated purpose of Paul's adult circumcision of Timothy was Jewish accommodation,[256] not Torah observance; this reveals that adult Gentile circumcision can be permissible (if not obligatory) in specific contexts. In fact, adult male circumcision is evidently commanded in case an uncircumcised adult desires to celebrate the Passover *and* eat of it;[257] this command, however, is apparently not presently in force, since the Passover can not be strictly observed as commanded in the Torah (due to the present nonexistence of a Temple). Contemporary Passover feasts may thus be viewed as commemorative celebrations which anticipate the coming Third Temple era, when a fuller measure of Torah observance will be enabled.

126.   Peter's teaching regarding the need for holiness[258] is derived from the Torah[259] where it is assumed that kosher dietary laws are a manifestation of that holiness.[260] Peter's urging of dietary holiness is not inconsistent with his

vision.[261] His vision meant not that we can eat whatever we want, but that the "unclean Gentiles" are now declared clean and accepted by God, if they fear him and do what is right.[262] That helps explain why the Holy Spirit also descended upon the uncircumcised Gentiles[263] who believed.

127. We should crave pure spiritual milk.[264] The Torah is holy, righteous, good, and spiritual.[265] Therefore, we should embrace the Torah as we mature in our salvation.[266]

128. We should be filled with thanksgiving as the word of God and prayer jointly function to consecrate our food.[267] The Torah is the word of God. Therefore, Torah kosher food laws remain in force.

129. A lifestyle of discipleship in Yeshua is characterized by Torah observance.[268] Therefore, Torah observance is a proper characteristic of disciples of Yeshua.

130. Shall we immediately saddle new or prospective converts to Yeshua with full Torah observance in all details? The verdict of the Council at Jerusalem was to make it easier for them[269] and gradually phase them in,[270] so long as they were able to routinely hear Moses preached in such places as the synagogues,[271] in the temple area,[272] or elsewhere outside the synagogues[273] as they matured into eventual attainment of maximal Torah observance. It should be emphasized that this verdict also included rejection of the claim that circumcision and Torah observance are necessary for salvation.[274] Torah observance is not a prerequisite for salvation, but may manifest deepening and ongoing Spirit-led sanctification as the Holy Spirit writes the Torah upon our hearts.[275]

131. In addition to the above evidence, the Torah-observant position for which I have argued has also been (persuasively, I submit) set forth in detail in the Torah-observant literature, including responses to objections raised by critics. For example, see the works authored by Timothy Hegg,[276] J.K. McKee,[277] David Friedman,[278] D. Thomas Lancaster,[279] Bruce R. Booker,[280] Aaron Eby,[281] and Tony Robinson.[282]

I submit that the above 131 lines of evidence in support of Torah observance constitute a compelling case, and this understanding justifies our pursuit of maximal obedience insofar as such obedience is possible and justifiable. Temple-dependent sacrificial laws, however, can not be presently strictly observed, since we still await the rebuilding of the third Jewish temple.[283] Also, observance of any laws predicated upon the establishment of a Torah-based theocracy can only be strictly observed in Torah-based governmental structures. In addition, laws are, of course, not binding which are clearly established as having only a localized regional application or a finite temporal application period that has now expired. Too, the consequences of violation of those laws which are practically impossible to observe due to the specific uniqueness of one's position, condition, finances, power, knowledge, etc., may be understood to be graciously forgiven[284] for those who are faith-filled in their obedience.[285] Also, there evidently exists hierarchical precedence in the commands of the Torah,[286] and such underlying principles as love, life, kindness, holiness, mercy, justice, humility, grace, and purity[287] must be cautiously applied to our judgments regarding law conflicts. So, we may work (individually and corporately) to obey as much of the Torah as presently possible,[288] knowing that a fuller expression of this faith-derived obedience[289] will be made available with the advent of the Third Temple,[290] both before the revelation of the Anti-Messiah[291] and especially during the Millennium[292] when the Torah will go out to the nations from Zion in Jerusalem.[293]

For a more detailed examination of the Biblical Scriptures from a Torah-observant perspective, one may consult works by J.K. McKee[294] and Timothy Hegg.[295] Also, for a helpful introduction to competing views on the relationship between law and Gospel, see Zondervan's published debate between scholars from several different points of view.[296]

Seven Challenged Systems

Messianic Israelism presents a direct challenge to seven widespread (and incorrect) systems of belief:

1.   ATHEISM. Since Messianic Israelism is theistic, atheism is false.

2.   ANTI-BIBLICALISM. Since Messianic Israelism entails that the Bible properly functions as a source of supreme authority, any anti-Biblical position is false, including all aberrant theological systems, all anti-Biblical religions, and all anti-Biblical philosophical systems.

3.   SUPERSESSIONISM. Since Israel is not replaced by any other church or people group, any such form of replacement theology is false.

4.   DISPENSATIONALISM.   Since Israel is the only Biblically authenticated people of YHVH, any theology which advocates an Israel/church distinction is false.

5.   JUDAISM. Since Yeshua is Israel's Messiah and Savior, any form of Judaism is false which rejects that Yeshua is Israel's Messiah and Savior.

6.   CHRISTIANITY.   Since Christian theological systems routinely explicitly reject Torah observance as obligatory for members of the New Covenant faith community, such systems are consequently false insofar as they reject the commands of YHVH.

7.   MESSIANIC JUDAISM. Since the prevailing theology within much (but not all) of Messianic Judaism denies that Torah observance is obligatory for non-Jewish members of the New Covenant faith community, Messianic Judaism is false insofar as it embraces that denial.

Response to Michael L. Brown

Messianic author Michael L. Brown has made a significant and valuable contribution to the Messianic literature,[297] and I appreciate his work and ministry. Some of his views, however, are inconsistent with MI (Messianic Israelism), and what follows is a critique of the position he expressed in a recent publication.[298]

It should not be controversial to take as plainly evident that Brown accepts some of the core truths of MI. In particular, Brown accepts the first core truth (he embraces theism), the second core truth (he accepts that YHVH is the creator-sustainer-designer of the physical world who exists as described in the Tanach), and the fourth core truth (Yeshua is Israel's Savior and Messiah).

BROWN ON ISRAEL

Brown does appear to disagree with the third MI core truth. He claims that Gentiles in Yeshua are in the family of God, but are not spiritual Israelites.[299] In response to this claim, we may agree that Gentiles in Yeshua are, by definition, not part of *physical* Israel as a physical descendant of Abraham through Jacob. However, such Gentiles are nevertheless clearly part of spiritual Israel (*living Israel* is my preferred term). It is clear that Gentiles in Yeshua may be included with citizenship (NIV) in the commonwealth (NKJV) of Israel.[300]

Brown strangely excluded Ephesians 2:12 from his quotation of this critical passage.[301] It follows that Gentiles in Yeshua are part of Israel. Since this is a spiritual (not strictly physical) reality, we may conclude that Gentiles in Yeshua are spiritual Israelites (i.e., part of living Israel).

Also, Gentiles in Yeshua are participants in the covenants (plural) of promise.[302] Since YHVH's covenants are made with Israel,[303] and since Gentiles in Yeshua are participants in the covenants (as Brown evidently would concede[304]), it follows that Gentiles in Yeshua *must* be a spiritual part of Israel (i.e., living Israel). Again, it is strange that Brown excludes Ephesians 2:12 from his quotation of this critical passage in Ephesians.[305] It is also strange that Brown acknowledges that Gentiles participate in a covenant (the New Covenant) between YHVH and Israel, yet Brown denies that Gentiles are spiritually part of Israel. After all, if Gentiles are neither physical nor spiritual Israel, then Gentiles can not participate in the New Covenant...yet Brown acknowledges that they do participate, while also claiming that Gentiles are neither physical nor spiritual Israel! This contradiction in Brown's theology must be resolved. A better solution is to reject his self-contradictory position in favor of the position here set forth: Gentiles in Yeshua are physical Gentiles, and they are also spiritual Israelites by virtue of being grafted into Israel so as to participate in the covenants of promise. We may agree that Gentiles need not become Jews in order to receive these blessings;[306] nevertheless, Gentiles must become spiritual Israelites (regardless of whether they are aware of this fact) in order to receive these blessings.

Moreover, Gentiles in Yeshua are Abraham's seed.[307] Since New Covenant faith in Yeshua clearly does not bring about a change in one's physical ethnicity, it follows that Gentiles in Yeshua are *spiritual* descendants of Abraham through Israel. Thus, Gentiles in Yeshua are spiritual Israelites (i.e., part of living Israel).

Another important observation comes from Isaiah 56:3, which entails that Gentiles can be included as part of YHVH's people. Since YHVH's people are Israel, it follows that Gentiles can be included as part of Israel (i.e., as spiritual Israelites).

Yet another important observation comes from Amos 3:1-2, where it is stated that the family of Israel is the only family YHVH has chosen or known. Since Brown would presumably acknowledge that Gentiles in Yeshua are in the family of YHVH, it follows that Brown should acknowledge that Gentiles in Yeshua are members of the family of Israel. Of course, this membership is a spiritual (not strictly physical) reality. Therefore, Gentiles in Yeshua are spiritual Israelites (i.e., members of living Israel).

Additionally, Brown notes that Gentiles in Yeshua are "fellow citizens" with the (redeemed Israelite) people of God.[308] Since the redeemed Israelite people of God are citizens of Israel, it follows that Gentiles in Yeshua are also citizens of Israel. Clearly, this citizenship is a spiritual (not strictly physical) reality. Therefore, Gentiles in Yeshua are spiritual Israelites (i.e., members of living Israel).

Still another important point pertains to Brown's acknowledgement that Gentiles in Yeshua are members of God's household.[309] Since God's household (house) may be taken to refer to YHVH's family, and since Brown would surely agree that Gentiles are included as members of that house,[310] and since that family is the family of Israel,[311] it follows that Gentiles in Yeshua are members of YHVH's house of Israel. Of course, this Gentile membership in Israel is a spiritual (not strictly physical) reality. Therefore, Gentiles in Yeshua are spiritual Israelites (i.e., living Israel).

In addition, since Gentiles in Yeshua are not part of physical Israel, but they *are* part of Israel, it follows that they must be spiritually grafted into Israel, as stated by Paul.[312] Brown thinks that Paul's reference to Gentiles in Yeshua as *Gentiles* requires the inference that such Gentiles are not spiritual Israelites.[313] In response, if physical Gentiles (i.e., physical non-Israelites) in Yeshua are spiritual Israelites, then reference to them as Gentiles does not deny their spiritual Israelite status, but merely references them by their physical non-Israelite status. That is, Gentiles who are spiritual Israelites are still Gentiles (i.e., still not physically Jewish or physically Israelite). Of course, Gentiles in Yeshua do not become physical Jews,[314] but they are, nevertheless, spiritual Israelites. Reference to Gentiles as *Gentiles*, therefore, does not prove that they are not spiritual Israelites.

Brown claims that Gentiles in Yeshua are never explicitly called spiritual Israel by Paul.[315] In response, even if this were true, it would be no fact of significant relevance to the issue here at hand, since truths may be implicitly inferred from a passage, even if those truths are not explicitly stated. Furthermore, my above discussion of this issue entails that Paul did teach that Gentiles in Yeshua are spiritual Israelites. Such Gentiles need not be erroneously labeled as "Jewish wannabes".[316] Rather, they may be viewed as having a correct Biblical understanding of their spiritual Israelite (not Jewish) status in Yeshua.

If Gentiles in Yeshua are "heirs together with Israel"[317] by virtue of being spiritually grafted into Israel as spiritual Israelites, then this fact does not establish that "Gentile believers do not become [spiritual] Israel".[318] To reason as Brown has reasoned is, therefore, to beg the question in favor of his position. We may respectfully reject such reasoning as unsound.

So we may agree that Gentiles in Yeshua do not become physical Israel.[319] Nevertheless, they do spiritually become part of Israel (i.e., part of *living Israel*).

Brown claims that the overwhelming majority of cases in which the terms Israel/Israelite appear in the Messianic Scriptures are cases in which reference is made to "the literal people of Israel".[320] In response, if it is a literal fact that Gentiles in Yeshua are spiritual Israelites (i.e., part of living Israel), then Brown's observation does nothing to support his attempted (but failed) refutation of the position I advocate.

Brown rightly warns of the dangers of supersessionism (Replacement Theology).[321] However, a correct Biblical understanding of Gentiles in Yeshua as spiritual Israelites does not lend support for supersessionism. It is simply incorrect to assume that "Gentiles are spiritual Israelites" implies "Israel is replaced by the Christian (or Gentile) church". The former emphasizes the Biblically essential nature of Israel and its role in the divine economy, whereas the latter flatly denies that very nature.

In summary, Brown has argued that Gentiles in Yeshua are not part of Israel. However, exclusion from Israel is accompanied by exclusion from the covenants of promise, exclusion from hope, and exclusion from God.[322] We must surely reject this significantly erroneous consequence of his theology, and I would respectfully urge him to modify his position so as to account for the critique here provided.

BROWN ON TORAH

Brown clearly rejects the fifth core truth of MI. He claims that it is confused, if not heretical,[323] to teach that Gentiles are obligated to obey Torah commands.[324] He also takes the position that only some Jewish people in Yeshua should be Torah-observant.[325] It would be helpful if Brown had addressed the 131 lines of Biblical evidence in support of my position that Torah obedience (independent of one's ethnicity) is the proper manifestation of New Covenant faith. Since Brown's analysis did not account for much of this evidence, his analysis is an incomplete and unsatisfactory basis for justifying his position. Also, the limited considerations within his analysis itself do not establish his position.

We may agree that Yeshua was fully Torah-observant[326] and did not abolish the Torah (or the Prophets).[327] But then, the Torah is not abolished! It must still be in force.[328] Moreover, the earth still exists; therefore, the Torah is still in force.[329] In addition, since the Torah is written upon the hearts of the participants in the New Covenant,[330] it is surely not abolished, but still in force. Also, since trained disciples imitate their teacher,[331] we who are His disciples should imitate Yeshua by also observing the Torah. See, also, the 131 lines of Biblical evidence provided above.

Brown cites Hebrews 8-10 as if it establishes that Torah laws pertaining to such things as sacrifice, priesthood, and the temple have been replaced.[332] In response, the revelation of a shadow-casting substance does not imply a shadow no longer exists. Also, in the future, the Torah will go out from Zion,[333] and the Torah includes laws pertaining to such things as sacrifice, priesthood, and the temple, even in the New Temple era to come.[334] In addition, the very portion of Scripture referenced by Brown clearly shows that the Torah-based Mosaic Covenant will soon disappear,[335] implying that it has not yet disappeared.

Regarding some Torah laws which carry the death penalty as a consequence of their violation, Brown claims they no longer bring the death penalty.[336] In response, if a national government chooses to uphold a Torah-based legal structure, then these Torah death penalties will be in force within the national jurisdiction of that structure. The nonexistence of Torah death penalties, therefore, results from governmental decisions, not from Yeshua's changing of our relationship to the Torah. Our obligation to be Torah-observant must be properly balanced by our obligation to respect governing authorities.[337] I do not know whether a fully Torah-observant governmental structure can be anywhere expected prior to Yeshua's return. When He returns, however, we may presume that Torah death penalties may be reinstituted.[338] In fact, a sword of judgment is a particularly striking feature of Yeshua's Torah-sanctioned[339] judgment of the nations[340] who do not serve YHVH.

We may agree that New Covenant participants are not *under* the Torah,[341] but this does not establish that such participants should not *observe* the Torah. Such participants can observe the Torah in Spirit-directed faithful obedience, even though they are not under its condemnation, and even though they are not justified through that observance. Also, "they are no longer under the Torah to bring them to Yeshua" does not entail "they should not be Torah-observant", since Torah-observance does not bring anyone to Yeshua. Rather, it is one's inability to fully obey the Torah without sin that requires that one come to Yeshua in faith,[342] recognizing He is our perfectly Torah-observant sacrificial Lamb whose death in our place may secure the free gift of righteousness for all who believe. Thus, Torah observance does not earn this righteousness that is by faith,[343] even though Torah observance may be a sufficient condition of knowing that one truly possesses that righteousness.[344]

Brown claims that Paul did not ever require that Gentile believers should observe the Torah.[345] In response, even Brown understands that Paul's life was characterized by Torah observance.[346] Paul also commanded that disciples (Gentiles and non-Gentiles) of Yeshua should imitate Paul.[347] It follows that Paul commanded Yeshua's disciples to be Torah-observant.

Also, Paul taught that love fulfills (not replaces or abolishes) the Torah.[348] If we need not be Torah-observant, then we need not fulfill the law. We need to fulfill the law (via love). Therefore, Paul taught that we need to be Torah-observant.

In addition, Paul was careful to meet ceremonial Torah requirements.[349] We should imitate Paul.[350] Therefore, we should also meet ceremonial Torah requirements insofar as such obedience is possible. Of course, we do not presently have a temple in place, but this Torah-observant imitation of Paul was clearly commanded.[351] and surely widely practiced in Paul's time[352] by disciples of Yeshua.

Paul said that he did nothing wrong against the Torah.[353] We should imitate Paul.[354] Therefore, we should do nothing wrong against the Torah.

If Brown were correct that Paul never required Gentiles to observe the Torah, then Paul would not command Gentiles to keep the Passover Festival. Paul commanded Gentiles to keep the Passover Festival.[355] Therefore, Brown's position is not correct.

Paul was careful to speak in obedience to Torah speech commands.[356] Paul commanded Gentiles to imitate Paul.[357] Therefore, Brown is wrong in claiming that Paul never commanded Gentiles to observe the Torah.

Paul used the Torah to identify applicable ethical principles[358] regarding material support and compensation. Paul commanded Gentiles to imitate Paul.[359] Therefore, Brown's position is wrong in claiming that Paul did not command Gentiles to observe the Torah.

I could recall much more of the 131 lines of Torah-observant Biblical evidence provided above, but the point has already been firmly established. Brown is wrong in claiming that Paul never required that Gentile believers should observe the Torah.

We may agree that disciples of Yeshua can not be justified or saved through Torah observance,[360] but this does nothing to prove that such disciples should not observe the Torah in Spirit-directed faith-filled obedience to YHVH's commands.

We may agree that disciples of Yeshua are not under the Torah to bring them to Yeshua.[361] However, this does not prove that such disciples are not required to obey the Torah in Spirit-directed faith-filled obedience to YHVH's commands after they have been brought to Yeshua.

We may agree that righteousness is not achieved through Torah observance. This fact, however, does not prove that disciples of Yeshua are not required to obey the Torah in Spirit-directed faith-filled obedience to YHVH's commands after they have received the free gift of righteousness by faith.

We may agree that disciples of Yeshua do not receive the Spirit through Torah observance. This fact, however, does not prove that disciples of Yeshua are not required to obey the Torah in Spirit-directed faith-filled obedience to YHVH's commands after they have received the Spirit.

We may agree that we are not under the Torah, but under grace. This fact, however, does not prove that we are not graciously delivered from the curse of Torah disobedience so that we can meet our Torah-observant obligations in faith-filled Spirit-directed obedience to YHVH's commands.

We may agree that uncircumcised adult male Gentile converts may be Torah-observant in their uncircumcision.[362] This fact, however, does not establish that adult male Gentile converts should not be Torah-observant in their uncircumcision.[363] In fact, Paul esteems the uncircumcised adult male Gentile convert who is Torah-observant.[364] Moreover, Paul claims that Torah observance is a sufficient (not abolished!) condition of our knowing that we will be declared righteous.[365] Brown's claim that Gentiles are not required to be Torah-observant, therefore, is not supported by circumcision considerations.

Brown provides his preferred interpretation of Acts 15:19-21.[366] He favors an interpretation that assumes that new Gentile converts had already heard the Torah read on numerous occasions in the synagogues. In response, if new Gentile converts are *new*, then we should not assume they have heard or learned much at all,[367] disconfirming Brown's favored interpretation.

Moreover, Brown rejects the "Gentiles should start with the four restrictions and continue to grow into full Torah observance" interpretation based, in part, upon the claim that Biblical scholars rarely accept that interpretation. In response, truth is not determined by vote, and since majority interpretations can be flawed for many reasons, scholarly consensus is an inadequate basis for justifying a theological argument.

Brown also rejects the "Gentiles should start with the four restrictions and continue to grow into full Torah observance" interpretation based, in part, upon the claim that such an interpretation is contrary to the overall context of Acts 15. In response, such an interpretation is not contrary to the overall context of Acts 15, since nothing in Acts 15 contradicts that interpretation. Granted, the context of Acts 15 focuses upon whether Torah observance and circumcision are required for salvation. The fact that Torah observance and circumcision are not required for salvation, however, does not support the claim that Torah observance (including Torah-observant circumcision) is not obligatory in the ongoing faith-filled Spirit-directed sanctification of disciples of Yeshua. We don't observe Torah with circumcision to be *saved*. However, this fact does not prove we should not observe Torah with circumcision in our *sanctification*.

Brown makes a confused claim that Paul referenced the Torah "not in a binding way".[368] In response, commands bind (i.e., generate a moral obligation upon) those to whom they apply. Since Paul issued commands, Paul's commands are binding. When Paul's commands are coincident with Torah commands, the coincident Torah commands are also binding. Therefore, Brown is incorrect in claiming that Paul's issuance of commands coincident with the Torah do not impose a binding Torah obligation upon those he commanded.

Brown is willing to approve of Gentile Torah observance, provided several conditions are satisfied.[369] We may agree that Torah observance does not increase one's spiritual standing as a recipient of the free gift of righteousness and eternal life by faith. Nevertheless, we will be rewarded according to our works, and since the Torah (along with the other Biblical Scriptures) is a supreme source of authority in determining what actions are acceptable, Torah observance (along with observance of all personally applicable Scripture) may be viewed as the means by which we may meet our reward-storing obligations. Moreover, Torah-lessness (lawlessness) is a characteristic of those whom Yeshua will cast away.[370] With this in mind, Brown's antinomian teachings would appear to have potentially catastrophic consequences for those who accept them.

We may agree that we should not judge one another on disputable matters,[371] but the obligation to be Torah-observant is not such a disputable matter. Thus, Paul did not hesitate to judge those who violate Torah commands,[372] and he commanded that the Torah-inclusive Scriptures be used to rebuke, train, teach, and correct others in Torah-observant works,[373] just as Yeshua also said that we live by every word of YHVH.[374] We should imitate Yeshua and Paul.[375] Should we reject the commands of YHVH? Paul commanded that we imitate (not reject) Him.[376]

We should not let unbelievers judge us in our Torah observance.[377] This point of emphasis, however, only serves to underscore Paul's Torah observant teachings.

Brown warns that Torah observance could be associated with nonessential concerns. In response, our theology of law[378] is of paramount concern, and should function as a central focus of understanding as we grow in Yeshua. Moreover, Yeshua is the purpose of the Torah,[379] so it is surely incorrect to suppose that Torah-relevant considerations are nonessential.

Brown suggests Gentiles are not judged for violation of Torah commands.[380] In fact, YHVH will not hesitate to judge the entire world for its Torah violations.[381] Likewise, Yeshua will cast away workers of lawlessness (Torah-lessness),[382] regardless of their ethnicity or spiritual status-claims, and He will bring the iron scepter of destructive rule[383] against the nations opposed to YHVH,[384] whose commands are found in the Torah. Therefore, Amos 1:1-2:3 does not establish that the Torah is not applicable to Gentiles. In fact, we are commanded to submit to God who is YHVH,[385] and YHVH's commands include those in the Torah. Therefore, we should submit to the commands of YHVH, as also to those of Yeshua[386] whose Torah-observant teachings we should imitate.[387]

Brown claims that Paul clearly did not teach that Gentiles should obey everything in the Torah.[388] In response, of course Gentiles should not obey *everything* in the Torah. After all, some commands apply to men, others to women, others to children, others to infants, others to priests, etc. Thus, Gentiles should obey all the Gentile-applicable Torah commands. Brown even agrees that some Torah commands are applicable to Gentiles,[389] so it seems that Brown believes that Gentiles should be at least *partially* Torah-observant after all. Sadly, he does not explain how to determine which Torah laws apply to Gentiles, but only refers to undefined "universal principles",[390] without clearly identifying this set of principles and without explaining how to use these unidentified principles to establish the morally binding content of, for example, Leviticus 18.[391]

Brown is willing to allow that all of YHVH's people are minimally obligated to obey those Torah portions that are applicable to the nations.[392] However, YHVH will not refrain from judging all nations for their violation of Torah laws, Torah statutes, and the everlasting covenant.[393] Therefore, Brown's allowance should lead him to embrace the position that Torah observance is a moral obligation for all the inhabitants of the earth.

If a command applies only to, say, Moses,[394] then it surely does not apply to Gentiles. Nevertheless, it should be very clear that Brown has failed to justify his belief that Gentiles should not be Torah-observant. I encourage Brown, and everyone, to examine the 131 Scriptural lines of evidence provided above.

Brown appears to fall short of clearly claiming that all believers are commanded to obey the moral components of the Torah. Rather, he merely writes that all believers should "be encouraged to follow" those components.[395] In response, "encouragement to follow" is not identical to "command to follow". Do not hesitate to clearly command what is already commanded in the Scriptures!

Moreover, Brown refers to the moral components of the Torah, as if anyone actually agrees on what those components actually are. Since no clear and concrete definition of "moral Torah precept" is provided, it is far from clear what commands Brown has in mind. Therefore, it is especially unclear which Torah commands Brown thinks are moral and, thus, applicable to New Covenant believers.

We may agree that no person must be under the Torah's condemnation, and we may agree that no person must observe the Torah to attain righteousness, justification, or salvation.[396] Nevertheless, these points of agreement do not confirm that Jewish (or any) believers must not observe the Torah so as to meet their obligations to live properly as continuously maturing New Covenant participants.

Brown approves of the Torah-observance of Jewish participants in the New Covenant, provided God writes it on their heart to so observe the Torah.[397] In response, all New Covenant participants should observe the Torah, since participation in the New Covenant involves the writing of the Torah upon one's heart[398] by the Holy Spirit.[399]

Brown claims that New Covenant participants (Jewish or not) who do not observe the Torah should not be "judged" for their nonobservance.[400] In response, the Torah should be used to correct other believers.[401] So, as the greater body of Yeshua is coming to experience the renewal of awareness of the proper role of the Torah in their lives, we may offer Torah-grounded firm correction to those opposed to such Torah observance, provided this correction is given in love, in a gentle attitude of humility and respect.[402]

In particular, we may offer a correction to Brown's views on the Sabbath, since obeying YHVH's commandments (including the Sabbath commandment) is not a disputable matter of the kind Paul discusses,[403] even though the relative degree to which the various days of the week ought to be esteemed as sacred *is* such a disputable matter.[404] Brown acknowledges that the seventh-day Sabbath is given to the people of Israel.[405] Since all New Covenant participants are part of Israel,[406] it follows that observance of the Sabbath is given to Gentile and non-Gentile participants in the New Covenant. Also, we should not let those who embrace worldly philosophy or mere traditions of men[407] judge us in our observance of the Sabbath commandment,[408] nor should we suppose that when we obey YHVH that we are somehow inappropriately legalistic and binding.[409] Obedience is not inappropriate, but commanded,[410] and seventh-day Sabbath observance is surely a command in the Torah and elsewhere in the Tanach.[411] Since legalism may be defined as faithless obedience so as to attain salvation by works, it follows that faith-derived obedience (including faith-derived obedience to the Sabbath commandment) is not legalistic. Moreover, Brown embraces multiple contradictions by admitting that Yeshua said that the Sabbath was made for man,[412] yet claiming that Gentiles are not commanded to observe the Sabbath,[413] while also judging that the Sabbath "should be set aside" by Gentiles[414] as a special day,[415] and while also asserting that such Sabbath judgments should not even be made.[416] Furthermore, we may conclude that Sabbath observance is not a matter of calling or conviction,[417] but is a matter of obedience to YHVH's law as affirmed by Yeshua, as commanded in the Tanach and Messianic Scriptures, and as promised to be an everlasting commandment,[418] which fact is even conceded by Brown himself.[419]

We may also offer correction to Brown's views on dietary laws. Simply put, Torah observance is a proper form of obedience to YHVH's commands for all those whose faith is in Yeshua. Since the dietary laws are Torah laws,[420] it follows that the dietary commands are applicable to New Covenant participants. We may agree that we are not under "bondage" to the dietary laws,[421] but this does not entail that such laws may be disregarded as nonessential or inapplicable. We obey YHVH's commands not because we are in bondage, but because it is our loving expression of obedience.[422] Obedience brings insight, understanding and wisdom,[423] not bondage! Disobedience brings YHVH's wrath,[424] so surely obedience is good. Since YHVH is quite clearly displeased with consumption of unclean meats,[425] we are well advised to eat in obedience to Scriptural dietary requirements and expectations,[426] including the presumption that we properly define "food" so that it may be consecrated by the word of God;[427] the Torah is the word of God. We may agree that the physical act of eating does not, in and of itself, bring spiritual uncleanness;[428] nevertheless, an evil heart which disregards YHVH's laws (including dietary laws) brings uncleanness.[429] Therefore, all foods are clean,[430] but not all eaten objects are food! It may be wise, however, to abstain from Scripturally sanctified foods in cases where the faith of a brother may be at stake.[431] We may agree that law conflicts can arise,[432] in which case a conflict resolution procedure must be cautiously employed so as to identify the appropriate course of action; however, exceptions to generalizations do not, in and of themselves, justify routine abandonment of the generalizations. We may conclude that since there appears to be no justification for the assumption that Scriptural dietary laws are removed by the cross,[433] individual convictions regarding this matter should not be honored,[434] but gently (yet firmly) corrected[435] in love.[436] We are not free in Yeshua to pick and choose to obey only those commands we feel like obeying![437] It is not advisable to follow Brown's approach of acknowledging the present-day applicability of Leviticus 18,[438] while denying the applicability of Leviticus 11. Rather, we in Yeshua are free to walk in the blessings of true life, love, and holiness, without being under the judgment of the Torah. Obedience to YHVH's commands is not a disputable matter,[439] but is an expected manifestation of true faith-derived righteousness.[440]

We may also offer correction to Brown's views regarding the Biblical feasts. Paul commanded imitation of his example,[441] and he (along with thousands of others[442]) clearly modeled an example of Torah observance[443] which he prayed others would emulate.[444] Moreover, he explicitly stated his expectation that those in Yeshua would follow his celebration of the Passover feast,[445] contradicting Brown's incorrect claim that Biblical feast celebration is not commanded in the Messianic Scriptures.[446] We may agree that Biblical feast celebration is inappropriate as a means by which one may be justified,[447] but this fact does not justify rejection of our Biblical feast-celebrating obligations. Granted, Biblical feast celebration may not be strictly possible in all details, given the present nonexistence of a functioning temple. Nevertheless, we may seek to practice a memorialized celebration of the feasts in eager anticipation of the coming Third Temple era[448] and Fourth Temple era,[449] when a greater measure of Torah observance will be possible.

Torah and Gospel

It is vitally important to understand the relationship between the Torah and the Biblical Gospel. The Biblical Gospel is a gospel of righteousness by faith.[450] Salvation is through faith by God's grace,[451] not by human works of obedience to the Torah. Living faith is accompanied by works,[452] but the righteousness of salvation is from faith, not works. Our righteousness is not by self-righteous, faithless, merit-based, rule-following legalistic works,[453] for although righteousness is available to those who perfectly follow the Torah,[454] the testimony of Scripture (as well as personal experience) is that no one actually achieves righteousness by this means.[455] Our sanctification, however, is facilitated by (and manifested through) Spirit-enabled growth[456] through faith-derived obedience[457] to that perfect and royal law which gives freedom[458] and which encapsulates the true essence and foundation upon which Torah observance is built.[459]

Yeshua did not observe the Torah so that New Covenant believers would not also need to observe the Torah. Rather, Yeshua's perfect obedience to the Torah ensured that He was a perfect sacrifice,[460] the Lamb of God who takes away the sins of the world,[461] thereby removing not the Torah, but the *curse* which rests upon those who fail to perfectly obey either the Torah[462] or whatever measure of law is written upon their hearts and consciences.[463] Having nailed to the cross the legal requirements, unsatisfiable by mere human effort,[464] which stood opposed to our attainment of righteousness,[465] we receive forgiveness of sins[466] and the justification of righteousness through Yeshua's blood,[467] so that the blessings of Torah observance may be enjoyed in the fullness of the abundant life which Yeshua came to bring.[468]

For those who are faith-filled, the Biblical Gospel removes the guilt and eternal punishment that result from sin, so that they may be free to obey the Torah and enjoy the blessed life[469] that accompanies obedience. Our moral obligation to live a Torah-observant life is not removed by the Biblical Gospel. Rather, the Biblical Gospel facilitates a blessed Torah-observant life that is motivated by a loving desire to please God in obedience to His commands which apply to New Covenant believers. So, since Yeshua lived in obedience to the Torah, we who are New Covenant believers are to be conformed into His image and do the same. We must live a life of love[470] which fulfills (not abolishes) the Torah, as we grow in the grace, knowledge, and Spirit-given wisdom that brings ever-increasing insight to the interpretation, significance, and proper function and application of the Torah.

The New Covenant[471] was initiated in the blood[472] of Yeshua. The New Covenant does not replace the Torah, but it reinforces it through the writing of the Torah on the hearts of the people of Israel.[473] The corporate assembly (church) of all New Covenant believers comprises the body of Yeshua,[474] which consists of both believing Jews,[475] as well as those Gentiles grafted into Israel,[476] who together form the "one new man"[477] which is God's household, the church. Thus, the church is *living*[478] Israel; the Israel that is broken off[479] is not *living* Israel. Living Israel is not identical to the physical descendants of Abraham.[480] Neither is it identical to the recently (1948 C.E.) formed Israeli nation-state, since the corporate assembly (church) of all true believers in the

God of Israel, of course, predates the year 1948. Also, the perpetuity of Israel as a nation before YHVH[481] proves that the Biblical nation (family) of Israel is not identical to the Israeli nation-state formed in 1948. So, the New Covenant does not abolish the divine covenant[482] made with Israel's physical descendants[483] and replace it with the church, as incorrectly taught in a theological system known as Replacement Theology. Neither does the New Covenant authenticate a postponement of God's dealing with Israel until an interjected and temporary church age is completed, as typically (and incorrectly) taught in a theological system often termed Dispensationalism. Nor does the New Covenant allow for any significant distinction between Gentile and non-Gentile insofar as the Torah-derived moral obligations for one's personal life are concerned.[484] Rather, the New Covenant is made *with Israel*[485] in which grafted Gentiles[486] and regrafted Jews/Israelites[487] who together[488] comprise the citizenship of living Israel,[489] share in the blessings of the promise,[490] and function as a light to bring salvation to the earth[491] as Torah observance brings global recognition of divinely manifested wisdom and greatness.[492]

Sin is lawlessness.[493] Sadly, to the extent that (regrettably large) segments of the Christian church reject observance of the law, they may actually function to promote the very sin (Torah-lessness) they ought to be seeking to overcome.[494] I am concerned that Yeshua's description of a wicked and adulterous generation[495] may be applicable even to those who erroneously think they are His disciples.[496] We may grant that God's behavioral expectations of us are conditional upon the measure of understanding and power we have been given,[497] and many genuine members of living Israel continue to be ignorant of much of the meat of the Scriptures[498] as was I in my earlier years of discipleship. However, if our own willfully self-imposed ignorance, defiance, foolishness, or procrastination limits our understanding, then negative consequences will surely result,[499] for God has overlooked forms of ignorance in the past,[500] but now issues the global command to repent from ignorant evil desires[501] by following the God of Israel whose commands are revealed in the Torah, and who will justly judge the world by Yeshua[502] through the Torah.[503] The Lord is slow to anger and rich in love,[504] but if the church rejects the Torah, then judgment may come upon her,[505] if she refuses to repent. Indeed, our nation is not healed, and how can judgment on our nation be avoided unless the resident followers of the God of Israel repent of their wicked ways[506] and turn to the Torah?[507] The Lord is patient, gracious, merciful, slow to anger, and abounding in love. However, the Lord is also just. May those who claim His Name (Hashem) repent and prove their repentance with works[508] lest they be cut off, regurgitated, and thrown into the fire![509]

It is my personal observation that Torah observance appears to be a central theological distinctive of a significant segment of the Messianic (and Hebrew

Roots) movements within the body of disciples of Yeshua. This "new" teaching is not really new at all, although it is evidently rapidly growing, so far as I can tell. I dare submit that much of Christian theology has been incorrect on this issue for much of the past two millennia, arguably due to the Gentile-dominated churches losing knowledge of their Hebrew roots. Many thousands of the first-century converts persisted as Hebrews who were zealous for the Torah.[510] Thus, the contemporary Christian churches of the world have apparently substantially deviated from this most authentic form of Biblical faith: Torah-observant, Gentile-inclusive, Biblically conservative Messianic Israelism.

As with movements in general, there is not uniformly accepted doctrinal agreement on all points of theology in all Torah-observant Biblically-conservative groups. While generally in agreement with conventional conservative Evangelical/Protestant Biblical theology, key emphasized features of these groups may frequently focus upon acceptance of Yeshua as Israel's Messiah, Torah-observant Biblical ethics, the identity of *living Israel* with the true and only church (corporate assembly) of God's people, appreciation of the Hebraic roots of genuine Biblical faith, and an eager eschatological expectation (in the Messianic age to come) of the fulfillment of the patriarchal land promises, along with full global implementation of the prophesied Kingdom of God.

So may the theological errors of Replacement Theology and Dispensationalism, as well as all anti-Semitism, be fully expunged from all churches as they rediscover that their nourishing growth is properly rooted[511] in the patriarchs, covenants, promises, Torah, temple worship, feasts, adoption, glory, Scriptures, Messiah, and the salvation that is of the Jews (Hebrews), the people of Israel[512] who, in the fullness of time, shall yet possess the promised land[513] as God swore by divine oath to the forefathers[514] long ago,[515] with Jerusalem as God's chosen city[516] from which the Torah shall go out to all the nations[517] for a millennium[518] under the global governance of the Messiah[519] with David as prince[520] of the temple of tribally (and politically) reunified and regathered Israel.[521]

Given the growth (numerically and in geographical distribution) of Torah-observant fellowships, and given reports from personal contacts in Israel, there are indications of trends over the past few decades of significant growth in recognition, by Jews (or Israelites), of Yeshua as Israel's Messiah. I have also seen indications of growing recognition on the part of grafted Gentiles of the value of understanding the Hebrew roots of their faith. This suggests that we may now be rapidly approaching the full manifestation of the prophesied time of God's restoration,[522] when all Israel shall be saved[523] as the hardening of heart is removed from them.[524] Now, as we see that many Jews have been gathered in Israel, we may anticipate an eventual greater movement of both

Jews and the Israelite tribes of Ephraim (as well as those Gentiles grafted into Israel) in a return to the land of Israel.[525]

Through global evangelism and discipleship[526] we may participate in the fulfillment of conditions necessary for the return of Yeshua[527] to Israel,[528] thereby hastening the prophesied resurrection,[529] when Yeshua will destroy the enemies of Jerusalem,[530] judge (with saints also judging) those who are in the world,[531] and reign as king over the whole earth[532] for a millennium with those who partake in this, the first and blessed resurrection.[533] However, those whose names are not written in the book of life shall be thrown into the lake of unquenchable fire[534] as a loathsome witness[535] to the nations[536] of the newly created heavens and earth.[537]

Let us understand Yeshua through the Torah and Prophets as we repent and seek to persuade others to do the same,[538] for we must all appear before His judgment seat[539] and give account for our words,[540] works,[541] desires,[542] beliefs,[543] even all our secret attitudes and thoughts[544] which are laid bare before Him.[545] We shall be rewarded or punished accordingly.[546]

Repent and follow Yeshua!

Conclusion

Messianic Israelism is not difficult to understand. A five-year-old child can perceive the basic elements. Let us work together to evangelize our children, our friends and family, and all nations in loving discipleship of Yeshua as we continue to refine and perfect the case for conservative Biblical theology in the public marketplace of ideas. May we be unified in the love of YHVH, whose love in His only begotten son, Yeshua, continues to mold us into His image by the Holy Spirit through the word of truth. May our love for others overflow in practical good works[547] so that the world may know and believe.[548]

Amen.

NOTES

1. Genesis 1:1; John 1:3; Colossians 1:16-17; Hebrews 1:2-3.
2. See Chapter 5 for details.
3. Amos 3:1-2.
4. John 8:37-40; Romans 9:6-7.
5. Genesis 17:14; Matthew 23:33; Acts 3:23; Romans 2:28; Romans 11:17.
6. Isaiah 56:3-8; Romans 3:29-30; Romans 9:24-29; Romans 11:17; Galatians 3:14; Ephesians 2:11-22; Ephesians 3:1-6.
7. Ephesians 2:19; Hebrews 3:6.
8. Galatians 3:29.
9. Matthew 16:18.
10. Acts 7:37-38; Hebrews 3:2-6.
11. Genesis 12; Genesis 15; Genesis 17; Deuteronomy 31:9-13; Jeremiah 31:31-37; Jeremiah 33:14-26.
12. Jeremiah 31:31-33; Luke 22:20; 1 Corinthians 11:25; Hebrews 8:7-13.
13. Isaiah 60; Acts 1:6-7.
14. Ephesians 2:13.
15. See Chapter 5 for details.
16. Matthew 1:21; Luke 2:11.
17. Matthew 16:16-17; John 4:26.
18. Luke 2:30-32.
19. See Chapter 5 for details.
20. The commands in the Messianic Scriptures number in the hundreds, or even more than 1000, depending on the grouping methodology employed.
21. Matthew 5:17.
22. Ibid.
23. Deuteronomy 4:2.
24. Matthew 5:18.
25. Luke 16:17.
26. Matthew 5:19.
27. Matthew 23:3; Matthew 23:23.
28. Matthew 6:10.
29. Psalm 40:8.
30. Matthew 19:17; Matthew 25:31-46.
31. Matthew 4:4; Deuteronomy 8:3.
32. Matthew 7:12.
33. Matthew 7:21-23.
34. Matthew 24:12.
35. John 10:35.
36. Matthew 24:20.
37. Matthew 12:8.
38. Matthew 12:11-12.
39. Luke 5:14; Luke 17:11-14; Leviticus 14.
40. Acts 3:19.
41. Matthew 4:17.
42. Matthew 11:7-10.

43. Matthew 3:2.
44. Acts 3:19.
45. Matthew 22:36.
46. Matthew 22:37.
47. Matthew 22:39.
48. John 17:20-21.
49. John 17:17.
50. John 14:15; 1 John 5:3.
51. Matthew 28:18-20.
52. Matthew 5:48.
53. Psalm 19:7.
54. Matthew 23:10.
55. Luke 6:40.
56. Luke 4:15-16.
57. Isaiah 42:4.
58. Leviticus 11; Deuteronomy 14.
59. Mark 7:19.
60. Leviticus 11; Deuteronomy 14.
61. Mark 7:1-5.
62. Acts 15:19-21; Acts 21:24-25; 1 Corinthians 9:19-23.
63. Romans 14:1-4; Romans 14:13-15; 1 Corinthians 8:9-13.
64. Acts 16:3.
65. Romans 10:4.
66. Luke 11:28.
67. Luke 8:44; Numbers 15:37-41.
68. Luke 6:40; 1 John 2:6.
69. John 1:14.
70. John 10:27.
71. Genesis 17:22.
72. Genesis 26:5.
73. John 8:39.
74. Matthew 6:20.
75. Psalm 19:11; Matthew 5:19.
76. John 8:17; Deuteronomy 19:15.
77. Luke 6:40; 1 John 2:6.
78. John 10:34; Psalm 82:6.
79. For example, see Psalm 119.
80. Matthew 8:19.
81. John 5:46-47.
82. John 3:2.
83. Luke 22:13-20.
84. John 5:47.
85. John 3:16; John 14:1.
86. John 5:46.
87. Acts 6:7.
88. Luke 6:40; John 14:23-24; 1 John 2:6.
89. Matthew 13:52.
90. Jeremiah 31:33; Hebrews 8:6. See the Complete Jewish Bible.

91. Isaiah 2:3; Micah 4:2.
92. Hebrews 8:13.
93. Galatians 5:14; Leviticus 19:18.
94. Luke 22:20; 1 Corinthians 11:25.
95. Hebrews 8:10; Jeremiah 31:33.
96. Ephesians 2:11-13.
97. Acts 20:21.
98. Romans 1:7; 2 Corinthians 1:1; Ephesians 1:1; Jude 1:3.
99. Psalm 30:4.
100. Psalm 119:172.
101. Psalm 119:164.
102. Romans 1:7; 2 Corinthians 1:1; Ephesians 1:1; Jude 1:3.
103. Psalm 31:23.
104. Deuteronomy 6:4-6.
105. Romans 1:7; 2 Corinthians 1:1; Ephesians 1:1; Jude 1:3.
106. Psalm 34:9.
107. Proverbs 8:13.
108. 2 Kings 17:13.
109. Romans 1:7; 2 Corinthians 1:1; Ephesians 1:1; Jude 1:3.
110. Psalm 34:9.
111. Psalm 119:120.
112. Romans 1:7; 2 Corinthians 1:1; Ephesians 1:1; Jude 1:3.
113. Revelation 14:12.
114. Deuteronomy 31:12.
115. Romans 15:9.
116. Psalm 119:132.
117. Isaiah 56:6.
118. Deuteronomy 28:1-14.
119. 2 Timothy 3:15.
120. 2 Timothy 3:16.
121. 1 Corinthians 11:1; Philippians 4:9.
122. Acts 21:24.
123. 1 Corinthians 11:1; Philippians 4:9.
124. Romans 13:8-10.
125. Romans 3:31.
126. 1 Corinthians 11:1; Philippians 4:9.
127. Romans 7:22.
128. 1 Corinthians 11:1; Philippians 4:9.
129. Acts 23:6.
130. Matthew 23:1-3; Matthew 23:23.
131. 1 Corinthians 11:1; Philippians 4:9.
132. Acts 24:18.
133. 1 Corinthians 11:1; Philippians 4:9.
134. Acts 24:14.
135. 1 Corinthians 11:1; Philippians 4:9.
136. Acts 25:8.
137. 1 Corinthians 11:1; Philippians 4:9.
138. 1 Corinthians 5:7-8.

139. Acts 23:5.
140. 1 Corinthians 11:1; Philippians 4:9.
141. 1 Corinthians 9:7-12.
142. 1 Corinthians 11:1; Philippians 4:9.
143. 1 Corinthians 14:33-35.
144. 1 Corinthians 11:1; Philippians 4:9.
145. Acts 26:29.
146. 1 Corinthians 11:1; Philippians 4:9.
147. Romans 2:13.
148. 2 Peter 1:10.
149. Acts 17:11.
150. Acts 17:12.
151. Acts 28:17.
152. 1 Corinthians 11:1; Philippians 4:9.
153. Romans 15:18.
154. 1 Corinthians 7:19.
155. 1 Corinthians 11:1; Philippians 4:9.
156. Acts 15:1-16:5.
157. 1 Corinthians 4:17.
158. 1 Corinthians 11:1; Philippians 4:9.
159. Romans 1:17.
160. Psalm 40:8-10.
161. Ephesians 2:8-9.
162. Romans 1:5; Ephesians 2:10; James 2:17.
163. Romans 8:5-8.
164. Romans 7:12.
165. 1 Peter 1:15-16.
166. Romans 7:12.
167. Ibid.
168. Romans 2:7.
169. 1 Corinthians 4:6.
170. Acts 6:13.
171. Acts 6:5; Acts 7:55.
172. Acts 6:8.
173. Acts 6:11-14.
174. Acts 6:5; Acts 7:55.
175. Acts 6:8.
176. Acts 7:53.
177. Acts 7:51.
178. James 2:12.
179. James 4:11-12.
180. James 1:22.
181. Psalm 119:44-45; James 1:25.
182. Malachi 4:4.
183. Ephesians 2:11-13; Ephesians 3:6.
184. Romans 15:27; Ephesians 1:3.
185. Psalm 19:7.
186. Ibid.

187. Psalm 19:8.
188. Ibid.
189. Ibid.
190. Psalm 19:9.
191. Psalm 119:151.
192. Psalm 148:11.
193. Psalm 119:164; Psalm 119:175.
194. Psalm 68:32.
195. Psalm 119:172.
196. Romans 15:11.
197. Psalm 105:45; Psalm 119:7; Psalm 119:108; Psalm 119:164; Psalm 119:175; Psalm 147:20; Acts 21:20.
198. Psalm 33:8.
199. Psalm 119:120.
200. Psalm 33:8.
201. Proverbs 8:13.
202. 2 Kings 17:13.
203. Matthew 6:6.
204. Proverbs 28:9.
205. Ecclesiastes 12:13.
206. Deuteronomy 1:3.
207. Isaiah 24:5-6.
208. Revelation 16:9; Revelation 16:11.
209. 2 Peter 3:9.
210. Deuteronomy 11:26-27; Deuteronomy 28:1-14; Deuteronomy 30; Psalm 19:11.
211. 2 Corinthians 1:20.
212. Psalm 19:7-11.
213. Ephesians 1:3.
214. 1 John 3:4.
215. Romans 6:1-2; Romans 6:15.
216. 2 Thessalonians 2:3-9.
217. Psalm 103:17.
218. Psalm 103:18.
219. Hebrews 8:13.
220. Isaiah 56:1-8.
221. Psalm 119:129.
222. Psalm 119:153.
223. Psalm 119:155.
224. Psalm 119:156.
225. Psalm 119:160.
226. Psalm 119:144.
227. Romans 2:20.
228. Psalm 89:30-31.
229. Jeremiah 33:19-21.
230. Hebrews 7:12.
231. Matthew 5:17.
232. Colossians 2:17.

233. See http://www.templeinstitute.org or http://www.templemountfaithful.org for more information on efforts to build the third Jewish temple. Also, see footnote 290 (below) for reasons to support its construction.

234. Ezekiel 40:46.

235. Zechariah 14:21.

236. Revelation 20:1-6.

237. Hebrews 9:11-14; Hebrews 9:28.

238. John 3:16.

239. John 15:9-17.

240. Matthew 5:18; Revelation 21:1.

241. New physical laws will also presumably be in place, given the gravitationally crushing impact that would result from present physical laws applied to the structural support materials of the New Jerusalem (Revelation 21:15-21). Credit to Hugh Ross for this insightful observation.

242. Hebrews 12:22; Revelation 21:2.

243. John 14:2.

244. Revelation 21:22.

245. Hebrews 8:5; Hebrews 9:24.

246. Revelation 21:3.

247. Matthew 5:18. Also, see Hebrews 8:13, which points to this time of disappearance or passing away.

248. Romans 2:26-27.

249. Genesis 17:12; Leviticus 12:3.

250. Genesis 17:23-27.

251. Genesis 17:12.

252. Genesis 15:6.

253. Romans 4:11.

254. Romans 2:26-27.

255. Romans 2:29; Colossians 2:11-12.

256. Acts 16:3.

257. Exodus 12:48.

258. 1 Peter 1:15.

259. Leviticus 11:44-45.

260. Leviticus 11:1-47.

261. Acts 10:9ff.

262. Acts 10:34-35.

263. Acts 10:45-46.

264. 1 Peter 2:2.

265. Romans 7:12-14.

266. 1 Peter 2:2.

267. 1 Timothy 4:1-5.

268. Revelation 12:17.

269. Acts 15:19.

270. Acts 15:20; Acts 21:25.

271. Acts 13:5; Acts 15:21.

272. Acts 2:46; Acts 5:12.

273. John 9:22; John 16:2; Acts 2:46; Acts 20:8.

274. Acts 15:5-6.

275. Hebrews 10:15-16.

276. Hegg, Timothy (2008). *The Letter Writer: Paul's Background and Torah Perspective.* Tacoma, WA: TorahResource. Hegg, Timothy (2006). *It Is Often Said: Comments and Comparisons of Traditional Christian Theology and Hebraic Thought.* Littleton, CO: First Fruits of Zion, vol. 1-4.

277. McKee, J.K. (2006). *Torah in the Balance Volume 1: The Validity of the Torah and Its Practical Life Applications.* Kissimmee, FL: TNN Press. McKee, J.K. (2008). *The New Testament Validates Torah: Does the New Testament Really Do Away with the Law?* Kissimmee, FL: TNN Press.

278. Friedman, David (2001). *They Loved the Torah: What Yeshua's First Followers Really Thought About the Law.* Clarksville, MD: Lederer Books.

279. Lancaster, D. Thomas (2006). *Restoration: Returning the Torah of God to the Disciples of Jesus.* Littleton, CO: First Fruits of Zion, 1st edition.

280. Booker, Bruce R. (2009). *Torah: Our Expression of Love to the Lord.* Scotts Valley, CA: CreateSpace. Booker, Bruce R. (2009). *The Problem with Paul: Why the Epistles of the Apostle Paul Cannot be Used to Justify the Non-Observance of the Torah.* Scotts Valley, CA: CreateSpace.

281. Eby, Aaron (2009). *Boundary Stones: Divine Parameters for Faith and Life.* Littleton, CO: First Fruits of Zion, 2nd edition.

282. See the online book published in 2001 by Robinson, Tony, "The Restoration of Torah", URL = http://www.restorationoftorah.org/TheRestorationOfTorah.pdf

283. It has been claimed that 202 of the 613 laws are temple-dependent. See http://www.templeinstitute.org

284. Hebrews 8:12; 1 John 1:8-10.

285. Matthew 11:28-30; Romans 1:5.

286. Matthew 12:9-13; Luke 13:15; Luke 14:5; John 5:8-11; John 7:23.

287. Exodus 20:13; Leviticus 11:44-45; Leviticus 19:18; Deuteronomy 30:19-20; Micah 6:8.

288. Philippians 2:12.

289. Romans 1:5.

290. On reasons for supporting construction of a third temple in Jerusalem, see Decker, David N. (2004). *"Revival from Zion!" 50 Reasons Why Christians Should Support The Building of the 3rd Jewish Temple.* Jerusalem: M.A.D.P.-Tarshish Ltd.

291. 2 Thessalonians 2:4.

292. Ezekiel 40-44.

293. Isaiah 2:3; Micah 4:2.

294. McKee, J.K. (2008). *A Survey of the Tanach for the Practical Messianic.* Kissimmee, FL: TNN Press. McKee, J.K. (2006). *A Survey of the Apostolic Scriptures for the Practical Messianic.* McKee, J.K. (2007). *Galatians for the Practical Messianic.* Kissimmee, FL: TNN Press. McKee, J.K. (2008). *Ephesians for the Practical Messianic.* Kissimmee, FL: TNN Press. McKee, J.K. (2007). *Philippians for the Practical Messianic.* Kissimmee, FL: TNN Press. McKee, J.K. (2006). *Hebrews for the Practical Messianic.* Kissimmee, FL: TNN Press. McKee, J.K. (2005). *James for the Practical Messianic.* Kissimmee, FL: TNN Press. Also, see http://www.tnnonline.net for more information online.

295. Hegg, Tim (2000). *Interpreting the Bible: An Introduction to Hermeneutics.* Tacoma, WA: TorahResource. Also, see http://www.torahresource.com for more information online.

296. Strickland, Wayne G. (1996). *Five Views on Law and Gospel.* Grand Rapids, MI: Zondervan. Although none of the contributing authors in this volume fully represents my point of view, this book does help to expose the wide disagreement amongst Evangelicals regarding the extent to which Torah observance is applicable to New Covenant participants. I submit that the Torah-observant position I have set forth best accounts for the available Biblical data, so far as I can tell.

297. Brown, Michael L. (2000). *Answering Jewish Objections to Jesus: General and Historical Objections.* Grand Rapids, MI: Baker. Brown, Michael L. (2000). *Answering Jewish Objections to Jesus: Theological Objections.* Grand Rapids, MI: Baker. Brown, Michael L. (2003). *Answering Jewish Objections to Jesus: Messianic Prophecy Objections.* Grand Rapids, MI: Baker. Brown, Michael L. (2007a). *Answering Jewish Objections to Jesus: New Testament Objections.* Grand Rapids, MI: Baker.

298. Brown, Michael L. (2007b). *What Do Jewish People Think About Jesus? And Other Questions Christians Ask About Jewish Beliefs, Practices, and History.* Grand Rapids, MI: Chosen Books.

299. Ibid., p. 237:13-17.

300. Ephesians 2:12.

301. Brown (2007b), p. 235.

302. Ephesians 2:12.

303. See Genesis 12; Genesis 15; Genesis 17; Deuteronomy 31:9-13; Jeremiah 31:31-37; Jeremiah 33:14-26.

304. Brown (2007b), p. 188:23-29.

305. Ibid., p. 235.

306. Ibid., p. 208:5-6.

307. Galatians 3:29.

308. Brown (2007b), p. 235:22-26.

309. Ibid.

310. Hebrews 3:6.

311. Amos 3:1-2.

312. Romans 11:17.

313. Brown (2007b), p. 237:13-17; p. 238:3-6.

314. Ibid., p. 237:21-24.

315. Ibid., p. 236:17-21.

316. Ibid., p. 255:25-28.

317. Ibid., p. 238:31-239:2.

318. Ibid., p. 239:2-5.

319. Ibid., p. 239:2-5; p. 268:30-31.

320. Ibid., p. 240:1-7.

321. Ibid., p. 240:15-17.

322. Ephesians 2:12.

323. Brown (2007b), p. 189:22-24.

324. Ibid., p. 190:1-3.

325. Ibid., p. 220:11-20.

326. Ibid., p. 206:13-14.

327. Ibid., p. 204:8-10; p. 205:8-11.

328. Matthew 5:17; Luke 16:17.

329. Matthew 5:18.

330. Jeremiah 31:31-34; Hebrews 8:10; Hebrews 10:16.

331. Luke 6:40; 1 John 2:6.
332. Brown (2007b), p. 205:19-30.
333. Isaiah 2:3; Micah 4:2.
334. Ezekiel 40-44; Zechariah 14:21.
335. Hebrews 8:13.
336. Brown (2007b), p. 209:16-19.
337. Romans 13:1-7.
338. Isaiah 65:20.
339. Psalm 2:9. (Evidently, the Psalms may also be considered part of the Torah. See Psalm 82:6; John 10:34.)
340. Isaiah 66:15-16; Revelation 19:15.
341. Brown (2007b), p. 213:3-7.
342. Galatians 3:24.
343. John 3:16-17; Romans 3:20.
344. Matthew 19:16-17; Romans 2:13; James 2:17.
345. Brown (2007b), p. 215:14-18.
346. Ibid., p. 212:32-213:3.
347. 1 Corinthians 11:1; Philippians 4:9. Also, see Acts 26:29.
348. Romans 13:8-10.
349. Acts 24:18.
350. 1 Corinthians 11:1; Philippians 4:9.
351. Ibid.
352. Acts 21:20.
353. Acts 25:8.
354. 1 Corinthians 11:1; Philippians 4:9.
355. 1 Corinthians 5:7-8.
356. Acts 23:5.
357. 1 Corinthians 11:1; Philippians 4:9.
358. 1 Corinthians 9:7-12.
359. 1 Corinthians 11:1; Philippians 4:9.
360. Brown (2007b), p. 216:3-17.
361. Galatians 3:23-25.
362. Romans 2:26.
363. Adult male Gentile convert circumcision is apparently not commanded in the Torah, so far as I can tell.
364. Romans 2:27.
365. Romans 2:13.
366. Brown (2007b), p. 217:10-28.
367. Cf. Hebrews 5:11-12.
368. Brown (2007b), p. 217:31-218:3.
369. Ibid., p. 218:20-33.
370. Matthew 7:23.
371. Romans 14:1.
372. E.g., 1 Corinthians 5:1-2. Cf. Leviticus 18:8.
373. 2 Timothy 3:16-17.
374. Matthew 4:4. Cf. Deuteronomy 8:3.
375. Luke 6:40; 1 Corinthians 11:1; Philippians 4:9; 1 John 2:6.
376. Ephesians 5:1.

377. Colossians 2:16.
378. Matthew 7:23.
379. Romans 10:4.
380. Brown (2007b), p. 106:24-31; p. 219:10-13.
381. Isaiah 24:1-6.
382. Matthew 7:23.
383. Psalm 2:7-12.
384. Revelation 19:15.
385. James 4:7.
386. John 14:15.
387. Luke 6:40; 1 John 2:6.
388. Brown (2007b), p. 218:16-19.
389. Ibid., p. 219:3-13.
390. Ibid., p. 219:3-5.
391. Ibid., p. 219:5-7.
392. Ibid., p. 219:7-9.
393. Isaiah 24:5.
394. E.g., Exodus 14:2.
395. Brown (2007b), p. 219:14-20.
396. Ibid., p. 219:21-33.
397. Ibid., p. 220:11-20.
398. Jeremiah 31:33; Hebrews 8:10; Hebrews 10:16.
399. Hebrews 10:15.
400. Brown (2007b), p. 220:11-20.
401. 2 Timothy 3:16-17.
402. 1 Peter 3:15.
403. Romans 14:1; Romans 14:16.
404. Romans 14:5-6.
405. Brown (2007b), p. 223:1-4.
406. Jeremiah 31:33.
407. Colossians 2:8; Colossians 2:21.
408. Colossians 2:16.
409. Brown (2007b), p. 224:31-225:2.
410. Matthew 5:17-19; Luke 6:40; John 14:15; Romans 2:13; 1 Corinthians 11:1; Philippians 4:9; 2 Timothy 3:16-17; 1 John 2:6; 1 John 5:30.
411. Exodus 20:8-11; Deuteronomy 5:12-15; Nehemiah 13:15-18; Isaiah 56:1-8.
412. Brown (2007b), p. 225:18-20.
413. Ibid., p. 224:20-24.
414. Ibid., p. 221:16-18.
415. Ibid., p. 225:17-18.
416. Ibid., p. 224:24-28.
417. Ibid., p. 226:5-10.
418. Isaiah 66:23.
419. Brown (2007b), p. 222:13-21.
420. E.g., see Leviticus 11 and Deuteronomy 14.
421. Brown (2007b), p. 226:16-20.
422. John 14:15; 1 John 2:6.
423. Psalm 119:97-99.

424. Isaiah 24:5-6.

425. Isaiah 65:4.

426. Mark 7:9.

427. 1 Timothy 4:5.

428. Mark 7:18.

429. Mark 7:20-23.

430. Mark 7:19; Romans 14:14.

431. 1 Corinthians 8:9-13.

432. Brown (2007b), p. 228:7-22.

433. Ibid., p. 227:26-27.

434. Ibid., p. 227:30-32.

435. 2 Timothy 3:16-17.

436. 1 Corinthians 13:2-3.

437. Such an arbitrary approach would clearly be vulnerable to the "Salad Bar Christianity" objection recently raised in Avakian, Bob (2008). *Away With All Gods! Unchaining the Mind and Radically Changing the World.* Chicago: Insight Press, pp. 32-33.

438. Brown (2007b), p. 219:5-7.

439. Romans 14:1.

440. Romans 1:13; James 2:17.

441. 1 Corinthians 11:1; Philippians 4:9.

442. Acts 21:20-24.

443. Acts 24:14; Acts 28:17.

444. Acts 26:29.

445. 1 Corinthians 5:8. Brown's resort to a metaphorical interpretation of this passage (p. 295:14-16) is unnecessary, and it violates the hermeneutical principle that a metaphorical interpretation should be avoided, if a non-metaphorical interpretation is adequate. A literal interpretation is preferred, as it coheres with Paul's Torah-observant example and teaching.

446. Brown (2007b), p. 231:9-11.

447. Galatians 4:8-11; Galatians 5:4.

448. The Third Temple era has not yet begun, and will be terminated by the actions of the anti-Messiah (Daniel 9:27; 2 Thessalonians 2:4).

449. The Fourth Temple era is the Millennial era which will be firmly established after the Messiah physically returns to earth (Ezekiel 43; Zechariah 14; Revelation 20:4-6).

450. Genesis 15:6; Romans 4:3; Hebrews 4:2.

451. Ephesians 2:8-9.

452. James 2:17.

453. Romans 3:20; Galatians 2:21; Ephesians 2:8-10.

454. Deuteronomy 6:25.

455. Psalm 14:3; Psalm 53:3; Ecclesiastes 7:20; Romans 3:9-20.

456. 2 Thessalonians 2:13.

457. Romans 1:5.

458. James 1:25; James 2:8.

459. Leviticus 19:18.

460. 1 Peter 1:19.

461. John 1:29.

462. Galatians 3:10-14.

463. Romans 1:12-16.

464. Romans 3:23.

465. Colossians 2:14.

466. Colossians 2:13.

467. Romans 5:9.

468. John 10:10.

469. Deuteronomy 30:19; John 10:10.

470. Ephesians 5:2.

471. Jeremiah 31:31-34; Hebrews 8-10.

472. Luke 22:20.

473. Jeremiah 31:33; Hebrews 8:10.

474. Romans 12:5; Ephesians 2:19; 1 Timothy 3:15.

475. Romans 2:29.

476. Romans 11:17-21.

477. Ephesians 2:14-22.

478. 1 John 5:12.

479. Romans 11:19.

480. Matthew 23:33; Romans 2:28-29.

481. Jeremiah 31:36.

482. Genesis 17.

483. Genesis 32:28; Genesis 35:23-26; Romans 15:8.

484. See Timothy Hegg's online articles in defense of the Torah being applicable to both Gentile and non-Gentile in the body of Yeshua (http://www.torahresource.com). One noteworthy exception that I have found, however, is that circumcision of adult physical descendants of Abraham (if not already circumcised) may be commanded in the Torah (Genesis 17:14) as a condition of participation in the Abrahamic Covenant, whereas adult Gentile circumcision is evidently not commanded in the Torah, as confirmed, also, by Paul's claim that uncircumcised Gentiles can be Torah-observant despite the fact that they are physically uncircumcised (Romans 2:27). Given the presumably poor quality of genealogical data justifying one's Abrahamic descent (or lack thereof), it is unclear how to implement this apparent genetically-contingent Torah distinction. Pending further research on my part, I am hesitant to advocate a better-safe-than-sorry solution to this issue, although such a solution does not appear to be without merit, provided a mature understanding of the doctrine of salvation-by-faith is clearly understood, thereby precluding any hint of the erroneous suggestion that works of the flesh can in any way secure one's attainment of righteousness or justification.

485. Jeremiah 31:31-34; Hebrews 8:8-12.

486. Romans 11:17.

487. Romans 11:23.

488. Ephesians 3:6.

489. Ephesians 2:12.

490. Ephesians 2:12; Romans 3:26-29.

491. Isaiah 49:6; John 8:12.

492. Deuteronomy 4:5-8.

493. 1 John 3:4.

494. Jude 4.

495. Mark 8:38. I have heard reports that American adultery rates within Biblically-churched populations are comparable to those in American unchurched populations.

Granted, forgiveness is available to the repentant, but I fear that many of those within American churches are utterly unaware of even the need for repentance.

496. Matthew 7:21-23.
497. Luke 12:48.
498. Hebrews 5:11.
499. Luke 12:47-48.
500. Acts 16:30.
501. 1 Peter 1:14.
502. Acts 16:31.
503. James 2:12.
504. Exodus 34:6.
505. Exodus 34:7; Amos 3:1-2; 1 Peter 4:17.
506. 2 Chronicles 7:14.
507. 2 Kings 17:13.
508. Matthew 7:20; Acts 26:20.
509. Revelation 3:16; Matthew 7:19-23.
510. Acts 2:22-42; Acts 21:20.
511. Romans 11:17.
512. Isaiah 49:6; John 4:22; Romans 3:1-2; Romans 9:3-5.
513. Genesis 15:18; Deuteronomy 1:7-8; Deuteronomy 11:22-32; Joshua 1:1-18; Joshua 23:9-13; Psalm 37:11; Ezekiel 47:13-48:29; Matthew 5:5; Romans 15:8.
514. Deuteronomy 7:13.
515. Micah 7:20.
516. Zechariah 2:12.
517. Isaiah 2:3; Micah 4:2.
518. Revelation 20:4-6.
519. Ezekiel 43:7; Zechariah 14:4-9.
520. Eze. 37:24-28.
521. Jeremiah 3:18; Ezekiel 37:15-23; Revelation 7:4-8; Revelation 14:3-4.
522. Acts 3:21.
523. Romans 11:26.
524. Ezekiel 11:17-20; Matthew 23:39; Romans 11:25.
525. Isaiah 11:12-16; Ezekiel 37:15-23; Zechariah 10:7-10.
526. Matthew 28:19-20.
527. Matthew 23:39; Matthew 24:14.
528. Ezekiel 43:4-7; Zechariah 14:3-4.
529. Ezekiel 37:12-14; Daniel 12:2; Zechariah 14:5; Romans 11:15; 1 Thessalonians 4:14-18; Revelation 20:4-6.
530. Isaiah 24:1-6; Isaiah 66:15-16; Zechariah 14:12-15; Revelation 19:15.
531. Matthew 19:28; 1 Corinthians 6:2; Revelation 19:13-16; Revelation 20:4.
532. Isaiah 24:23; Zechariah 14:9.
533. Revelation 20:6.
534. Isaiah 66:24; Mark 9:47-48; Revelation 20:15.
535. Isaiah 66:24; Revelation 20:8.
536. Isaiah 66:24; Revelation 22:2.
537. Isaiah 66:22; Revelation 21:1.
538. Acts 26:1-29; Acts 28:23-31; 2 Corinthians 5:11; Titus 1:9; 1 Peter 3:15; Jude 1:3.

539. 2 Corinthians 5:10.
540. Matthew 12:36-37.
541. 1 Corinthians 3:13-15.
542. E.g., Matthew 5:28.
543. John 3:18.
544. Romans 2:16; Ecclesiastes 12:14.
545. Hebrews 4:12-13.
546. Romans 2:5-11.
547. Galatians 6:10.
548. Matthew 5:16.

BIBLIOGRAPHY

BOOKS ARGUING FOR ATHEISM

Angeles, Peter A. (1986). *The Problem of God: A Short Introduction*. Buffalo, NY: Prometheus Books.

Angeles, Peter A. (1997). *Critiques of God: Making the Case Against Belief in God*. Amherst, NY: Prometheus Books.

Avakian, Bob (2008). *Away With All Gods! Unchaining the Mind and Radically Changing the World*. Chicago: Insight Press

Baggini, Julian (2003). *Atheism: A Very Short Introduction*. Oxford: Oxford University Press.

Barker, Dan (1992). *Losing Faith in Faith: From Preacher to Atheist*. Madison, WI: Freedom From Religion Foundation.

Barker, Dan (2008). *Godless: How an Evangelical Preacher Became One of America's Leading Atheists*. Berkeley, CA: Ulysses Press.

Blackford, Russell and Schueklenk, Udo, eds. (2009). *50 Voices of Disbelief: Why We Are Atheists*. Malden, MA: Wiley-Blackwell.

Carrier, Richard (2005). *Sense and Goodness Without God: A Defense of Metaphysical Naturalism*. Bloomington, IN: AuthorHouse.

Cave, Peter (2009). *Humanism: A Beginner's Guide*. Oxford: Oneworld Publications.

Comte-Sponville, Andre (2007). *The Little Book of Atheist Spirituality*. New York: Penguin Books.

Dawkins, Richard (2006). *The God Delusion*. Boston: Houghton Mifflin Company.

Drange, Theodore (1998). Nonbelief *& Evil: Two Arguments for the Nonexistence of God*. Amherst, NY: Prometheus Books.

Edis, Taner (2002). *The Ghost in the Universe: God in Light of Modern Science*. Amherst, NY: Prometheus Books.

Eller, David (2004). *Natural Atheism*. Cranford, NJ: American Atheist Press.

Everitt, Nicholas (2004). *The Non-existence of God*. New York: Routledge.

Flew, Antony (2005). *God and Philosophy*. Amherst, NY: Prometheus Books.

Gale, Richard (1993). *On the Nature and Existence of God*. Cambridge: Cambridge University Press.

Johnson, B. C. (1983). *Atheist Debater's Handbook*. Amherst, NY: Prometheus Books.

Joshi, S. T. (2003). *God's Defenders: What They Believe and Why They Are Wrong*. Amherst, NY: Prometheus Books.

Krueger, Douglas (1998). *What is Atheism?* Amherst, NY: Prometheus Books.

Le Poidevin, Robin (1996). *Arguing for Atheism: An Introduction to the Philosophy of Religion*. New York: Routledge.

Loftus, John W. (2008). *Why I Became an Atheist: A Former Preacher Rejects Christianity*. Amherst, NY: Prometheus Books.

Loftus, John W. (2008). *Why I Became an Atheist: Personal Reflections and Additional Arguments*. Victoria, BC: Trafford Publishing.

Mackie, J. L. (1982). *The Miracle of Theism: Arguments For and Against the Existence of God.* Oxford: Oxford University Press.

Martin, Michael (1990). *Atheism: A Philosophical Justification.* Philadelphia: Temple University Press.

Martin, Michael and Monnier, Ricki, eds. (2003). *The Impossibility of God.* Amherst, NY: Prometheus Books.

Martin, Michael and Monnier, Ricki, eds. (2006). *The Improbability of God.* Amherst, NY: Prometheus Books.

Martin, Michael, ed. (2007). *The Cambridge Companion to Atheism.* Cambridge: Cambridge University Press.

Matson, Wallace (1965). *The Existence of God.* Ithaca, NY: Cornell University Press.

Mills, David (2006). *Atheist Universe.* Berkeley, CA: Ulysses Press.

Narciso, Dianna (2005). *Like Rolling Uphill: Realizing the Honesty of Atheism.* Coral Springs, FL: Llumina Press.

Nielsen, Kai (2001). *Naturalism and Religion.* Amherst, NY: Prometheus Books.

Nielsen, Kai (2005). *Atheism and Philosophy.* Amherst, NY: Prometheus Books.

O'Hair, Madalyn Murray, 2nd rev. ed. (1991). *Why I Am An Atheist.* Austin, TX: American Atheist Press.

Oppy, Graham (2006). *Arguing About Gods.* Cambridge: Cambridge University Press.

Paulos, John Allen (2008). *Irreligion: A Mathematician Explains Why the Arguments for God Just Don't Add Up.* New York, NY: Hill and Wang.

Pigliucci, Massimo (2000). *Tales of the Rational: Skeptical Essays About Nature and Science.* Smyrna, GA: Freethought Press.

Schellenberg, J. L. (2006). *Divine Hiddenness and Human Reason.* Ithaca, NY: Cornell University Press.

Schellenberg, J. L. (2007). *Wisdom to Doubt.* Ithaca, NY: Cornell University Press.

Scriven, Michael (1966). *Primary Philosophy.* New York: McGraw-Hill Book Company.

Shermer, Michael (2003). *How We Believe: Science, Skepticism, and the Search for God.* New York: Owl Books.

Smith, George (1989). *Atheism: The Case Against God.* Buffalo, NY: Prometheus Books.

Sobel, Jordan Howard (2003). *Logic and Theism: Arguments For and Against Beliefs in God.* Cambridge: Cambridge University Press.

Steele, David Ramsay (2008). *Atheism Explained: From Folly to Philosophy.* Chicago, IL: Open Court.

Stenger, Victor (2003). *Has Science Found God? The Latest Results in the Search for Purpose in the Universe.* Amherst, NY: Prometheus Books.

Stenger, Victor (2007). *God: The Failed Hypothesis: How Science Shows That God Does Not Exist.* Amherst, NY: Prometheus Books.

Stenger, Victor (2009). *The New Atheism: Taking a Stand for Science and Reason.* Amherst, NY: Prometheus Books.

Tremblay, Francois (2003). *Handbook of Atheistic Apologetics.* Morrisville, NC: Lulu Press.

Tremblay, Francois (2004). *Short Handbook of Atheistic Apologetics.* Morrisville, NC: Lulu Press.

Weisberger, A. M. (1999). Suffering Belief: Evil and the Anglo-American Defense of Theism. New York: Peter Lang.

White, Hugh (2002). *What's Real? God is not: A Realistic View on Belief in Gods and Religions.* Bloomington, IN: 1stBooks Library.

Young, Matt (2001). *No Sense of Obligation: Science and Religion in an Impersonal Universe.* Bloomington, IN: 1stBooks Library.

OTHER WORKS CITED OR RECOMMENDED

Abanes, Richard (2003). *One Nation Under Gods: A History of the Mormon Church.* New York: Basic Books.

Abanes, Richard (2004). *Becoming Gods.* Eugene, OR: Harvest House.

Abdul-Haqq, Abdiyah Akbar (1980). *Sharing Your Faith with a Muslim.* Minneapolis, MN: Bethany House.

Alston, William P. (1993). *Perceiving God: The Epistemology of Religious Experience.* Ithaca, NY: Cornell University Press.

Ankerberg, John (1989). *The Case for Jesus the Messiah.* Eugene, OR: Harvest House.

Ankerberg, John and Weldon, John (1992). *Everything You Ever Wanted to Know About Mormonism.* Eugene, OR: Harvest House.

Ankerberg, John and Weldon, John (2003). *Fast Facts on Jehovah's Witnesses.* Eugene, OR: Harvest House.

Babinski, Edward T. (1995). *Leaving the Fold: Testimonies of Former Fundamentalists.* Amherst, NY: Prometheus Books.

Barker, Dan (2008). *Godless: How an Evangelical Preacher Became One of America's Leading Atheists.* Berkeley, CA: Ulysses Press.

Beckwith, Francis J., Mosser, Carl, and Owen, Paul eds. (2002). *The New Mormon Challenge: Responding to the Latest Defenses of a Fast-Growing Movement.* Grand Rapids, MI: Zondervan.

Behe, Michael J. (1996). *Darwin's Black Box: The Biochemical Challenge to Evolution.* New York, NY: Free Press.

Behe, Michael J. (2007). *The Edge of Evolution: The Search for the Limits of Darwinism.* New York: Free Press.

Berry, Harold J. (1992). *The Truth Twisters: What They Believe.* Lincoln, NE: Back to the Bible.

Black, David Alan (1994). *New Testament Textual Criticism: A Concise Guide.* Grand Rapids, MI: Baker.

Black, David Alan, ed. (2002). *Rethinking New Testament Textual Criticism.* Grand Rapids, MI: Baker.

Blanchard, John (1995). *Whatever Happened to Hell?* Wheaton, IL: Crossway Books.

Blomberg, Craig L. (1997). *Jesus and the Gospels: An Introduction and Survey.* Nashville, TN: Broadman and Holman.

Blomberg, Craig L. (2007). *The Historical Reliability of the Gospels.* Downers Grove, IL: InterVarsity Press.

Bock, Darrell L. (2002). *Studying the Historical Jesus: A Guide to Sources and Methods.* Grand Rapids, MI: Baker.

Bock, Darrell L. (2002). *Jesus According to Scripture: Restoring the Portrait from the Gospels.* Grand Rapids, MI: Baker.

Bock, Darrell L. (2006). *The Missing Gospels: Unearthing the Truth Behind Alternative Christianities.* Nashville, TN: Thomas Nelson.

Bock, Darrell L. and Wallace, Daniel B. (2007). *Dethroning Jesus: Exposing Popular Culture's Quest to Unseat the Biblical Christ*. Nashville, TN: Thomas Nelson.

Booker, Bruce R. (2009). *Torah: Our Expression of Love to the Lord*. Scotts Valley, CA: CreateSpace.

Booker, Bruce R. (2009). *The Problem with Paul: Why the Epistles of the Apostle Paul Cannot be used to Justify the Non-Observance of the Torah*. Scotts Valley, CA: CreateSpace.

Bowman, Robert M. (1995). *Jehovah's Witnesses*. Grand Rapids, MI: Zondervan.

Brotzman, Ellis R. (1994). *Old Testament Textual Criticism: A Practical Introduction*. Grand Rapids, MI: Baker.

Brown, Michael L. (2000). *Answering Jewish Objections to Jesus: General and Historical Objections*. Grand Rapids, MI: Baker.

Brown, Michael L. (2000). *Answering Jewish Objections to Jesus: Theological Objections*. Grand Rapids, MI: Baker.

Brown, Michael L. (2003). *Answering Jewish Objections to Jesus: Messianic Prophecy Objections*. Grand Rapids, MI: Baker.

Brown, Michael L. (2007). *Answering Jewish Objections to Jesus: New Testament Objections*. Grand Rapids, MI: Baker.

Brown, Michael L. (2007). *What Do Jewish People Think About Jesus? And Other Questions Christians Ask About Jewish Beliefs, Practices, and History*. Grand Rapids, MI: Chosen Books.

Bruce, F. F. (1981). *The New Testament Documents: Are They Reliable?* Grand Rapids, MI: Eerdmans.

Bunge, Mario (2009). *Causality and Modern Science*. New Brunswick, NJ: Transaction Publishers.

Campbell, William F. (1992). *The Quran and the Bible in the Light of History and Science*. Published by Middle East Resources.

Carrier, Richard (2009). *Not the Impossible Faith: Why Christianity Didn't Need a Miracle to Succeed*. Morrisville, NC: Lulu Press.

Carson, D.A. and Moo, Douglas J. (2005). *An Introduction to the New Testament*. Grand Rapids, MI: Zondervan.

Collins, Francis S. (2007). *The Language of God: A Scientist Presents Evidence for Belief*. New York: Free Press.

Collins, John C. (2003). *Science and Faith: Friends or Foes?* Wheaton, IL: Crossway Books.

Comfort, Philip (2005). *Encountering the Manuscripts: An Introduction to New Testament Paleography & Textual Criticism*. Nashville, TN: Broadman & Holman.

Comfort, Ray and Cameron, Kirk (2006). *The Way of the Master*. Orlando, FL: Bridge-Logos.

Craig, William Lane (2008). *Reasonable Faith: Christian Truth and Apologetics*, 3rd ed. Wheaton, IL: Crossway Books.

Craig, William Lane (2001). *Time and Eternity: Exploring God's Relationship to Time*. Wheaton, IL: Crossway Books.

Craig, William Lane and Sinnott-Armstrong, Walter (2004). *God? A Debate Between a Christian and an Atheist*. Oxford: Oxford University Press.

Dauer, Francis Watanabe (1996). *Critical Thinking: An Introduction to Reasoning*. New York: Barnes & Noble.

Davis, Mike (2008). *The Atheist's Introduction to the New Testament: How the Bible Undermines the Basic Teachings of Christianity*. Denver, CO: Outskirts Press.

Dawkins, Richard (2009). *The Greatest Show on Earth: The Evidence for Evolution.* New York: Free Press.

Decker, David N. (2004). *"Revival from Zion!" 50 Reasons Why Christians Should Support The Building of the 3rd Jewish Temple.* Jerusalem: M.A.D.P.-Tarshish Ltd.

Dembski, William A. (1998). *The Design Inference: Eliminating Chance Through Small Probabilities.* Cambridge: Cambridge University Press.

Dembski, William A. (2002). *No Free Lunch: Why Specified Complexity Cannot Be Purchased without Intelligence.* Lanham, MD: Rowman & Littlefield.

Dembski, William A. and McDowell, Sean (2008). *Understanding Intelligent Design: Everything You Need to Know in Plain Language.* Eugene, OR: Harvest House.

Dockery, David S., Mathews, Kenneth A., and Sloan, Robert B. eds. (1994). *Foundations for Biblical Interpretation.* Nashville, TN: Broadman & Holman Publishers.

D'Souza, Dinesh (2007). *What's So Great About Christianity.* Washington, DC: Regnery Publishing.

Eby, Aaron (2009). *Boundary Stones: Divine Parameters for Faith and Life.* Littleton, CO: First Fruits of Zion, 2nd edition.

Eddy, Paul Rhodes and Boyd, Gregory A. (2007). *The Jesus Legend: A Case for the Historical Reliability of the Synoptic Jesus Tradition.* Grand Rapids, MI: Baker.

Edis, Taner (2008). *Science and Nonbelief.* Amherst, NY: Prometheus Books.

Ehrman, Bart D. (2008). *God's Problem: How the Bible Fails to Answer Our Most Important Question—Why We Suffer.* New York, NY: HarperCollins Publishers.

Elwell, Walter A., ed. (1989). *Evangelical Commentary on the Bible.* Grand Rapids, MI: Baker.

Evans, Craig A. (2006). *Fabricating Jesus: How Modern Scholars Distort the Gospels.* Downers Grove, IL: InterVarsity Press.

Fogelin, Robert J., ed. (1980). *Logic: Techniques of Formal Reasoning.* Fort Worth, TX: Harcourt Brace Jovanovich.

France, R.T. (1986). *The Evidence for Jesus.* Downers Grove, IL: InterVarsity Press.

Friedman, David (2001). *They Loved the Torah: What Yeshua's First Followers Really Thought About the Law.* Clarksville, MD: Lederer Books.

Futuyma, Douglas J. (1995). *Science on Trial: The Case for Evolution.* Sunderland, MA: Sinauer Associates, Inc.

Geisler, Norman L., ed. (1980). *Inerrancy.* Grand Rapids, MI: Zondervan.

Geisler, Norman L. and MacKenzie, Ralph E. (1995). *Roman Catholics and Evangelicals: Agreements and Differences.* Grand Rapids, MI: Baker.

Geisler, Norman L., ed. (1998). *The Counterfeit Gospel of Mormonism.* Eugene, OR: Harvest House.

Geisler, Norman L. and Hoffman, Paul K. (2001). *Why I Am A Christian.* Grand Rapids, MI: Baker.

Geisler, Norman L. and Saleeb, Abdul (2002). *Answering Islam: The Crescent in Light of the Cross.* Grand Rapids, MI: Baker.

Geivett, R. Douglas and Habermas, Gary R. (1997). *In Defense of Miracles: A Comprehensive Case for God's Action in History.* Downers Grove, IL: InterVarsity Press.

Griffel, Frank (2009). *Al-Ghazali's Philosophical Theology.* Oxford: Oxford University Press.

Grudem, Wayne (1994). *Systematic Theology: An Introduction to Biblical Doctrine.* Grand Rapids, MI: Zondervan.

Gruss, Edmond (1976). *Apostles of Denial.* Grand Rapids, MI: Baker.

Habermas, Gary R. (1996). *The Historical Jesus: Ancient Evidence for the Life of Christ.* Joplin, MO: College Press.

Habermas, Gary R. and Licona, Michael R. (2004). *The Case for the Resurrection of Jesus.* Grand Rapids, MI: Kregel.

Habermas, Gary R. and Moreland, J.P. (2004). *Beyond Death: Exploring the Evidence for Immortality.* Eugene, OR: Wipf & Stock Publishers.

Hackett, Stuart C. (1984). *Reconstruction of the Christian Revelation Claim: A Philosophical and Critical Apologetic.* Grand Rapids, MI: Baker.

Hagopian, David G., ed. (2000). *The Genesis Debate: Three Views on the Days of Creation.* McLean, VA: Global Publishing Services.

Halpern, Joseph Y. (2003). *Reasoning About Uncertainty.* Cambridge, MA: MIT Press.

Halverson, Dean C. (1996). *The Compact Guide to World Religions.* Minneapolis, MN: Bethany House.

Hansen, Carol (1999). *Reorganized Latter Day Saint Church: Is It Christian?* Independence, MO: Life Line Ministries.

Hegg, Timothy (2000). *Interpreting the Bible: An Introduction to Hermeneutics.* Tacoma, WA: TorahResource.

Hegg, Timothy (2006). *It Is Often Said: Comments and Comparisons of Traditional Christian Theology and Hebraic Thought.* Littleton, CO: First Fruits of Zion, vol. 1-4.

Hegg, Timothy (2008). *The Letter Writer: Paul's Background and Torah Perspective.* Tacoma, WA: TorahResource.

Holman, Joe E. (2008). *Project Bible Truth: A Minister Turns Atheist and Tells All.* Morrisville, NC: Lulu Press.

Huey, William and McKee, J.K. (2009). *Hebraic Roots: An Introductory Study.* Kissimmee, FL: TNN Press.

Hutchinson, Janis (1995). *The Mormon Missionaries.* Grand Rapids, MI: Kregel.

Isaak, Mark (2007). *The Counter-Creationism Handbook.* Berkeley, CA: University of California Press.

Jeffrey, Richard C. (1983). *The Logic of Decision.* Chicago: University of Chicago Press.

Johnson, Luke Timothy (1996). *The Real Jesus: The Misguided Quest for the Historical Jesus and the Truth of the Traditional Gospels.* New York, NY: HarperCollins.

Kac, Arthur (1986). *The Messiahship of Jesus: Are Jews Changing Their Attitude Toward Jesus?* Grand Rapids, MI: Baker.

Kafatos, Minas C. and Henry, Richard B. C., eds. (1985). *The Crab Nebula and Related Supernova Remnants.* Cambridge: Cambridge University Press.

Kaiser, Walter C. (1995). *The Messiah in the Old Testament.* Grand Rapids, MI: Zondervan.

Kaiser, Walter C., Davids, Peter H., Bruce, F. F., and Brauch, Manfred T. (1996). *Hard Sayings of the Bible.* Downers Grove, IL: InterVarsity Press.

Kaiser, Walter C. (2001). *The Old Testament Documents: Are They Reliable and Relevant?* Downers Grove, IL: InterVarsity Press.

Koch, Kurt (1969). *Occult Practices and Beliefs.* Grand Rapids, MI: Kregel Publications.

Koch, Kurt (1972). *Occult Bondage and Deliverance.* Grand Rapids, MI: Kregel Publications.

Koenig, William R. (2004). *Eye to Eye: Facing the Consequences of Dividing Israel.* Alexandria, VA: About Him.

Komoszewski, J. Ed, and Sawyer, M. James, and Wallace, Daniel B. (2006). *Reinventing Jesus: How Contemporary Skeptics Miss the Real Jesus and Mislead Popular Culture.* Grand Rapids, MI: Kregel Publications.

Kyburg, Henry E., and Teng, Choh Man (2001). *Uncertain Inference.* Cambridge: Cambridge University Press.

Lancaster, D. Thomas (2006). *Restoration: Returning the Torah of God to the Disciples of Jesus.* Littleton, CO: First Fruits of Zion.

Lingle, Wilbur (2004). *Approaching Jehovah's Witnesses in Love: How to Witness Effectively Without Arguing.* Fort Washington, PA: CLC Publications.

Lockyer, Herbert (1991). *All the Teachings of Jesus.* Peabody, MA: Hendrickson.

Loftus, John W. (2006). *Why I Rejected Christianity: A Former Apologist Explains.* Victoria, BC: Trafford Publishing.

Long, Jason (2005). *Biblical Nonsense: A Review of the Bible for Doubting Christians.* New York: iUniverse.

Longman III, Tremper, and Dillard, Raymond B. (2006). *An Introduction to the Old Testament.* Grand Rapids, MI: Zondervan.

Love, Charles (2005). *20 Questions Jehovah's Witnesses Cannot Answer.* Longwood, FL: Xulon Press.

McDowell, Josh and Gilchrist, John (1983). *The Islam Debate.* San Bernardino, CA: Here's Life.

McDowell, Josh and Stewart, Don (1983). *Handbook of Today's Religions.* Nashville, TN: Thomas Nelson.

McElveen, Floyd (1997). *The Mormon Illusion.* Grand Rapids, MI: Kregel.

McGrath, P. J. (1987). *Atheism or Agnosticism.* Analysis, v. 47, pp. 54-57.

McKee, J.K. (2005). *James for the Practical Messianic.* Kissimmee, FL: TNN Press.

McKee, J.K. (2006). *A Survey of the Apostolic Scriptures for the Practical Messianic.* Kissimmee, FL: TNN Press.

McKee, J.K. (2006). *Torah in the Balance Volume 1: The Validity of the Torah and Its Practical Life Applications.* Kissimmee, FL: TNN Press.

McKee, J.K. (2006). *Hebrews for the Practical Messianic.* Kissimmee, FL: TNN Press.

McKee, J.K. (2007). *Galatians for the Practical Messianic.* Kissimmee, FL: TNN Press.

McKee, J.K. (2007). *Philippians for the Practical Messianic.* Kissimmee, FL: TNN Press.

McKee, J.K. (2008). *The New Testament Validates Torah: Does the New Testament Really Do Away with the Law?* Kissimmee, FL: TNN Press.

McKee, J.K. (2008). *A Survey of the Tanach for the Practical Messianic.* Kissimmee, FL: TNN Press.

McKee, J.K. (2008). *Ephesians for the Practical Messianic.* Kissimmee, FL: TNN Press.

McKee, J.K. (2009). *Introduction to Things Messianic.* Kissimmee, FL: TNN Press.

McKeever, Bill (1991). *Answering Mormons' Questions.* Minneapolis, MN: Bethany House

McKeever, Bill and Johnson, Eric (2000). *Mormonism 101: Examining the Religion of the Latter-day Saints.* Grand Rapids, MI: Baker.

McKinsey, C. Dennis (1995). *Encyclopedia of Biblical Errancy.* Amherst, NY: Prometheus Books.

McTernan, John P (2006). *As America Has Done to Israel.* Longwood, FL: Xulon Press.

Menuge, Angus (2004). *Agents Under Fire: Materialism and the Rationality of Science.* Lanham, MD: Rowman & Littlefield.

Montgomery, John Warwick (1986). *History and Christianity.* Minneapolis, MN: Bethany House.

Moreland, J. P. (1997). *Love Your God With All Your Mind: The Role of Reason in the Life of the Soul.* Colorado Springs, CO: Navpress.

Moreland, J. P. and Rae, Scott B. (2000). *Body & Soul: Human Nature & the Crisis in Ethics.* Downers Grove, IL: InterVarsity Press.

Moreland, J. P. and Craig, William Lane (2003). *Philosophical Foundations for a Christian Worldview.* Downers Grove, IL: InterVarsity Press.

Morey, Robert A. (1980). *How to Answer a Jehovah's Witness.* Minneapolis, MN: Bethany House.

Morley, Donna (2003). *A Christian Woman's Guide to Understanding Mormonism.* Eugene, OR: Harvest House.

Moss, Claude Beaufort (2005). *The Christian Faith: An Introduction to Dogmatic Theology.* Eugene, OR: Wipf & Stock Publishers.

Murphy, Ed (2003). *The Handbook For Spiritual Warfare.* Nashville, TN: Thomas Nelson Publishers.

Murray, Michael J., ed. (1999). *Reason for the Hope Within.* Grand Rapids, MI: Eerdmans Publishing Company.

Osborne, Grant R. (1991). *The Hermeneutical Spiral: A Comprehensive Introduction to Biblical Interpretation.* Downers Grove, IL: InterVarsity Press.

Packer, J. I. (1993). *Knowing God.* Downers Grove, IL: InterVarsity Press.

Parshall, Phil (1983). *Bridges to Islam.* Grand Rapids, MI: Baker.

Parshall, Phil (1985). *Beyond the Mosque.* Grand Rapids, MI: Baker.

Payne, J. Barton (1980). *Encyclopedia of Biblical Prophecy.* Grand Rapids, MI: Baker.

Pentecost, J. Dwight (1981). *The Words and Works of Jesus Christ.* Grand Rapids, MI: Zondervan.

Peppers-Bates, Susan (2009). *Nicolas Malebranche: Freedom in an Occasionalist World.* London: Continuum International.

Perakh, Mark (2004). *Unintelligent Design.* Amherst, NY: Prometheus Books.

Perrin, Nicholas (2007). *Lost in Transmission? What We Can Know about the Words of Jesus.* Nashville, TN: Thomas Nelson.

Plantinga, Alvin (1999). *Warranted Christian Belief.* Oxford: Oxford University Press.

Rana, Fazale (2008). *The Cell's Design: How Chemistry Reveals the Creator's Artistry.* Grand Rapids, MI: Baker.

Rawlings, Maurice S. (1993). *To Hell and Back.* Nashville, TN: Thomas Nelson.

Reed, David A. (1986). *Jehovah's Witnesses Answered Verse by Verse.* Grand Rapids, MI: Baker.

Reed, David A., ed. (1990). *Index of Watchtower Errors.* Grand Rapids, MI: Baker.

Reed, David A. and Farkas, John R. (1992). *Mormons Answered Verse by Verse.* Grand Rapids, MI: Baker.

Reed, David A. (1996). *Answering Jehovah's Witnesses Subject by Subject.* Grand Rapids, MI: Baker.

Rhodes, Ron (1993). *Reasoning from the Scriptures with the Jehovah's Witnesses.* Eugene, OR: Harvest House.

Rhodes, Ron (2001). *The 10 Most Important Things You Can Say to a Jehovah's Witness.* Eugene, OR: Harvest House.

Rhodes, Ron (2002). *Reasoning from the Scriptures with Muslims.* Eugene, OR: Harvest House.

Rische, Jill Martin (2008). *The Kingdom of the Occult.* Nashville, TN: Thomas Nelson.

Roberts, R. Philip (1998). *Mormonism Unmasked: Confronting the Contradictions Between Mormon Beliefs and True Christianity.* Nashville, TN: Broadman and Holman.

Ross, Hugh (1994). *Creation and Time.* Colorado Springs, CO: Navpress.

Ross, Hugh (2001). *The Genesis Question: Scientific Advances and the Accuracy of Genesis.* Colorado Springs, CO: Navpress.

Ross, Hugh (2001). *Creator and the Cosmos: How the Greatest Scientific Discoveries of the Century Reveal God.* Colorado Springs, CO: Navpress, 3rd edition.

Ross, Hugh (2004). *Matter of Days: Resolving A Creation Controversy.* Colorado Springs, CO: Navpress.

Ross, Hugh (2004). *Origins of Life: Biblical and Evolutionary Models Face Off.* Colorado Springs, CO: Navpress.

Ross, Hugh (2006). *Creation as Science: A Testable Model Approach to End the Creation/Evolution Wars.* Colorado Springs, CO: Navpress.

Ross, Hugh (2008). *Why The Universe Is The Way It Is.* Grand Rapids, MI: Baker.

Rundle, Bede (2006). *Why There Is Something Rather Than Nothing.* Oxford: Oxford University Press.

Ruse, Michael (2000). *Can a Darwinian be a Christian? The Relationship Between Science and Religion.* Cambridge: Cambridge University Press.

Ruse, Michael (2006). *Darwinism and Its Discontents.* Cambridge: Cambridge University Press.

Russell, Robert John, ed. (1993). *Quantum Cosmology and the Laws of Nature: Scientific Perspectives on Divine Action.* Vatican City State: Vatican Observatory Publications and Berkeley, CA: The Center for Theology and the Natural Sciences.

Salmon, Merrilee H. (1995). *Introduction to Logic and Critical Thinking.* Forth Worth, TX: Harcourt Brace College Publishers.

Scott, Eugenie C. (2004). *Evolution vs. Creationism: An Introduction.* Berkeley, CA: University of California Press.

Shanks, Niall (2006). *God, the Devil, and Darwin: A Critique of Intelligent Design Theory.* Oxford: Oxford University Press.

Shorrosh, Anis A. (1988). *Islam Revealed: A Christian Arab's View of Islam.* Nashville, TN: Thomas Nelson.

Sire, James W. (1980). *Scripture Twisting: 20 Ways the Cults Misread the Bible.* Downers Grove, IL: InterVarsity Press.

Skyrms, Brian (2000). *Choice and Chance: An Introduction to Inductive Logic.* Belmont, CA: Wadsworth/Thomson Learning.

Sloman, Steven (2005). *Causal Models: How People Think About the World and Its Alternatives.* Oxford: Oxford University Press.

Smith, James E. (1993). *What the Bible Teaches about the Promised Messiah.* Nashville, TN: Thomas Nelson.

Snoke, David (2006). *A Biblical Case for an Old Earth.* Grand Rapids, MI: Baker.

Sobel, Jordan Howard (2009). *Modus Ponens and Modus Tollens for Conditional Probabilities, and Updating on Uncertain Evidence.* Theory and Decision, v. 66, pp. 139-141.

Sober, Elliott (2000). *Philosophy of Biology.* Boulder, CO: Westview Press.

Sober, Elliott (2002). *Intelligent Design and Probability Reasoning.* International Journal for Philosophy of Religion, v. 52, pp. 65-80.

Sober, Elliott (2005). *Core Questions in Philosophy: A Text With Readings.* Upper Saddle River, NJ: Pearson Prentice Hall.

Sober, Elliott (2008). *Evidence and Evolution: The Logic Behind the Science.* Cambridge: Cambridge University Press.

Spencer, Robert (2006). *The Truth About Muhammad: Founder of the World's Most Intolerant Religion.* Washington: Regnery.

Stein, Gordon (1990). *God Pro and Con: A Bibliography of Atheism.* New York: Garland Publishing, Inc.

Stein, Robert H. (1994). *The Method and Message of Jesus' Teachings.* Louisville, KY: Westminster John Knox Press.

Stenger, Victor (2006). *The Comprehensible Cosmos: Where Do the Laws of Physics Come From?* Amherst, NY: Prometheus Books.

Stern, David H. (1998). *Complete Jewish Bible.* Clarksville, MD: Jewish New Testament Publications.

Stoner, Don (1992). *A New Look at an Old Earth: What the Creation Institutes Are Not Telling You About Genesis.* Paramount, CA: Schroeder Publishing.

Strickland, Wayne G. (1996). *Five Views on Law and Gospel.* Grand Rapids, MI: Zondervan.

Tanner, Jerald and Sandra (2008). *Mormonism—Shadow or Reality.* Salt Lake City, UT: Utah Lighthouse Ministry.

Tegmark, Max (1998). *Is "the Theory of Everything" Merely the Ultimate Ensemble Theory?* Annals of Physics, v. 270, pp. 1-51.

Tobin, Paul (2009). *The Rejection of Pascal's Wager.* Bedfordshire, England: Authors OnLine.

Tov, Emanuel (1992). *Textual Criticism of the Hebrew Bible.* Minneapolis, MN: Fortress Press.

Trask, Paul (2005). *Part Way To Utah: The Forgotten Mormons.* Independence, MO: Refiner's Fire Ministries.

Unger, Merrill F. (1971). *Demons in the World Today.* Wheaton, IL: Tyndale House.

Unger, Merrill F. (1994). *Biblical Demonology: A Study of Spiritual Forces at Work Today.* Grand Rapids, MI: Kregel Publications.

Wagner, Carl G. (2004). *Modus Tollens Probabilized.* British Journal for the Philosophy of Science, v. 55, pp. 747-753.

Walvoord, John F. (1999). *Every Prophecy of the Bible.* Colorado Springs, CO: Chariot Victor Publishing.

Wegner, Paul D. (2006). *A Student's Guide to Textual Criticism of the Bible: Its History, Methods, & Results.* Downers Grove, IL: InterVarsity Press.

Wells, G.A. (1982). *The Historical Evidence for Jesus.* Buffalo, NY: Prometheus Books.

White, James R. (1993). *Letters to a Mormon Elder.* Minneapolis, MN: Bethany House.

Whorton, Mark S. (2005). *Peril in Paradise: Theology, Science, and the Age of the Earth.* Carlisle, U.K.: Authentic Media.

Wiese, Bill (2006). *23 Minutes in Hell.* Lake Mary, FL: Charisma House.

Wilkins, Michael J. and Moreland, J. P., eds. (1994). *Jesus Under Fire: Modern Scholarship Reinvents the Historical Jesus.* Grand Rapids, MI: Zondervan.

Wilson, Diane (2002). *Awakening of a Jehovah's Witness: Escape from the Watchtower Society.* Amherst, NY: Prometheus Books.

Woodward, James (2003). *Making Things Happen: A Theory of Causal Explanation.* Oxford: Oxford University Press.

Wooten, Angus (2002). *Take Two Tablets Daily: The 10 Commandments and 613 Laws.* Saint Cloud, FL: Key of David.

Wright, N. T. (2003). *The Resurrection of the Son of God.* Minneapolis, MN: Augsburg Fortress Publishers.

Würthwein, Ernst (1995). *The Text of the Old Testament.* Grand Rapids, MI: Eerdmans.

Young, Davis A. and Stearley, Ralph F. (2008). *The Bible, Rocks and Time: Geological Evidence for the Age of the Earth*. Downers Grove, IL: InterVarsity Press.

Young, Matt and Edis, Taner, eds. (2004). *Why Intelligent Design Fails: A Scientific Critique of the New Creationism*. Piscataway, NJ: Rutgers University Press.

Youngblood, Ronald, ed. (1984). *Evangelicals and Inerrancy*. Nashville, TN: Thomas Nelson Publishers.

Zacharias, Ravi, ed. (2003). *The Kingdom of the Cults*. Minneapolis, MN: Bethany House.